D0622582

Decolonization and the Struggle for National Liberation in India (1909–1971)

ANGLO-AMERIKANISCHE STUDIEN
ANGLO-AMERICAN STUDIES

Herausgegeben von
Rüdiger Ahrens, Maria Eisenmann und Laurenz Volkmann

Band 48

Zu Qualitätssicherung und Peer Review der vorliegenden Publikation

Die Qualität der in dieser Reihe erscheinenden Arbeiten wird vor der Publikation durch Herausgeber der Reihe geprüft.

Notes on the quality assurance and peer review of this publication

Prior to publication, the quality of the work published in this series is reviewed by editors of the series.

Thierry Di Costanzo / Guillaume Ducœur (eds.)

Decolonization and the Struggle for National Liberation in India (1909–1971)

Historical, Political, Economic, Religious and Architectural Aspects

PETER LANG
EDITION

Bibliographic Information published by the Deutsche Nationalbibliothek
The Deutsche Nationalbibliothek lists this publication in the Deutsche National-bibliografie; detailed bibliographic data is available in the internet at http://dnb.d-nb.de.

Library of Congress Cataloging-in-Publication Data

Decolonization and the struggle for national liberation in India (1909-1971) : historical, political, economic, religious and architectural aspects / Thierry Di Costanzo, Guillaume Ducoeur (eds.).
    pages cm
Includes bibliographical references.
ISBN 978-3-631-65466-8 -- ISBN 978-3-653-04714-1 (ebook) 1. India--History--Autonomy and independence movements. 2. National liberation movements--India--History--20th century. 3. Decolonization--India--History--20th century. 4. India--History--British occupation, 1765-1947. 5. India--Politics and government--20th century. 6. India--Economic conditions--20th century. 7. Religion and politics--India--History--20th century. 8. Architecture--Political aspects--India--History--20th century. I. Di Costanzo, Thierry. II. Ducoeur, Guillaume.
DS480.45.D353 2014
954.03'5--dc23

2014033098

ISSN 0177-6959
ISBN 978-3-631-65466-8 (Print)
E-ISBN 978-3-653-04714-1 (E-Book)
DOI 10.3726/978-3-653-04714-1

© Peter Lang GmbH
Internationaler Verlag der Wissenschaften
Frankfurt am Main 2014
All rights reserved.
Peter Lang Edition is an Imprint of Peter Lang GmbH.

Peter Lang – Frankfurt am Main · Bern · Bruxelles · New York · Oxford · Warszawa · Wien

All parts of this publication are protected by copyright. Any utilisation outside the strict limits of the copyright law, without the permission of the publisher, is forbidden and liable to prosecution. This applies in particular to reproductions, translations, microfilming, and storage and processing in electronic retrieval systems.

This publication has been peer reviewed.

www.peterlang.com

Contents

6   Contents

Acknowledgments

We would like to thank the following people for having contributed in one way or another to this collection of articles:

Professor Michelguglielmo Torri, from the University of Turin, was a great help in critically checking our introduction. Professor Nupur Chaudhuri, from Texas Southern University, is to be thanked for her moral support she gave during summer 2013 when carefully selecting among many submitted articles and checking three of the articles appearing in this book. Also, Professor Geetha Ganapathy-Doré from the University of Paris enthusiastically supported this project from the outset, together with our colleagues from the Department of English or at the Institute of Political Studies of the University of Strasbourg, Professor Ghislain Potriquet, Professor Hélène Ibata and Professor Virginie Roiron, who checked the remaining articles.

Professor Marc Cluet gave us wonderful friendly support and encouragements; Professor Julia Hegewald, Dr Sonia Cordera and Dr Ingrid Sankey had unshakable confidence in the project; colleagues encountered during Dr Di Costanzo's 2013-Fellowship at JNIAS (*Jawaharlal Nehru Institute of Advanced Studies*) proved solid in their promise to provide a piece for this projected collection of articles: Professor Sucheta Mahajan, Dr. Agnes Maillot, Professor Salil Misra, Professor Aditya Mukherjee and Professor Saradindu Mukherji. Our many special thanks to Professor Aditya Mukherjee who made JNIAS happen, the result being this book and our discovery of Bipan Chandra's works. Bless him and his wonderful family!

We must also profusely thank Professor Dr. Dr. h.c. Ruediger Ahrens, OBE, from the University of Würzburg in Franconia, who selected our manuscript to appear in the collection that he directs at Peter Lang. His tremendous support has indeed made it possible for us to complete the long-term project that had actually started in May 2012.

Thierry Di Costanzo
Université de Strasbourg

Le débat sur l'indépendance de l'Inde : entre décolonisation orchestrée et débâcle britannique

Introduction

La décolonisation politique de l'Empire des Indes britanniques est l'un des événements historiques les plus marquants du XXe siècle. Les Indes[1] ne représentent qu'une petite partie de la superficie de l'Empire britannique, équivalent tout de même à la moitié de la superficie des États-Unis d'Amérique[2], mais leur population rassemble les trois-quarts de la population impériale, soit un peu moins de quatre-cent millions d'habitants à la date du retrait britannique en 1947. Si le terme de « décolonisation » apparaît bien après la crise de 1929, ce sont toutefois les termes de « transfert de pouvoir » et de « fin d'Empire » qui s'imposent dans le contexte indien. Le phénomène indien a ainsi un caractère exceptionnel, la plupart des pays de l'Afrique et de l'Asie colonisée devant patienter encore une dizaine d'années pour obtenir leur indépendance retardée par la Guerre froide[3].

Le phénomène de décolonisation des Indes représente un très court moment dans l'histoire britannique, mais il a pourtant toute son importance. Il avait fallu

---

1 « Les Indes » tant que les Britanniques en restent maîtres, puis lorsqu'elles deviennent indépendantes, « l'Inde » et le « Pakistan ». « Les Indes » sont un « empire » ; non un « dominion », ni une « colonie » dans la classification impériale britannique. Ceylan et la Birmanie sont des colonies. Ceylan est une « colonie de la Couronne », ce qui lui vaut de n'être jamais rattaché aux Indes britanniques, et même d'obtenir le suffrage universel dès 1932, mais n'a pas le statut de « dominion ». La Birmanie fait partie des Indes jusqu'en 1938.

2 La superficie de l'Empire des Indes britanniques en 1947 est équivalente à celle de l'Union européenne de 2013.

3 Le sort des colonies comme Ceylan et la Birmanie ne sera pas abordé ici, dans un recueil consacré exclusivement à l'émancipation de l'Empire des Indes, constitué de l'Inde britannique sous administration directe et de l'Inde princière, sous tutelle indirecte. Le Népal n'est pas de notre ressort non plus.

plus de trois siècles aux Britanniques pour consolider leur Empire indien[4] ; mais il suffit de quelques années pour que les Indiens se libèrent. Moins de trois décennies sont nécessaires à cette possession britannique majeure, centre du monde colonisé, pièce maîtresse de la stratégie asiatique impériale, pour s'affranchir de la tutelle coloniale. Le processus est difficile à dater de façon précise ; les historiens retiennent 1947 comme date symbolique de la décolonisation indienne, mais il faudrait plutôt indiquer les multiples faits marquants de son déclenchement. Ainsi, l'histoire de cet Empire retient généralement une dizaine d'événements marquants : la première réforme constitutionnelle d'envergure menée par le ministre des Indes, celle du Libéral Edwin Montagu (1879–1924) et du vice-roi Chelmsford (1868–1933) ; la venue de la commission d'enquête dirigée par John Simon (1873–1954) sur l'application de cette loi en 1927 ; l'organisation de trois conférences de la Table ronde à Londres et la réforme des collèges électoraux par le gouvernement d'union nationale de Ramsay MacDonald (1866–1937) entre 1930 et 1932 ; la seconde réforme constitutionnelle du vice-roi Linlithgow (1887–1952) en 1935 ; les premières élections générales de 1937, la mission gouvernementale du Travailliste Stafford Cripps (1889–1952) en 1942 ; la conférence de Simla organisée par le vice-roi Wavell (1883–1950) ; les secondes élections générales de 1945 ; la seconde mission Cripps de 1946 ; l'annonce faite par le Premier ministre Travailliste Clement Attlee (1883–1967) du retrait britannique définitif en février 1947 ; l'annonce du Plan de Louis Mountbatten (1900–1979) de la partition des Indes en juin de cette même année.

Le caractère exceptionnel de la situation indienne réside aussi dans la vigueur et la longévité du mouvement anticolonial dans cette colonie. Les crises économiques à répétition fragilisent à l'extrême l'ensemble de la société indienne. Les grandes villes sont saturées de mendiants, les campagnes décimées par la famine. L'alphabétisation touche une toute petite partie des couches les mieux loties de la société colonisée. Les impôts sont lourds et les revenus engrangés par le régime colonial desservent le développement du pays. L'étude de ce mouvement est donc primordiale pour comprendre pleinement le processus final de la colonisation aux Indes.

Les colonisateurs promettent l'autonomie aux Indiens lors du premier conflit mondial, mais les réformes constitutionnelles dyarchiques de 1919 déçoivent l'opinion indienne. Le gouvernement central restant entièrement aux mains des Britanniques, le mouvement anticolonial indien mené par Mohandas Gandhi (1869–1948) se radicalise. Les autorités mènent une très sévère répression. Il faut

---

4   Les Britanniques arrivèrent en 1599 aux Indes. Voir à ce propos la chronologie de Riddick 2006.

retenir au moins cinq grands « moments » dans l'histoire du mouvement national indien : « non-coopération » et mouvement Khilafat au début des années vingt ; déclaration d'indépendance unilatérale, marche du sel et opposition aux réformes concernant les collèges électoraux séparés entre 1930 et 1932 ; opposition à l'entrée en guerre sans consultation ; mouvement *Quit India* de 1942 ; mouvements de grèves et campagne électorale à la fin de la guerre. Puis en 1947, ce sont deux nouvelles nations qui acquièrent leur indépendance politique : l'Union indienne et le Pakistan[5].

Le processus de décolonisation ne s'arrête toutefois pas en 1947, date de l'indépendance de l'Inde et du Pakistan, États-nations successeurs du *Raj* britannique ou Empire des Indes. La complexité de la domination coloniale nous échappe si nous nous arrêtons seulement à ces années de « transfert du pouvoir »[6]. Un simple exemple : les « décolonisés » prennent en main les rênes du pouvoir tout en acceptant le tracé des frontières hérités de la conquête coloniale et de la partition des Indes qui a lieu au même moment que l'indépendance ; de nombreux contentieux en résultent au Cachemire, au Bengale oriental et dans les régions du nord-est de l'Inde. Notre chronologie se terminera donc avec la mort du « premier » Pakistan, nation se projetant exclusivement comme le pays de tous les musulmans de l'Inde. La sécession du Bangladesh reconnue par la communauté internationale en pleine Guerre froide va contredire l'idéal panislamique indien sur lequel se fonde le Pakistan formé de deux « ailes », géographiquement et culturellement très éloignées l'une de l'autre.

Le nouveau gouvernement pakistanais hérite de structures étatiques coloniales inadaptées et n'a, au départ, aucune tradition de gestion du pouvoir. Ses élites ont, certes, un solide passé militaire, mais la terre est aux mains de notables conservateurs latifundiaires, et les industriels ou les bureaucrates, principalement originaires du Punjab ou de Karachi, contrôlent le reste de l'économie. L'Ouest du Pakistan, conservateur, rejette tout changement et déclare la loi martiale en 1958. La politique autoritaire des militaires génère corruption et instabilité. La Ligue Awami devient le principal parti au Pakistan oriental. En 1966, son chef, Sheikh Mujibur Rahman, préconise l'autonomie pour le Pakistan oriental. Et en 1970, lorsque le pays organise les premières élections de son histoire, c'est ce parti régionaliste qui remporte la majorité absolue au niveau national. Les troupes du gouvernement central répriment durement la province rebelle tandis que la Ligue Awami déclare l'indépendance du Pakistan oriental (Bangladesh), contre l'avis

---

5   Ceylan et la Birmanie deviennent indépendantes l'année suivante en 1948.
6   Bandyopadhyay 2009, p. 1–6.

des États-Unis[7]. C'est finalement l'armée indienne qui libère le Bangladesh, après une troisième guerre avec son voisin pakistanais. L'Inde acquiert ainsi le statut de puissance régionale[8].

Le phénomène de décolonisation des Indes a évidemment donné lieu à d'abondants commentaires fortement teintés d'idéologie. Aucune école historique n'est absolument homogène ou figée dans ses certitudes. Il existe de nombreuses versions de l'histoire de la décolonisation. Si certaines font l'apologie des décisions prises lors du « transfert de pouvoir » aux Indiens ou aux Pakistanais, d'autres vont jusqu'à mythifier la lutte anticoloniale. Il existe toutefois des versions de l'histoire plus nuancées. La brève enquête à laquelle nous nous livrons dans cet ouvrage se limitera ainsi à donner quelques exemples parmi les approches les plus connues[9].

L'école nationaliste hagiographique

Pourquoi les autres nations colonisées par les Britanniques n'ont-elles pas produit de grands récits nationalistes à l'exemple de l'Inde ? Il y a probablement quelque raison à cela : les Indes ont déjà une vieille tradition historiographique à l'époque coloniale. Les universités indiennes possèdent des départements d'histoire et de nombreux intellectuels indiens ont pu étudier l'histoire dans les meilleures universités britanniques ou américaines. Il y a donc en Inde (et au Pakistan), après l'indépendance, un milieu bien formé, acquis aux méthodes les plus modernes de l'expertise historique. Cette tradition n'existe pas encore dans le reste de l'Empire où, en l'absence d'historiens, ce sont souvent des poètes, des romanciers et des intellectuels qui tenteront de projeter leur conception de l'histoire nationale

---

7　Ahsan 2014 ; Bass 2013 ; Baxter & Rahman 1996 ; Chatterji 2007 ; Cohen 2004 ; Shaikh 2009 ; Jalal 1995 ; Khan 1999 et 2002 ; Lewis 2011 ; Oldenburg 1985 ; Raghavan 2014 ; Van Schendel 2009.

8　Le Commonwealth ne parvient pas à créer une troisième force dans le monde de la Guerre froide, le mouvement des Non-Alignés non plus. L'Inde et le Pakistan se font trois guerres, l'Inde et la Chine une courte guerre au Cachemire en 1962. L'Inde se rapproche un temps de l'Union soviétique pendant que le Pakistan voit les États-Unis et la Chine comme des alliés de poids. La région se nucléarise sans signer aucun traité international de non-prolifération. Les rébellions maoïstes, séparatistes et la violence religieuse freinent le développement de nombreuses régions de l'Inde et du Pakistan.

9　Iggers & Wang 2008, p. 227–249 et 284–290 ; Gottlob 2003 ; Brasted & Bridge 1994, p. 93–114.

ou de la reconstruire[10]. Les historiens originaires de l'ancien Empire des Indes donnent une version assez bien documentée de la lutte pour l'indépendance. Peu de temps après l'indépendance, le gouvernement indien charge d'ailleurs une poignée d'entre eux de rédiger une histoire nationale à partir des années 1950.

Cette version officielle ou semi-officielle de l'histoire indienne propose une vision de l'Inde marchant de manière inexorable vers la libération nationale et le progrès social ou la démocratie parlementaire ; elle affirme que les héros de la lutte anticoloniale, moralement supérieurs aux colonisateurs, ne peuvent que vaincre la puissance britannique ou leurs « alliés » séparatistes musulmans fondateurs du Pakistan, adversaires de la paix et de la laïcité.

Ramesh Chandra Majumdar (1888–1980), parfois appelé le doyen des historiens indiens, écrit un tel récit sur la lutte anticoloniale qui fait la part belle à la classe moyenne anglicisée du Bengale qui se révolte contre la décision du Vice-Roi Curzon de réorganiser les frontières administratives de la colonie en 1905 et lance un mouvement de boycott des produits britanniques. Majumdar défend deux thèses fondamentales dans son ouvrage sur la lutte anticoloniale : la première est que le gouvernement de l'Inde indépendante aurait largement exagéré le rôle de Gandhi ; la seconde, que les dirigeants indo-musulmans se préoccupent plus des problèmes du monde musulman que de la question indienne. À titre d'exemple, Majumdar cite l'épisode où Gandhi défend les frères Jauhar et Shaukat Ali, les leaders du mouvement Khilafat lorsque ceux-ci affirment qu'il vaut mieux une domination musulmane de l'Inde qu'une domination des Britanniques. Majumdar défend aussi les apports de l'hindouisme politique face à la colonisation britannique, si bien que ses idées déplaisent tellement à ses sponsors du ministère de l'éducation que tout soutien financier après 1955 lui est retiré. Majumdar parvient tout de même, au début des années 1960, à publier ses thèses en trois épais ouvrages intitulés *History of the Freedom Movement in India*[11].

Le gouvernement, par l'intermédiaire de l'*Indian Historical Records Commission* transmet alors le projet de rédaction de grand manuel d'histoire/récit officiel à un éminent archéologue, Tara Chand (1888–1973). Cet ancien ambassadeur de l'Inde en Iran, quant à lui, s'intéresse de près aux apports de la culture indo-musulmane. Entre 1965 et 1983, Chand produit quatre volumes sur le mouvement

---

10 Voir à ce sujet l'entretien donné à Yvon Jablonka par l'historien sénégalais Mamadou Diouf le 9 janvier 2009 pour « La vie des idées » : *L'Afrique et le renouvellement des sciences humaines*, (http://www.laviedesidees.fr/L-Afrique-et-le-renouvellement-des. html).

11 Majumdar 1962–1963.

anticolonial[12] en accordant une attention toute particulière aux ressemblances culturelles entre hindous et musulmans ou autres minorités de l'Inde. Certes, Chand insiste sur les méfaits de la colonisation britannique, mais aussi sur le caractère composite et pluraliste de la nation indienne : il met ainsi à l'honneur les nationalistes indiens d'origine musulmane que Majumdar avait négligé. Toutefois, il est possible d'affirmer, à l'instar de Bipan Chandra, que ces grands récits, celui de Majumdar et celui de Chand, défendent une sorte de saga nationaliste, sorte de vision « *whiggish* »[13] de l'histoire de la libération de l'Inde. Nous reviendrons plus loin sur ce point de vue.

L' école de Cambridge : « métropolitains », « périphériques » et « relations internationales »

Au contraire de ces deux érudits indiens, d'autres historiens, en général originaires de Grande-Bretagne, pensent que l'initiative de décoloniser revient à la puissance impériale plutôt qu'aux colonisés, et que Westminster est à l'origine de réformes constitutionnelles complexes mises en place dans le but de transférer le pouvoir aux Indiens de façon tout à fait pacifique[14]. C'est souvent le point de vue d'historiens utilisant les archives de l'*India Office* ou celles de politiciens impliqués dans ce long processus.

L'Empire des Indes est la première colonie à s'émanciper, mais ce n'est qu'une fois le retrait terminé en Afrique que les autorités britanniques permettent et encouragent la publication des archives de l'*India Office*, l'ancien ministère chargé des affaires indiennes, sur le transfert du pouvoir aux Indes. En 1967, Harold Wilson (1916–1995) nomme Nicholas Mansergh (1869–1979), un spécialiste de l'Irlande, à la tête d'une équipe d'historiens chargée de réunir une documentation conséquente sur la question[15]. Mansergh choisit la date d'août 1940 comme point de départ de la décolonisation des Indes (lorsque Londres invite les dirigeants nationalistes à former un gouvernement d'union nationale local, ce qu'ils refusent), les colonisateurs britanniques rejetant toute idée d'indépendance tant que dure le conflit mondial. Pour Mansergh, le transfert définitif du pouvoir advient à partir de ce moment-là, de façon inévitable, dans la douleur ; et la Partition sera encore bien plus tragique, vu la complexité de la situation indienne, que dans l'Irlande de 1920.

---

12 Chand 1961–1970.
13 Ses représentants sont Guha 2007 et 2011 ; Bandyopadhyay 2004.
14 Kendle 1997, p. 149.
15 Mansergh, Rawson & Moon, 1970–1983.

Bien que Londres rechigne à diviser les Indes en deux, Mansergh soutient que le contexte de quasi guerre civile oblige la Couronne à une partition hâtive, son but étant louable : rétablir l'ordre au plus vite[16]. Mansergh documente d'ailleurs en détail les multiples efforts déployés de toute part pour éviter la Partition. Les documents présentés sont presque tous les produits du niveau le plus élevé de la hiérarchie politique, c'est-à-dire qu'ils incluent la correspondance entre le Gouvernement britannique et le Gouvernement des Indes ainsi qu'occasionnellement la correspondance entre le vice-roi et les gouverneurs des provinces indiennes. Les actions des dirigeants indiens comme Jawaharlal Nehru (1889–1964), Mohandas Gandhi, Vallabhai Patel (1875–1950) ou Muhammad Ali Jinnah (1876–1948) n'apparaissent toutefois que dans la mesure où elles sont consignées dans la correspondance officielle.

L'approche métropolitaine fournit un aperçu plutôt clair de la nature des intérêts de la puissance impériale qui vont bien au-delà des limites de l'Empire des Indes. Toutefois, le travail des historiens se basant uniquement sur ces sources en reflète trop souvent la partialité, même s'ils sont peu nombreux à écarter totalement le mouvement nationaliste indien dans le processus de décolonisation. Toutefois, le point de vue des nationalistes indiens n'apparaît qu'en filigrane de tous ces documents reflétant la version officielle britannique de la décolonisation des Indes[17].

Si certains historiens métropolitains attribuent le pilotage de la décolonisation aux dirigeants métropolitains (c'est bien ce qu'affirme l'école de *Transfer of Power* de Mansergh), d'autres en Grande-Bretagne, après 1968, adoptent un point de vue différent dit « ex-centré » ou « périphérique ». Ils soulignent le rôle primordial, non pas des dirigeants britanniques, mais de l'administration locale (les collaborateurs indiens du régime) dans le phénomène. Encouragé par John Andrew Gallagher (1919–1980) et Ronald Robinson (1920–1999), cette thèse,

---

16 Les Britanniques proposaient de nombreux modèles d'organisation territoriale pour décoloniser l'Inde : modèle fédéral à l'américaine, modèle confédéral à la canadienne, mais c'est en quelque sorte le modèle irlandais de partition qui advient. Le vieux modèle européen de nettoyage ethnique connaîtra malheureusement beaucoup de succès dans la suite immédiate des indépendances. Voir Di Costanzo 2011a, 2011b, 2011c et 2012.

17 Ce travail sur la décolonisation indienne fait partie intégrante de l'histoire de la Grande-Bretagne. Il faut inclure dans l'école « Transfer of Power » les travaux de David C. Potter sur la haute administration coloniale, de l'Australien Robin James Moore sur la mission Cripps, des Américains Morris D. Morris sur l'économie coloniale, Stanley Wolpert sur la décolonisation, Lloyd et Susanne Rupolph sur l'héritage politique.

renforcée par Anil Seal après 1973, défend l'idée que le régime colonial aux Indes fait preuve de profondes discriminations envers ses collaborateurs locaux et précipite sa propre chute à la fin de la Deuxième guerre[18]. L'historien italien Michelguglielmo Torri souligne que c'est en 1973, avec la monographie publiée par *Modern Asian Studies* que commence véritablement la propagation des thèses de l'école périphérique[19]. Lorsque Seal écrit le chapitre introductif de *Modern Asian Studies*, il se base moins sur ses travaux antérieurs, d'orientation nationaliste, que sur celui de ses étudiants et sur celui de son collègue John Gallagher[20].

L'école « périphérique » a publié de nombreux ouvrages, souvent incontournables, comme ceux de la *New Cambridge History of India*. Ses historiens animent la revue *Modern Asian Studies* où une génération entière a diffusé ses travaux novateurs. Cette introduction exige de citer quelques noms appartenant à cette école : B.R. (Tom) Tomlinson ou Tirthankar Roy (histoire économique), Gordon Johnson (politique du gouvernement colonial), Thomas Metcalf (idéologie coloniale), Sugata Bose (monde paysan), Barbara Ramusack (Inde princière), Joya Chatterji ou Anil Seal (transfert du pouvoir et Partition), Judith Brown (Gandhi) ou Anthony Low (relations Londres-Congrès), et Ayesha Jalal (Jinnah). Subrata Kumar Mitra, indien de nationalité française en poste à l'université de Heidelberg a récemment offert une perspective allant dans le sens de l'école « périphérique » sur le concept de « réutilisation » des institutions britanniques dans l'Inde indépendante[21].

La riposte indienne des partisans de la débâcle

Tout au contraire des historiens de l'école de Cambridge ou des hagiographes nationalistes comme Chand et Majumdar, Bipan Chandra (1928-), un historien indien formé à Stanford et Delhi et orienté cette fois en partie par le marxisme, offre une lecture totalement différente de l'histoire de la décolonisation de l'Inde dès la fin des années soixante. Chandra soutient en quelque sorte que les partisans de l'indépendance mènent une lutte difficile et inégale pour

---

18 Gallagher, Johnson & Seal 1973.
19 Torri 1989 ; 1991 et 1996.
20 Seal 1973, p. 321. La monographie d'Anil Seal sur le nationalisme n'est pas fondatrice de cette école. Anil Seal fait auparavant partie de l'approche nationaliste de l'histoire indienne (Seal 1968) tout comme Mehotra 1965, Pandey 1969 et Broomfield 1968. Certes Broomfield est américain, mais sa monographie appartient au courant nationaliste indien.
21 Mitra 2011, p. 21–42.

une libération nationale au résultat tragique (partition). Si progrès et démocratie il y a, ils restent fragiles et la lutte de personnages-clés du Congrès reste prégnante, le combat mené par Gandhi est avant tout une lutte politique qui continue même après l'indépendance, dans le contexte difficile de la montée du *communalism*.

La création de la toute nouvelle université *Jawaharlal Nehru University* au sud de New Delhi après 1968 permettra à Bipan Chandra d'initier une nouvelle génération à l'histoire économique ou politique (il renouvèle les études gandhiennes et nehruviennes) et publie lui aussi un grand récit sur la libération des Indes sous la forme de plusieurs manuels[22]. Il est bien dommage que Bipan Chandra soit si méconnu dans les milieux universitaires occidentaux, au contraire de R. C. Majumdar (qui a largement bénéficié du soutien de l'administration coloniale à son époque) ou des historiens de l'école de Cambridge et des subalternistes qui n'ont pas, eux, au contraire de Bipan Chandra, fait toute leur carrière en Inde. Dans sa mouvance toutefois, des historiens indiens de toutes tendances, enseignant dans les meilleures universités fédérales du pays, renouvèlent, dès lors, de fond en comble la vision indienne de la décolonisation. Cette nouvelle génération s'implique dans l'étude du mouvement nationaliste à travers le projet de *Towards Freedom* subventionné par l'*Indian Council of Historical Research* – réponse indienne à la publication de Mansergh[23].

Towards Freedom prend comme date de départ 1937, l'année où l'Empire des Indes obtient l'autonomie de ses provinces (et non 1940 comme Mansergh). Le choix de cette date signifie que les nationalistes indiens sont alors prêts à participer aux responsabilités au gouvernement de la colonie. S'ils se retirent du gouvernement au début de la guerre, c'est que le gouvernement britannique n'est pas disposé à promettre l'indépendance. Les historiens derrière ce projet soutiennent donc la thèse d'une « débâcle » : le mouvement nationaliste indien infligerait une véritable défaite aux Britanniques, surtout à partir de 1944, le régime colonial décidant finalement de négocier son retrait définitif, en toute hâte.

Si la mise en œuvre de *Transfer of Power* a nécessité plus d'une douzaine d'années, le projet *Towards Freedom* prend plus de vingt-sept ans à se réaliser. Il a

---

22 Ces historiens « de la JNU » produiront eux aussi de grands récits sur la décolonisation de l'Inde. Voir Chandra 1981 ; Chandra, Mukherjee, Mahajan, Mukherjee & Panikkar 1988 ; Chandra, Mukherjee & Mukherjee 2008 ; Chandra 2009 et 2012.

23 Plusieurs régions de l'Inde publient aussi leur propre série d'archives sur la décolonisation. Le gouvernement fédéral parraine également un énorme recueil en cent volumes regroupant la correspondance, les articles et l'œuvre intégrale de Gandhi.

posé de nombreux problèmes dans son organisation du fait d'une alternance gouvernementale qui bloque toute publication entre 1998 et 2004, le parti alors au pouvoir étant peu favorable, pour des raisons politiques, aux historiens chargés du projet[24]. Le premier volume concernant l'année 1937 sort en 1986 ; le dernier portant sur 1947 vient de sortir en 2013[25]. L'équipe chargée de ce travail titanesque regroupe de très grands historiens indiens comme P.N. Chopra, Basudev Chatterjee, Mushirul Hasan, K.N. Panikkar, Sabyasachi Bhattacharya, Amit Kumar Gupta et Dev Arjun, Partha Sarathi Gupta, Bimal Prasad, Sumit Sarkar et Sucheta Mahajan.

Les écoles subalterniste et postcoloniale

Les débats historiques sur la fin de l'Empire britannique, les récits de « transfert de pouvoir » planifié, d'exploits nationalistes ou de luttes des classes triomphantes demeureraient-ils lacunaires ? Est-il vrai qu'aucune approche ne fournit d'explications suffisantes concernant le processus de décolonisation aux Indes ? La nécessité de compléter les grands récits explicatifs est-elle logique ? L'histoire sociale et culturelle contribue-t-elle à apporter une plus fine compréhension du phénomène de décolonisation ?

Au début des années 1980, de retour de Grande-Bretagne, Ranajit Guha (1922-) invite Edward Palmer Thomson (1924–1993) à faire une série de conférences en Inde. Influencé par les travaux de l'intellectuel italien antifasciste Antonio Gramsci (1891–1937), Guha produit une série d'études en net désaccord avec l'histoire « élitiste » de Majumdar, Chand et Chandra. Il dénonce, tout comme Bipan Chandra, l'école dite de Cambridge qui circonscrirait le mouvement anticolonialiste indien à de simples rivalités entre individus et entre groupes ambitieux ou assoiffés de pouvoir désirant apprendre de leurs maîtres britanniques la « bonne » pratique de la politique moderne avant que ceux-ci ne décident de quitter les Indes de leur propre gré.

Guha écarte tout autant le bien-fondé des sagas hagiographiques nationalistes mettant uniquement en scène, selon lui, les élites indiennes « éclairées » menant de façon inévitable « leur » peuple sur le chemin de la liberté. Il récuse, enfin et surtout, de façon surprenante, les thèses d'un historien pourtant proche de lui par les idées

---

24 Le parti au pouvoir alors, le *Bharatiya Janata Party* (BJP), encourage sa propre version de l'histoire, ouvertement anti-laïque, sous l'influence de l'historien B. R. Grover qui met à l'honneur des idéologues de l'exclusivisme hindou des années trente comme K.B. Hedgewar, M.S. Golwalkar et V.D. Savarkar.

25 Mahajan & Bhattacharya (ed.) 2013.

comme Bipan Chandra. Selon Guha, Chandra et son groupe se limiterait à décrire les actions salvatrices de Jawaharlal Nehru ou de Mohandas Gandhi, ou principalement celles des membres du Comité directeur du *Congrès national indien*[26].

Guha remettrait ainsi à l'honneur les « sans-grade », les paysans révoltés (comme entre 1942 et 1947), qu'il nomme « subalternes »[27]. Les auteurs « subalternistes », souvent bengalis comme Guha, regroupent huit chercheurs qui sont les disciples de Guha lorsque celui-ci réside et professe en Grande-Bretagne : Sumit Sarkar, Shahid Amin, Gyanendra Pandey, Partha Chatterjee, Gautam Bhadra, Dipesh Chakrabarty, David Arnold et David Hardiman (les deux seuls Britanniques du groupe)[28].

Si dans les dix volumes qu'ils publient en Inde, les « subalternistes » participent au renouvellement des recherches sur la (dé)colonisation des Indes, ils ne sont guère, en fait, les seuls à renouveler ces études[29] : tous les courants historiques se penchent sur les conséquences dues à la disparition de l'Empire en Grande-Bretagne ou dans ses anciennes colonies. Ce nouveau courant de la recherche délaisse alors l'étude de l'État colonial tout-puissant ou de la direction centrale du Congrès et se porte sur les multiples aspects qui lient les colonies entre elles et à la métropole, plutôt que sur les relations purement bilatérales entre la métropole britannique et la colonie indienne[30].

De façon générale, les chercheurs dans leur ensemble s'orientent aussi vers une histoire régionale moins traditionnelle, autre que celle du Bengale et du nord des Indes. Ce renouveau des études historiques, initié par Guha, sur la colonisation tardive (ou non) permet finalement de mieux cerner les différences entre les notions d'impérialisme, de capitalisme et les prémisses de la mondialisation. Ces recherches soulignent les effets, dans les localités des Indes colonisées, du progrès, de la modernité et de la toute-puissance du rouleau-compresseur colonial[31]. Les « Subaltern Studies » ne sont pas, répétons-le, les seules à se lancer

---

26 Pourtant les historiens de la *Bipan Chandra School* n'oublient en rien les mouvements organisés par la base militante non-violente du Congrès dans les milieux paysans et ouvriers, cela bien avant les mouvements organisés par les communistes indiens. Ces historiens excellent aussi dans l'analyse du concept de *communalism*. Voir Chandra 1984, p. 1–33 ; Mahajan 2000 ; Misra 2001 ; Batabyal 2005.

27 Sur le cheminement intellectuel de Guha, voir Merle 2004. Guha écrit six articles et sept livres fondamentaux sur la colonisation/décolonisation. Son dernier ouvrage date de 2003.

28 Retenons ici les ouvrages de Sarkar 1983a, 1983b et 1985.

29 Bose 2003.

30 Kennedy & Ghosh 2006.

31 Ludden 2002.

dans ce mouvement, mais elles font toutefois beaucoup pour populariser cette orientation du monde de la recherche.

À partir de la fin des années 1980, Chatterjee, Arnold, Pandey et Chakarbarty réorientent les travaux de leur groupe, élargissant leur corpus sous l'influence de l'anthropologie culturelle, des études littéraires (Gayatri Spivak) et de la psychanalyse (Ashis Nandy), etc. Sumit Sarkar, Shahid Amin et David Hardiman décident de quitter le groupe, car ces derniers restent attachés à l'histoire sociale. Si les « Subaltern Studies » désignent à l'origine une école historique, ses membres finiront par se confondre avec le nouveau courant dit « postcolonialiste »[32]. Dipesh Chakrabarty est celui qui incarne le mieux cette évolution, depuis les années 2000. Selon lui, l'Europe continue de façon inévitable de hanter les esprits indiens et il suffirait de la « provincialiser » pour qu'elle recouvre la liberté[33].

Ces « Subalternistes tardifs » ou « postcolonialistes » se tournent donc vers le thème de l'identité indienne malmenée et fragile, conséquence directe du choc colonial, de l'impossibilité tragique qu'a l'Inde de se libérer, de « se décoloniser » totalement du point de vue culturel et linguistique. L'indépendance politico-économique chèrement acquise depuis 1947 ne suffit pas, selon eux, à la libérer des chaines du colonialisme. En véritables militants, ils affirment lutter pour l'indépendance intellectuelle totale d'une Inde encore soumise à la domination occidentale. Des intellectuels occidentaux se revendiquant comme appartenant à la gauche, comme Perry Anderson le frère de Benedict Anderson, s'adonnent eux aussi au « Gandhi/Nehru/Congress-bashing » cher à cette école[34].

Les tenants de l'histoire sociale comme Sarkar, l'école « néo-impériale » de Cambridge et les marxistes comme Chandra dénoncent l'ambiguïté des « postcolonialistes », dont certains membres, comme Nandy, sont accusés de

---

32 Les « Subalternistes » n'écrivent plus aujourd'hui d'ouvrages militants : ils ont atteint une telle notoriété ! La publication en 2005 de l'ouvrage suivant constitue un nouveau tournant : Mayaram, Pandian & Skaria 2005. La plupart des départements d'études postcoloniales des universités occidentales sont à la base des départements d'études anglaises associant sciences humaines, sciences sociales et littérature.

33 Chakrabarty 2000. Pour une première approche sur cette « école », voir Peers & Gooptu 2012, p. 1–6.

34 Voir Perry Anderson sur « l'idéologie indienne » (anticolonialiste, exclusiviste ou laïque) dans la *London Review of Books* qui a publié ces trois essais en juillet-août 2012 sous les titre *Gandhi Centre Stage* (vol. 34/13, p. 3–11 ; www.lrb.co.uk/v34/n13/perry-anderson/gandhi-centre-stage) ; *Why Partition* (vol. 34/14, p. 11–19 ; www.lrb.co.uk/v34/n14/perry-anderson/why-partition) ; *After Nehru* (vol. 34/15, p. 21–36 ; www.lrb.co.uk/v34/n15/perry-anderson/after-nehru). Ces essais sont maintenant publiés en Inde : Anderson 2012.

critiquer sans nuance l'État-nation, le libéralisme politique, la modernité et les récits d'émancipation issus des Lumières, fournissant ainsi des arguments aux forces antidémocratiques, et encourageant même de façon indirecte, curieuse ironie, le renouveau du *communalism* en Inde[35]. Les « Postcolonial Studies » sont donc un champ d'études flou et non une discipline à part entière, et, selon eux, ce projet impose trop de limites aux sciences sociales[36]. L'ouvrage de Crispin Bates offrira une synthèse complète et objective de ce champ historique souvent riche et parfois contradictoire[37]. En fin de compte, c'est l'ouvrage de Michael Dusche qui offrira la meilleure synthèse, et la plus vivante, de l'évolution de la discipline historique[38], bien qu'il existe en Europe deux autres historiens, moins jeunes, de l'Inde britannique : l'Allemand Dietmar Rothermund ou l'Italien Michelguglielmo Torri, qui aussi ont l'avantage d'offrir d'excellentes synthèses (en anglais) sur la question de la décolonisation des Indes[39].

Finalement, la décolonisation fait aussi partie intégrante de l'histoire des relations internationales. L'historien américain Erez Manela étudie les doléances des Indiens auprès de la Ligue des Nations et du président Wilson et souligne le profond mécontentement des Indiens suite à l'énorme sacrifice méconnu de cette colonie sur les champs de bataille européen et moyen-orientaux ; l'Australien Auriol Weigold, de son côté, aborde un aspect peu connu de la politique étrangère américaine, celui de la propagande rooseveltienne aux Indes face à Churchill pendant la Seconde Guerre mondiale. Anita Inder Singh évoque, quant à elle, le rôle grandissant des États-Unis au début de la Guerre froide, entre 1946 et 1957, période de déclin rapide de l'influence britannique dans la région suite à l'inattendue et surprenante Partition des Indes[40].

---

35 Nandy 1983.

36 En France, le débat oppose des anglicistes à des politologues. Voir Bayart 2010 et l'excellent débat qui en a résulté avec Laetitia Zecchini (Zecchini 2011) ; Zecchini 2009 ; Pouchepadass 2010.

37 Bates 2002.

38 Dusche 2010.

39 Le recueil suivant, le plus précis sur la question indienne, est sans conteste Rothermund 2006, p. 21–32, 53–71 et 279–281, mais Torri 2007 donnera un très complet et synthétique tour d'horizon du processus de décolonisation indien. Voir aussi le recueil plus général sur la décolonisation de Duara 2004. Il regroupe quelques-unes des meilleures signatures sur la décolonisation. Son ouvrage contient non seulement des déclarations de nature historique faites par Jawaharlal Nehru, mais de multiples références sur les conséquences de la Première Guerre Mondiale pour le nationalisme indien, sur la Guerre froide et la Partition des Indes.

40 Manela 2007 ; Weigold 2008 ; Singh 1993 et 2006.

22   Thierry Di Costanzo

Perspectives

Le but du recueil qui suit, intitulé *Decolonization and the Struggle for National Liberation in India*, n'est pas de faire l'impasse sur ces divers courants historiographiques. Les anciennes limites imposées par l'histoire politique et institutionnelle ont depuis longtemps laissé une place à l'histoire de la société et de la culture liée à la colonisation et à la décolonisation de l'Empire des Indes et le débat est bien toujours vivant sur la décolonisation. Chaque école s'y ressource.

L'ouvrage permet d'aborder la décolonisation/libération des Indes sous plusieurs angles particuliers, et de s'initier au débat entre historiens sur la question de la décolonisation des Indes britanniques. Nous chercherons à savoir qui, dans le débat en question, est plus ou moins en faveur de la thèse de la débâcle ou celle de la transition douce et bien menée. Nous avons choisi de couvrir une très courte partie du XXe siècle, entre la date de la mise en place de la première constitution coloniale de l'Inde vers 1909, pour aller jusqu'en 1971, au lendemain de la sécession du Pakistan oriental, ce qui correspond, à peu près, à la vie de trois générations d'Indiens.

Dans ce recueil d'articles, notre objectif n'a pas été d'élucider l'entière complexité de l'histoire globale de la décolonisation de l'Inde. Si l'étude exhaustive de cette question dépasse de loin un tel ouvrage, nous espérons en revanche que la bibliographie générale se révélera d'une grande utilité pour les étudiants et les chercheurs ainsi que pour tout lecteur curieux. Quoi qu'il en soit, tous constateront que le fil conducteur de ces contributions les mènera à s'interroger sur une problématique commune touchant au projet d'indépendance de l'Inde et aux débats qui l'ont animé. Nous avons porté, en particulier, notre attention sur le fait que cette décolonisation a pu être soit orchestrée par la puissance coloniale, soit déclenchée par la lutte menée par les forces anti-impérialistes, elles-mêmes fédérées par le Congrès national indien. Notre seconde visée a été de déterminer dans ces débats à quel moment la décolonisation s'est accélérée. Par cette approche, nous avons tenté de saisir l'ensemble des contours des débats historiographiques actuels. En effet, le lecteur remarquera aisément que ces articles ici sélectionnés reproduisent divers tendances liées à l'historiographie de la question. Les contributions, contenues dans ce recueil et organisées selon un ordre chronologique, reflètent, toutes sans exception, chacune à leur manière, les thèses défendues par une « école » historiographique présentée dans cet article introductif. Nous espérons qu'étudiants et chercheurs pourront ainsi compléter leurs propres connaissances sur cette vaste question qu'est l'histoire de l'Empire britannique et de sa décolonisation.

Les thèmes abordés se succèdent donc comme suit : le système économique indien à la fin de la période de la domination coloniale (A. Mukherjee) ;

l'exemple irlandais de résistance passive et sa réutilisation en Inde par Gandhi (A. Maillot) ; le destin de l'aristocratie indienne entre le gouvernorat-général de Curzon et la réforme constitutionnelle de 1935 (I. Sankey) ; conçue entre 1912 et 1930, la construction de la dernière capitale du Raj, la « Nouvelle-Delhi », par Luytens, le « plus grand architecte britannique » (J. Hegewald) ; la réorientation historique que propose, à l'appui des travaux des indianistes européens, le philosophe comparatiste Radhakrishnan revendiquant, au *summum* de l'idéologie colonialiste entre 1921 et 1942, l'apport de l'Inde dans l'histoire des civilisations et plus particulièrement celle de l'Europe (G. Ducœur) ; la peur de disparaître saisit avec angoisse la principale minorité religieuse de l'Inde, les musulmans, au moment où les Anglais quittent les Indes (S. Misra) ; les premières émeutes qui ravagent les Indes dès 1946 à Calcutta (S. Mukherji) ; la conclusion récente de la grande aventure du contre-projet indien sur les sources historiques par l'un de ses participants (S. Mahajan) ; la décolonisation de l'urbanisme indien par le projet novateur de Le Corbusier à Chandigarh à partir des années cinquante (M. Cluet) ; enfin, la guerre de 1971 et ses conséquences internationales (S. Cordera). Tous les contributeurs exercent une activité d'enseignant-chercheur soit dans des universités françaises ou européennes soit indiennes. Parmi eux, quatre sont des historiens indiens rattachés par leur formation et leur enseignement à diverses universités de la capitale indienne. L'analyse globale de ces articles fait ressortir que les préoccupations principales de ces chercheurs concernent aussi l'avenir de l'Inde britannique, la question musulmane et hindoue, la création du Pakistan, la nature du gouvernement colonial etc. et qu'elles tournent toutes autour de cette date-clé que fut l'année 1947. Ainsi, les résultats de ce recueil d'articles permettront au lecteur de mieux se familiariser avec le débat historiographique actuel sur cette fin de l'époque coloniale.

Enfin, cet ouvrage est aussi le résultat d'un travail de recherche personnel. L'idée de sa réalisation a pris naissance à l'université Jawarharlal Nehru de New Delhi, où nous avons séjourné en tant que *Fellow,* des mois de janvier à avril 2013. Au vu des recherches actuelles, nous pouvons affirmer, sans hésitation aucune, que, dans le cas de l'Inde, la Partition fut une véritable catastrophe et que les responsables avérés du séparatisme communautaire le plus fermé furent les politiques coloniales des Britanniques qui procédèrent dès 1857 à une communautarisation de la société indienne. Ironie de cette terrible fraction de l'histoire de l'Inde, ce furent ces mêmes Britanniques qui les premiers vinrent à regretter la partition de 1947 et ses conséquences plus ou moins lointaines, comme la guerre du Bangladesh.

Aditya Mukherjee
Jawaharlal Nehru University

Decolonization or the Last Phase of Colonialism?[1]

Introduction

This paper will focus on the last phase of colonialism in India particularly since the First World War. The period saw some growth of indigenous industry and a substantial growth of the indigenous capitalist class. Apart from this the period witnessed several other 'positive' developments which diverge from the classical colonial pattern that had got established in India[2]. This has led to one group of colonial writers seeing these as the result of colonialism and its policies,[3] which created conditions for rapid economic advance later[4]. Morris D. Morris too sees the period after 1914 as one during which "rather substantial structural modifications occurred" when "the *base was laid* for a renewed upward surge after independence"; unfortunately, despite all the "growth benefits of nineteenth century" the "nineteenth century as a period was *too brief* to achieve all the structural changes needed to provide the preconditions for an industrial revolution."[5] The implication in their writings is that the impetus of the changes during 1914–1947 remained colonial and post-Independence India could just build on them, without involving any fundamental break from colonialism. Other colonial scholars see this period as one of 'decolonization' where colonialism was gradually pulling out, handing over to Indian interests.[6]

---

1 This article is a revised version of the Presidential Address (Modern India) delivered at Sixty Eighth session of Indian History Congress, New Delhi, 2007.
2 For a detailed enumeration of the 'positive' changes seen in the Indian economy since WWI upto independence in 1947 see Mukherjee 2002.
3 For example Roy 2000.
4 Gordon 1978; Anstey 1957 and Roy 2000, see for example p. 51, 116–117, 136–137, 152–153, etc.
5 See for example Aditya Mukherjee, "Indian Economy, 1947–65: The Nehruvian Legacy", in Chandra, Mukherjee and Mukherjee 2000.
6 See Dewey 1978 and 1979; Gordon 1978.

Some even see this period as one where England was being exploited by India![7]
I shall question this range of colonial views[8].

Before I do a critique of the colonial view of this period let me give just
one example of the kind of 'positive' non-colonial development the Indian
economy witnessed between 1914 and 1947. There was indigenous industrial
growth leading to considerable import substitution especially in consumer
goods industries. The most dramatic change was that the Indian cotton textile
industry essentially regained the domestic market, which it had lost to Britain.
(See Table 1).

Table 1: Sea-Borne Imports Into British India, 1900–1945[9]

	I	II	III	IV
	1900–1	1920–21	1936–37	1944–45
Cotton piece-goods (million yards)	2003	1510	764	5
Sugar (thousand tons)	–	344	23	Nil (net imports-17)*
Soap (thousand cwt., i.e. 1000 hundredweight = 50 tons)	–	313	48	3

---

7   Drummond 1972.
8   I shall not discuss here the "Left" variant of the decolonization thesis which was
    argued initially in the late 1920s to explain this period seeing it as one where
    imperialism continued in an altered form encouraging industrialization and
    therefore the colonial bourgeoisie had no basic contradictions with it. See Aditya
    Mukherjee, "The Workers' and Peasants' Parties, 1926–1930: An Aspect of Com-
    munism in India", in Chandra 1983, for a brief summary of the communist view.
    I have critiqued this view extensively elsewhere. See, for example, Mukherjee and
    Mukherjee 1988.
9   Sources: Columns II, III and IV from Subramanian and Homfray 1946, p. 48–49 and
    p. 6–8. Column I from Bagchi 1972, p. 238, 295 and 354. For *, see Ray 1979, p. 138.
    By 1937 India had started *exporting* sugar. Note: Up to 1936–1937, figures included
    Burma.

	I	II	III	IV
	1900–1	1920–21	1936–37	1944–45
Matches (thousand gross boxes)	–	12399	55 (by 1938–39, 95% of imports met indigenously)	During war, imports rise due to shortages. No figures available for 1944–45).
Cement (thousand tons)	165 [1914]	131	51	5 [1940–41], insignificant in 1944–45 being one fifth of 1940–41 in value terms at current prices.
Paper and paste-board (million rupees)		73	39.4	261
Iron and steel (thousand tons)	286	712	363	

Further, during World War II, when Britain made large war purchases in India, India ceased to be a debtor country and by 1946 had accumulated as *credit* against Britain a whopping sterling balance of nearly Rs. 17,000 million.

The question now was: how to understand these positive changes? As mentioned earlier the colonial view was to see these changes as the beneficial result of colonialism or as the result of imperialism voluntarily pulling out. Colonial scholars have focused on the increasing import substitution in consumer goods industry in India (see Table 1) and the sharp decline in the British market in India, particularly in cotton textiles, to basically argue that Britain was now '*surrendering*' its interests in India in favour of Indian industrial interests. The 1919 'Fiscal Autonomy Convention' was described as "a British self-denying ordinance"[10] which led to the "deliberate surrender of the largest export market in the world for a staple British manufacture."[11] The fact that in the changed circumstances since the First World War India was able to achieve a somewhat better bargain in the trade agreements of the 1930s (the Ottawa Agreement, 1932, the Mody-Lees Pact, 1934 and the Indo-British Trade Agreements of 1935 and 1939), compared to the total surrender to British industrial and financial interests earlier, was interpreted as_ "the

---

10 Drummond 1972, p. 124.
11 Dewey 1978, p. 36.

clever and powerful Indians (having) forced a disadvantageous trade treaty upon the weak and inept English."[12] The 1939 agreement was described by Drummond as: "a 'capitulation' — the sort of thing which Marxists tell us the evil imperialist Western governments force on the weak and helpless countries of the Third World. But in this case, as at Ottawa...it was Britain who had capitulated, sacrificing most of her preferential advantages.... The reader is left to ask himself who was exploiting whom."[13]

It was further argued that not only was Britain not exploiting India but it was actually encouraging Indian industrialization[14]. The fact that India still did not industrialize was because the Indian entrepreneur was incapable of taking advantage of the government initiative, it was just not up to taking on the immense challenge[15]

Also, somewhat like what Tirthankar Roy was to echo later, Dewey accused Marxists and nationalists of being simplistic and indulging in "a conspiracy theory of imperialist exploitation"[16]. He accused them of ascribing "Indian tariff policy to a single dominant determinant, principally the Lancashire cotton lobby..." and not recognizing the "remarkable metamorphosis" that had occurred since the First World War, where "the power-struggles within the India Office and the Government of India were resolved in favour of factions allied with the Bombay mill owners, while the factions allied with Lancashire were reduced to virtual impotence." It was said, "in the 1870s the Secretary of State allied with Lancashire against the Government of India, while in the years after 1917 the Government of India aligned itself with Indian nationalists against the India Office...." In their battle with the Secretary of State the Government of India's "alliance with the *nominal* nationalist enemies" proved useful as did "the public opinion they helped *manufacture*" and the "upsurge of

---

12 Drummond 1972, p. 132.
13 Drummond 1972, p. 140. It is to be noted that the loss of 'preferential advantage' by Britain is seen as exploitation.
14 Drummond 1972, p. 122–123 and Dewey 1979.
15 Dewey 1979, p. 249–252. Given the massive economic upsurge of Indian business in recent years at least doubts should arise about the various alleged incapacities of the Indian entrepreneur.
16 Dewey 1978, p. 38 and Roy 2000, p. 10–18 and 309–311. Roy e.g., accuses Marxists and 'left-nationalist' scholars of picking up the arguments of the early nationalists "that were for them not much more than political tools" and then "reestablishing" them "as correct and valid descriptions".

political unrest in India."[17] It seems some 'manufactured' political unrest by the 'nominal nationalist enemies' was still necessary despite the assertion that "an important attribute of sovereignty had passed from England to India, *twenty-five years before* independence"[18]. A.D.D. Gordon argued a similar position saying that the Government of India was influenced by the Home government on the one hand and the fiscal demands of the local business interests on the other, with the government of India increasingly giving in to the latter, 'nurturing' Indian industrialists rather than industrialists of Britain. Subsequent events, it was claimed, were to "illustrate this point" as with the "*granting* of independence" in 1947, manufacturing industry was to grow from "strength to strength"[19]. Evident again is the tendency to see continuity between developments since the First World War and those after independence and the failure to understand the decisive structural break that 1947 represented in the political economy of the colonial situation in India.

While all this is bad economic history it is even worse political history. It goes one step further backwards from the so called "Cambridge School", which saw Indian nationalism as a '*tamasha*' 'manufactured' by the Indian elite, and argues the early 19th century Whig or liberal imperialist position, which saw the role of British rule as gradually training Indians for self-government[20]. It was now the Government of India which was helping to 'manufacture' nationalist opposition!

---

17 Dewey 1978, p. 50, 55–56, emphasis mine. Somewhat inexplicably Dewey in the same work talks of rival factions within the India Office and the Government of India and again a few pages later sees the two themselves as rival factions. Tirthankar Roy too sees the Secretary of State and the Viceroy representing Imperial and Indian interests with "the balance tilting in favour of India in the twentieth century". He goes one step further and adds a third layer, that of the provincial Governors "who were concerned with local developmental or welfare related issues". Roy 2000, p. 247. This third layer of colonial Governance presumably would tilt the balance even further in India's favour.

18 Dewey 1978, p. 67, emphasis mine.

19 Gordon 1978, p. 238–241, emphasis mine. See also a critique of Gordon in Mukherjee 1981. B. R. Tomlinson also sees the Government of India balancing the "imperial and domestic commitment" and the former dominated till the First World War and presumably the latter after that Tomlinson 1979, p. 28.

20 B. R. Tomlinson, for example, sees "British rule in India" as having "successfully achieved by 1947" the nineteenth century objective of Elphinstone: "We must not dream of perpetual possession, but must apply ourselves to bring the natives into a state that will admit of their governing themselves in a manner that may be beneficial to our interests as well as their own…". Tomlinson 1979, p. 152.

The colonial people are robbed even of their own liberation struggle. With elements of 'sovereignty' already being passed on to India with Government help one is left wondering what the Gandhian mass movement phase of the Indian national movement, between World War I and 1947, costing tens of thousands of lives and involving untold sacrifices by millions, was all about. Significantly, the colonialists have little objection to seeing this movement as the 'official' movement of the 'elite' keeping down the real aspirations of the Indian people, a position favoured by the so called 'Subaltern school.'

The altered colonial exploitation of India

In my understanding, there is a completely different explanation for the developments in the twentieth century, particularly between World War I and 1947. Instead of decolonization, what this period witnessed was not only the continuation of colonial exploitation (though in an altered form) but its blatant intensification in many respects at great cost to the Indian economy and its people.

Britain did not after World War I abandon its most important market for textiles in India, so ruthlessly captured in the 19th century, as a result of their now giving in to Indian industrial interests or merely due to Indian nationalist pressure. Britain was *forced* to concede substantially her imperial *industrial* interest in the colonial market in favour of imperial *financial* interest, i.e., using the colony as a source of capital through unrequited remittance or 'drain'. It was a switch from one imperial interest to another, not a switch from imperial to Indian national interest.

The tussle between the two *imperial* interests had already surfaced by the late 19th century when the Government of India was facing some difficulty in raising the revenue necessary for meeting the sterling remittance requirements[21]. The Government of India, unable economically and politically to raise the required revenue from any other source like land revenue, salt tax, etc., was keen to levy

---

21 The Government of India's sterling obligation or remittances were met by utilizing an equivalent amount in Rupee out of the Government's revenues to purchase the necessary hard currency earned by India through her export surplus. Smooth remittance therefore could occur only if the Government of India could generate a *budgetary* surplus equal to the *remittance*, and the export surplus was sufficient to convert the former into the latter. When these conditions did not prevail, the Government was forced to adopt measures such as introducing revenue tariffs, borrowing at home and/or abroad, using up India's currency reserves, altering the Rs./Stg. Exchange rate or resorting to a combination of fiscal and monetary manipulation. More on this later.

some revenue duties on Indian imports (not protective duties) which the Secretary of State under pressure from British textile manufacturing interests was adamant in not allowing. It is important to note that Government of India was not bending to national interest but was only trying to facilitate remittance and 'drain', a critical imperial financial interest. Eventually, in the 1890s the dilemma was resolved, expectedly at India's cost, by levying revenue duties on imports along with countervailing excise duties of the same amount on Indian manufacture of textiles to avoid even a semblance of any protection to Indian industry.

The dilemma of adjusting the two imperial interests, of finance and industry, followed a somewhat different trajectory in the 20th century, particularly since 1914. British financial demands on India increased manifold since W.W. I. For example, Home Charges[22] increased from approximately £ 20 million in 1913–14 to £ 32 million in 1924–25. Military expenditure doubled from £ 5 million to £ 10 million and interest charges on external public debt increased from about £ 6 million to £ 14.3 million between 1913–14 and 1934–5[23]. In 1917 India supplied goods worth £ 100 million without any payment and in 1918 decided to make another gift of £ 45 million to the British war effort[24]. During World War II defence expenditure increased by over nine times, from about Rs. 50 crores in 1939–40 to Rs. 458 crores in 1944. The proportion of the total expenditure of the Central Government accounted for by the Defence Services (an expenditure Tirthankar Roy fully approves) was about 55 per cent in 1920–21 rising to 75 per cent by the end of World War II[25]. Far from decolonizing, retaining India had become even more critical for Britain.

---

22 The Home Charges were the sterling expenses of Government of India incurred in Britain including cost of maintaining the Secretary of State's office, civil and military charges, interest on public debt and the guaranteed interest on Railway investments, pension and furlough to British civil and military officers, etc. The Home Charges represented to a very large extent what the early nationalists in India correctly described as drain of resources or capital from India.

23 Ray 1979, p. 11–13.

24 Levkovsky 1966, p. 96.

25 Subramanian and Homfray 1946, p. 15 and 72; Tomlinson 1979, p. 93. The early nationalists focused their critique on the huge defence expenditure incurred by India to meet *British* imperial designs pointing out that India's defence expenditure as a proportion of annual revenue was larger than that spent by advanced and militaristic nations like Britain and Czarist Russia. See Chandra 1966, pp. 580 ff. Tirthankar Roy however approves of this expenditure by arguing that the colonial government "spent less on luxuries and more on the *genuine duties* of the state such as defence…", Roy 2000, p. 273, emphasis mine.

The huge rise in India's sterling 'obligations' or 'commitments' (often used as an euphemism for, if not denial of drain)[26] or the 'external drain' required large increases in the revenues raised by Government of India or the 'internal drain' in order to pay for the external drain. Again, the only possible area where revenue could be increased substantially was customs revenue, which primarily meant import duties. Thus between 1901–5 and 1936–7 while the total revenue raised by Government of India more than doubled, *customs alone met about 72 per cent of the increase* in total revenue. Customs which had overtaken land revenue as the principal source of revenue by 1921–25 was thus critical in the maintenance of the rapidly increasing remittances of the Government of India on account of home charges, military expenditure, etc.[27].

The import duties on cotton goods had gone up from 3.5 per cent in the 1890s to 25 per cent for British cotton goods in 1931. (Duty on non-British, mainly Japanese goods had risen to 75 per cent by 1933). The countervailing excise of 3.5 per cent levied in 1896 however could not be increased in the changed political circumstances with a powerful anti-imperialist mass movement having come up in the meantime. Significantly, this change in scenario was not seen by the British government as the *surrender* of imperial interest, even if that may have been the view of some imperialist scholars. Samuel Hoare, the Secretary of State for India, quite conscious of the crucial role played by import duties in maintaining imperial interests, argued against the Lancashire agitation for removal of cotton duties. Apart from the "disastrous" political consequences such a course of action would produce, he urged that it must be recognized that "the present level of tariff on British cotton goods" was necessary for revenue purposes for "without this revenue India would be unable to discharge its financial obligations in this country and provide for military expenditure."[28]

---

26 It is, for example, said that "we do not need a conspiracy theory of imperialism" to explain the Government of India's "day-to-day running of its own business" which "in financial terms meant two things only — obtaining adequate revenue to meet its commitments in India and Britain, and securing enough remittance to pay its sterling debts" or obligations. See Tomlinson 1979, p. 25–6. Tirthankar Roy's favoured euphemism was government's "expenditure commitments". Roy 2000, p. 254. The point, however, is to question the very legitimacy of the 'commitments' or 'obligations' to begin with.

27 See Thomas 1939, p. 500–501 and Mukherjee 2002, p. 177–180, Tables 6.1 and 6.2.

28 Samuel Hoare to Kirpatrick, M.P., 3 February 1933, *Secretary of State's Private Office Papers,* L/PO/270, India Office Records (IOR), London. For a detailed discussion on the fiscal policy since W.W.I and maintenance of imperial interest, see Mukherjee 2002, Chs 5–8 on Tariffs, Trade and Industry from 1916 to 1947, the figures in this para are from p. 180.

Maintenance of remittance from India to Britain at any cost became the centre piece of British economic policy in this period for yet another reason. Britain, having lost its industrial supremacy in the world (first in consumer goods and later in capital goods as well) by the end of the 19th century and particularly by the beginning of the 20th century, was increasingly emerging as the major financial centre of the world with the pound sterling as its foundation[29] – a position that Britain was able to maintain till W.W.II to a large extent with the aid of India, by manipulating blatantly her currency, exchange and budgetary and financial policy.

It is small wonder, then, that finance was one portfolio the British refused to part with (even in the limited sense of appointing an Indian of *their* choice to the Viceroy's Executive Council) till the very end, i.e., till the formation of the Interim Government in 1946. Several other economic portfolios such as those of commerce, industry, planning and development, and supply were given to Indian members long before that. Even when the colonial Government set up the Reserve Bank of India in 1935, it was barely given any autonomy, with the British government insisting on "the last word" on financial matters. The bank, seen as an *instrument* for safeguarding imperial financial interests, was not to be allowed to be misused by Indians who "like a spoilt, wilful, naughty child" would instantly want to use it to demand financial responsibility[30].

An India Office document of December 1930, marked 'secret' and called "The Position of the Secretary of State in Relation to Indian Finance,"[31] brings out clearly some of the reasons for the crucial importance attached to the issue of finance by the British. It was stated that about 60 per cent of the Indian Government's budget, i.e., about £60 million out of £100 million, was absorbed by military expenditure, sterling debt charges and liabilities in respect of salaries and pensions for officials for which the Secretary of State was responsible. Of this, defence expenditure alone absorbed 45 per cent of

---

29 Hobsbawm 1969, Chapter 7, particularly, p. 148–153.

30 Neville Chamberlain, Chancellor of Exchequer and Samuel Hoare, Secretary of State at a cabinet meeting, Minutes of Meeting of the Cabinet Committee regarding Financial Safeguards, 4 November 1932, *Financial Collection,* L/F/5/191, India Office Records, London. The 'naughty child' statement is Chamberlain's. For a detailed discussion on the Reserve Bank, see Mukherjee 1992 and 2002, ch. 4, sec. V.

31 8 Dec. 1930, *Finance Department* (L/F)/5/191, IOR, London. See also another similar document dated June 17, 1931, signed by R.A. Mont, H. Strakosch, L.J. Kershaw and C.H. Kisch, L/F/5/191, IOR, London.

the central revenues. [32] When such a large proportion of the revenue was ear-marked for charges for which the Secretary of State was responsible, it was pointed out that "it is hardly open to doubt that Parliament should retain the power to secure that its obligations are duly honoured"[33]. Since the "revenues from which these commitments must be met are collected in rupees", and the 'commitments' were in sterling, it was "incumbent" upon the Secretary of State to see "that currency and exchange are being so managed" as to "permit of the remittances of the requisite funds from India to London". Also, he had to ensure that the revenue and expenditure of the Government of India were balanced[34]. In other words, the Secretary of State needed the "power to *impose* on the Indian Executive such measures as are needed to *provide the funds* and to *facilitate their transfer*… from India to London[35]. Some decolonization!

Before I go on to outline other aspects of the fiscal and monetary policy followed by Britain in this period to meet its growing imperial *financial* interests, it must be noted that the rising tariffs did not mean that Britain was ready to withdraw from trying to maintain its *industrial* interest in the colonial market, i.e., decolonize even in this limited sense. While it is true that British exports to India were shrinking rapidly since W.W.I, (except in chemicals where they increased) India still remained, as late as 1938, the *largest* single market for British exports of cotton piece-goods as it did for general machinery and other items[36]. The Indian market though shrinking was thus far from redundant, on the contrary its importance *increased* as British share in world trade kept declining. Basudev Chatterjee has ably demonstrated how Lancashire was desperate to hang on to

---

32 Basudev Chatterjee citing the June 1931 document says that "the aggregate annual charges under the heads of defence, debt servicing and salaries and pension […] 'would […] absorb three quarters of the total revenues of the Federation'". Chatterjee 1992.

33 'The position of the Secretary of State…', 8 Dec. 1930, L/F/5/191, *op. cit.*, p. 3, 8. Assurances that the Indian Federal Government would meet these obligations as a first charge on the government budget were clearly not considered enough. The note anticipated and rejected parallels with Australia in this regard that were repeatedly drawn by Indian capitalist and nationalist leaders with the argument, rarely made publicly, that "Australia, however, is a country where the government is of *our own kith and kin*." *ibid.*, p. 9 emphasis mine. Many colonial scholars like Drummond and more recently Ferguson 2003, fail to note the critical differences between British presence in USA, Canada, Australia and in colonies like India or West Indies when talking of the British 'empire'.

34 *Ibid.*, p. 2, 4.

35 *Ibid.*, p. 11, emphasis mine.

36 Tomlinson 1979, p. 46.

the Indian market and Britain tried to ensure that it did, as much as the new circumstances would permit. [37] By introducing the principle of Imperial Preference at Ottawa and through the various trade agreements of the 1930s Britain was making a last ditch effort to retain as much of the Indian market as was possible at a time when Britain was no longer able to compete effectively with other countries in various commodities, such as Japan in cotton textiles. There were however limits to how much imperial preference could be given to British goods as it could lead to retaliation by other countries, which in turn would affect Indian exports. This could not be permitted as India had to generate an export surplus at any cost so that the smooth flow of remittance to Britain could be sustained as imperial financial interests would not countenance any interruption in that process[38].

It is to ensure that India remained a constant source of capital to Britain through remittances, during a period when Britain just flitted from one crisis to the other (especially the two world wars and the depression), that the most gross use of imperial authority was made to turn the instruments of economic policy in her favour and against Indian interest.

To the great anguish of Indian nationalist opinion, the colonial government, in order to "manage" the currency and exchange in such a manner that the process of raising revenue in India and its remittance to Britain remained undisturbed, constantly followed a deflationary policy in India, including by severely contracting the currency in circulation, in order to push up the exchange value of the Rupee which it tried to keep at 1s. 6d. by virtual decree. A fiscal and monetary deflationary policy including severe cuts in Government capital expenditure was followed even during the Depression years, severely aggravating its negative consequences[39].

With the onset of the Great Depression, the situation in India changed drastically. World prices, especially those of primary produce, plummeted and

---

37 Chatterjee 1992.

38 See Mukherjee 2002, Chs 5–7 on Tariffs, Trade and Industry from 1916 to 1939 for a detailed discussion of the various trade agreements in the inter-war period.

39 See Mukherjee 2007; Aditya Mukherjee, "The Depression Years: Indian Capitalists' Critique of British Monetary and Financial Policy in India, 1929–39", in Bagchi 2002 and Mukherjee 2002, chs. 3–4 on Finance and Monetary Policy 1926–39, for a detailed discussion of British policy and Indian response on this question. Much of the advantage that Indian industry got due to the rise in tariffs in this period was smothered by the deflationary fiscal and monetary policy of the government. See Bagchi 1972, p. 66.

India's export earnings collapsed. With agricultural prices being so low, the Government was unable to collect full revenue[40]. Also, with the fall in export earnings, there was great difficulty in securing remittance to meet India's sterling obligations or the Home Charges[41]. With both revenue and remittance in jeopardy, the colonial Government was in the throes of a major financial crisis. Under continuous pressure from London,[42] the Government of India sought to ease remittance by resorting to severe deflation, contracting currency repeatedly, causing havoc in the Indian economy, especially in the money market.

A total breakdown of the remittance mechanism was averted by the massive export of gold from India that the government encouraged in this period. The gold exports were crucial in compensating for the drastic drop in India's export surplus on commodity transactions[43]. Between 1931–32 and 1938–39, on an average, more than half (about 55 per cent) of the total visible (positive) balance of trade (i.e. balance of transactions in merchandise and treasure) was met through the net exports of treasure, with the exports of gold increasing sharply in years when the commodity balance of trade was particularly low. For example, in 1932–33, *gold exports constituted about 95 per cent of the total visible positive balance of trade*[44]. Clearly remittance had to be maintained at all costs, if the export surplus in commodities (necessary to convert the rupee revenues into remittance) fell short it was made up through export of gold.

Apart from the role of gold exports in India's maintaining a smooth flow of remittance of the 'sterling obligations' or the Home Charges as well as the other invisibles such as profits, dividends and interests earned on foreign investments, it played another critical role for British interests at home. At a time when Britain

---

40 Schuster, Finance Member to Irwin, Viceroy, 1 June 1931, *Private Office Papers*, (L/PO)/269, IOR, London.

41 *Ibid.*

42 George Schuster, the Finance Member, wrote to Irwin on 1 June 1931: "We have been getting the usual telegrams from London trying to force us to contract, contract, contract and put up the bank rate – in their own words 'to create a money famine', which will make it impossible for people here to get rupees to sell for sterling. They say if you only do that you will get remittance". *L/PO/269*, IOR, London.

43 See Bannerji 1962, p. 22 and 27. Subramanian and Homfray 1946, p. 45–46 and Birla 1944, p. 17.

44 The above figures have been computed from Subramanian and Homfray 1946, Table XII, p. 45–46. C.B. Mehta of Bombay Bullion Exchange, cites similar figures for 1931 to 1938, Federation of Indian Chambers of Commerce and Industry, *Annual Report*, (hereafter FICCI, *A.R.*,) 1938, pp. 46–50. See also Kasturbhai Lalbhai, President, FICCI, A.R., 1935, p. 6.

was facing a balance of payment crisis it played a major part in strengthening the value of sterling vis-à-vis gold and other currencies[45].

It was small wonder then that the gold export from India was one issue on which the British home government remained very firm, though many countries including Britain were following an opposite strategy themselves. It appears that the Governor of the Reserve Bank of India, Osborne Smith, had to resign partially because of his taking a position on this question which was far too independent of the India Office and the Finance Department. He took a position similar to the nationalist demand for devaluation of the rupee to prevent outflow of hoarded gold from India[46].

However the blatant and cynical manner in which Britain used Indian finances for its own benefit during the Second World War was breathtaking in its audacity. It puts paid to any notion of imperialism withdrawing or decolonization having occurred till the bitter end of colonial rule. Britain took massive forced loans from India (popularly called the Sterling Balance) of about Rs.17,000 million (estimated at seventeen times the annual revenue of the Government of India and one-fifth of Britain's gross national product in 1947)[47] at a time when over three million Indians died of famine!

The Sterling Balances got accumulated as a result of the "large purchases of goods and services…made by the British Government, in India", against sterling bills or securities placed in reserve in London. For these large exports of goods and services, India, thus, received no "tangible quid pro quo" other than "I.O.U.s of His Majesty's Government"[48]. The procedure was similar to

---

45 See Balachandran 1996, particularly p. 178f.; Rothermund 1992; Walchand Hirachand, President, FICCI, A.R., 1933, p. 5; C.B. Mehta and M.R. Parikh, FICCI, A.R., 1933, p. 423; N.R. Sarkar, 5 Feb. 1932, *Purshotamdas Thakurdas Papers,* (PT Papers), press clippings, fl.11, NMML, and Purshotamdas, 5 May 1934, *PT Papers,* fl.76.

46 *L/PO/321*, IOR. For a detailed account of the unusually strong difference (expressed not quite with the celebrated British gentlemanly understatement) between Osborne Smith and the Government of India, especially the Finance Member, James Grigg, where Smith ended up calling the Viceroy a "weak ass, terrified of failure" and Grigg "a liar, undercover slanderer and mongrel…a dirty scurrilous swine", etc., see exchange of telegrams between the Secretary of State and the Viceroy, Sept.-Oct. 1936, *L/PO/321* and Osborne Smith to Purshotamdas, 16 Nov. and 24 Oct. 1936, *PT Papers,* fl.105.

47 Tomlinson 1979, p. 140.

48 Birla 1944, p. 18–21. See also, conclusions of War Cabinet meeting, 27 July 1943, *L/PO/325*, IOR, London.

that adopted during World War I – the Reserve Bank of India expanded currency or issued notes against its sterling holdings held in reserve in London to pay for the British war purchases in India[49]. The rapid expansion of currency that occurred as a result (the total notes issued increased by nearly four times between 1939 and 1944) combined with the fact that large quantities of goods and services were made available to England for which no goods or services came back to India in return, led to severe shortages and a runaway inflation[50]. What was shocking was that this policy could be pursued at a time when famine conditions prevailed in India. To cap it all, after the War was over, Britain made a serious bid towards defaulting on repayment of the loans raised at such tremendous cost to India[51].

The Second World War also saw British colonialism deny India yet another opportunity to make an industrial breakthrough an opportunity seized by the 'White' colonies. Indian entrepreneurs, who had already in the inter-war years shattered the bogey of India facing a lack of capital or entrepreneurship, or of Indian capital being 'shy' and unwilling to take risks, by growing rapidly, much faster than foreign capital in India and venturing into new areas,[52] were poised for a major industrial push during the Second World War.

The persistent efforts of Indian entrepreneurs to enter frontier areas of industry in India such as automobile, aircraft and locomotive manufacture, shipbuilding, manufacture of armaments, engineering goods, machine tools, etc., were smothered by the colonial state using fiscal, monetary and other instruments of

---

49 Secretary of State, L.S. Amery, Secret Note on Economic Situation in India, 11 Aug. 1943, *War Staff Papers* (L/WS), 1/581, IOR, London and War Cabinet Note on Indian Sterling Balances, 1 Aug. 1942, *L/PO/*325, IOR, London.

50 See L.S. Amery, Note on Economic Situation in India, 11 Aug., 1943, *L/WS/*1/581, IOR. *The Eastern Economist* (EE) criticized the Government of India for using the RBI to finance British expenditures without raising corresponding funds, e.g., by issuing rupee loans, but by simply issuing notes against sterling in England. This, the journal argued, was the worst form of inflationary finance, and the sterling credits represented the involuntary, forced savings inflicted on the Indian people, 26 Nov. 1943, p. 981.

51 For a full discussion of this issue see Mukherjee 1990 and 2002, ch. 5.

52 In fact, one of the crucial problems faced by the Indian capitalists was the "realization problem" – it was not shortage of resources but how to create conditions for converting the available resources into productive investment which bothered them. One may perhaps show a linkage between the more belligerent phases of Indian capitalists vis-à-vis the colonial government and their unrealized accumulations. See Mukherjee 2002, particularly ch. 9.

state policy such as the 'Capital Issues Control', all in the name of the "War effort," but in actuality in deference to imperial interests and even the interest of the white colonies[53].

The issue of the non-colonial type of development in late colonial India

To return to the question of the positive 'non-colonial' type of developments since the war, clearly they were not the result of any process of decolonization because, as I argue above, there was no such process occurring. Neither were these developments the *result* of colonialism itself. They were the product of space *wrenched* from it. As I have argued extensively elsewhere[54] it is easily demonstrable that all the developments listed above, occurred (to list some of the causes) either (a) as a result of the *struggle*, political and economic, against imperialism, whether through the national movement, legislative assemblies, business chambers or directly by entrepreneurs, as most demonstrably in the case of shipping, [55] or (b) when the grip of imperialism weakened or loosened due to world factors autonomous of the logic of the colonial system in the colony, such as the World Wars and the Great Depression,[56] or (c) when the principal metropolis Britain, lost out in competition to other metropolitan centres and preferred to permit indigenous enterprise in the colony to grow rather than allow other foreign powers to capture the colonial market, e.g., protection to cotton, iron and steel, matches and sugar was related respectively, to competition from Japan, Belgium and Germany, Sweden, and Java, a Dutch colony,[57] or (d) due to the inner contradictions of colonialism itself, e.g., the increasing need for revenue from the colony to meet imperial financial interests could no more be met from a by now stagnating or even declining agriculture but had to be met through revenue tariffs on

---

53 I have dealt with this at some length in Mukherjee 2002, ch. 9.

54 Mukherjee 2002, ch. 9.

55 There was a direct correlation between surges in the Indian national movement and economic concessions conceded by the colonial state. I have in great detail documented the efforts collectively as well as individually of Indian business to resist the 'collective monopoly' of British capital and wreak concessions from the colonial state in Mukherjee 2002. See also Bagchi 1972, ch. 6.

56 Bipan Chandra has documented how the spurts of growth experienced by Indian industry in this period was a result of the "loosening of the link" with colonialism during the two wars and the Great depression in "Colonialism and Modernisation" in Chandra 1979, pp. 1–37.

57 See the classic study by Adarkar 1939, p. 468–473 and Mukherjee 2002, ch. 6.

imports, which provided indigenous manufacture certain amount of protection against imperial industrial interests[58]. In other words, the specific non-colonial type of developments in the 20th century occurred *not as a result of colonialism but in spite of or in opposition to it.*

The very limited growth of the positive, non-colonial developments was occurring in an embryonic form in the hostile womb of colonialism whose continuation was making the birth of capitalism in India more and more difficult. The structural distortions created by colonialism made the future transition to self-sustained growth much more difficult. It required the overthrow of colonialism, and the 'un-structuring' of the colonial structure for India to start its attempt to build independent capitalism after colonialism for nearly two hundred years ravaged its economy and society and deprived it of the opportunity of participating in the process of modern industrial transformation occurring in other parts of the world. Despite the post W.W.I positive developments the Indian economy till 1947 remained essentially backward and structurally colonial. The Indian economy at independence was still basically dependent on a stagnating, low productivity, 'semi-feudal' agriculture with modern industry (in 1950) contributing a mere 6 to 8 per cent of the national income and (in 1951) employing 2.3 per cent of the labour force[59].

What India inherited after two hundred years of colonial 'benevolence', which allegedly gave India the 'advantages' of 'commercialization', 'exposure to the world market', 'transport and communication', 'a strong state', 'western scientific skills', etc., benefits that Tirthankar Roy could hardly stop listing, was a very sorry state of affairs indeed.

As Angus Maddison's monumental work shows, India was the largest economy of the world for the entire thousand years of the first millennium accounting for close to 30 per cent of the world's GDP. Till as late as the beginning of the 18th century India's was still the largest economy with about 25 per cent of the world's GDP, more than *eight times* that of the United Kingdom. The decline started soon after and at the end of nearly two hundred years of colonial rule (during which Tirthankar Roy claims "colonial India experienced positive economic growth")[60] India's share had been reduced to a mere 4.2 per cent in 1950. It was a few decades before India could sufficiently shrug off the colonial legacy and begin to gradually claw her way back into improving her share of the global pie[61].

---

58 As discussed in section II above.
59 Goldsmith 1983, p. 68 and Bipan Chandra, "The Colonial Legacy", in Jalan 1993, p. 8–9.
60 Roy 2000, p. 14.
61 Maddison 2007, table 8b, p. 641.

The impact of colonialism in human terms was traumatic and all too visible. At independence the *average* life expectancy was barely 30 years. The poor obviously died much younger. India was faced with acute food shortages creating near famine conditions repeatedly in different areas. The Bengal famine of 1943, just four years before the British left, claimed more than *three million* lives[62]. (A great tragedy which Tirthankar Roy predictably underplays, putting the famine deaths only at "some half a million", a figure much lower than even the official famine Inquiry Commission and other government estimates.)[63] Between 1946–53 about 14 million tons of food grains worth Rs.10,000 million had to be imported, seriously affecting India's planned development after independence. In 1951, 84 percent of the people (92 percent women) were illiterate. The legacy of colonialism which Tirthankar Roy misjudged so completely was anticipated by the poet Rabindranath Tagore, shortly before his death in 1941, in his inimitable way:[64]

The wheels of fate will some day compel the English to give up their Indian Empire. What kind of India will they leave behind, what stark misery? When the stream of their centuries' administration runs dry at last, what a waste of mud and filth will they leave behind them.

Post-Independence development

The growth that India witnessed *after* independence was not all about carrying on the 'good' work started during colonialism. It was a product of a structural break painstakingly crafted through a multi pronged planned effort — an unique effort of trying to industrialize and build capitalism with democracy and civil liberties. Jawaharlal Nehru and other leaders were deeply aware that India was experimenting with a hitherto uncharted path as none of the industrialized countries of the world had democracy and civil liberties during the initial period of transition to capitalism and industrialization. I have evaluated elsewhere the nature of this stupendous effort since

---

62 See Sen 1982, Appendix D, p. 195–216 for a comprehensive exercise in estimation of famine deaths during the Bengal famine. While the Famine Inquiry Commission put it at 1.5 million Sen convincingly argues why the figure is closer to around 3 million. See also Greenough 1982 where he argues a higher figure, and Batabyal 2005.

63 Sen 1982, Appendix D, p. 195–216 and Roy 2000, p. 257.

64 Quoted in Chandra, Mukherjee and Mukherjee 2000, p. 19.

independence[65]. I will only outline here a brief comparison of some of the features of the colonial period, especially the period of so called decolonization and positive growth since World War I with those of the period after independence. This may help underline the enormity of the break required, and to a considerable extent achieved.

The growth of per capita income in India in the colonial period was either zero or very low, remaining way below that of the independent countries of Europe, USA and Japan between 1820 and 1913. (See table 2.) In the last decades of colonial rule after colonialism had had its full impact, the *per capita* income in India actually *declined* at an annual rate of -0.22 per cent between 1913- 1950.[66] After independence, on the other hand, it grew at 1.4 per cent in the first couple of decades (about 3 times faster than the *best* phase, 1870–1913, under colonialism) and much faster at 3.01 per cent in the next 30 years, 1973–2001 (a rate considerably higher than that achieved by West Europe,[67] USA or Japan) and in the last four years (2003–4 to 2006–7) at an astounding 7 per cent (it was over 8 per cent in 2006–7) comparable to the explosive rates achieved by Japan (though in very special circumstances) between 1950–73[68].

---

65 Chandra, Mukherjee and Mukherjee 2000, p. 19; Mukherjee and Mukherjee 1988; Also reprinted in Shah 1990 and Chandra, Mukherjee and Mukherjee 2008, chs. 25–33. See also "Aspects of the Transformation Period of the Modern and Contemporary World", Chandra 2012.

66 The figures are all from Table 2 which is based on Maddison 2007, p. 643 except where indicated. Sivasubramonian and Heston's estimates show an annual growth rate of per capita income between 1914 to 1946 which is somewhat higher at 0.26 and 0.13 respectively but nevertheless prove our point reflecting the sharp contrast between before and after independence. M. Mukherjee's estimates of income growth are much lower than even Maddison's. See Goldsmith 1983, Table 1.2, p. 4.

67 West Europe as a whole grew at 1.88 per cent between 1973–2001. Maddison 2007, p. 643.

68 Figures for 2001–2007 are based on *Economic Survey, 2006–07*, Government of India, New Delhi 2007, Table 1.2, S-4, and Aditya Mukherjee, "Indian Economy in the New Millennium," in Chandra, Mukherjee and Mukherjee 2008. I have taken the per capita income growth rate for 2006–2007 at a conservative 8 per cent. S. Sivasubramonian's comprehensive and detailed study confirms the sharp break in aggregate growth rates as well as in different sectors of the economy between 1900–1947 and 1947–2000. See, e.g., Sivasubramonian 2000, Table 9.35, Fig. 9.5, p. 622–628.

Table 2: Rate of growth of per capita GDP (annual average compound growth rates)[69]

	1	2	3	4	5	6
	1820–1870	1870–1913	1913–1950	1950–1973	1973–2001	2001–2007
France	1.01	1.45	1.12	4.04	1.71	
UK	1.26	1.01	0.93	2.42	1.86	
USA	1.34	1.82	1.61	2.45	1.86	
Japan	0.19	1.48	0.88	8.06	2.14	
India	0.00	0.54	-0.22	1.40	3.01	5.65*

Similarly, the colonial period saw a process of de-industrialisation where traditional industry was largely destroyed and modern industry grew very slowly. Despite the growth of modern industry since W.W. I, at about 3.8 per cent per annum, it contributed a mere 6 to 8 per cent of the national product in 1950, having started from an extremely low level of 4 per cent of national product in 1913[70]. Moreover, modern industry was yet dominated by consumer goods industry with a near total and debilitating dependence on the advanced countries for capital goods and technology. Contrast this with the period after independence. Industry during the first three plans (1951–65) grew at 7.1 per cent per annum. More important, "the *three-fold* increase in aggregate index of industrial production between 1951 and 1969 was the result of a 70 per cent increase in consumer goods industries, a *quadrupling* of the intermediate goods production and a *ten-fold* increase in the output of capital goods."[71] This pattern of industrial development led to a structural transformation of the colonial legacy. From a situation where to make any capital investment, virtually the entire equipment had to be imported (in 1950, India met nearly 90 per cent of its needs of even machine tools through imports) the share of imported equipment in the total fixed investment in the form of equipment in India had come down to 43 per cent in 1960 and a mere 9 per cent in 1974, whereas the value of the fixed investment in India increased by about two and a half times

---

69 Source: Column 1 to 5 from Maddison 2007, Table 8b, p. 643. Column 6 is based on *Economic Survey, 2006–2007,* Government of India, New Delhi 2007, and Aditya Mukherjee, "Indian Economy in the New Millennium," in Chandra, Mukherjee and Mukherjee 2008. * : per capita net national product.

70 Goldsmith 1983, p. 68 and Bipan Chandra, "Colonial Legacy" in Chandra, Mukherjee and Mukherjee 2008, p. 8–9.

71 A. Vaidyanathan, "The Indian Economy Since Independence (1947–1970)", in Kumar 1983, p. 961, emphasis mine.

over this period (1960–74)[72]. This was a major achievement, and it considerably increased India's autonomy from the advanced countries in determining her own rate of capital accumulation or growth.

Agriculture, the largest sector of the Indian economy, was in a state of ruin under colonialism. Per-capita agricultural output actually *fell* at the rate of 0.72 per cent per year during 1911–1941. Per-capita food grains output fell even more sharply by 1.14 per cent per year, a 29 per cent fall over the period[73]. All crop *yields* per acre declined by 0.01 per cent per year between 1891–1946 and again food grain yields declined more rapidly by 0.18 per cent, and even more sharply by 0.44 per cent per year between 1921–46[74]. No wonder the food shortages and famine conditions mentioned above. After independence, a combination of institutional changes (land reforms) and massive state sponsored technological change transformed this situation[75]. During the first three plans (leaving out 1965–66, a drought year), Indian agriculture grew at an annual rate of over 3 per cent, a growth rate more than *eight times faster* than the annual growth rate of 0.37 per cent achieved during the half a century (1891–1946) of the last phase of colonialism in India[76]. The Green Revolution in the late 1960s maintained a rate of growth ranging from about 2.5 to 3.5 per cent (primarily through increases in yield) till the mid 1990s[77] The Green Revolution areas like Punjab and Haryana did not have any *continuities* with trends in the colonial period as Tirthankar Roy, for example, argues[78]. Haryana was largely an extremely backward area in colonial times and even Punjab showed meager growth rates in terms of all-crop yields per acre of 0.36 per cent per annum between 1901–1941 by one estimate and of only 0.06 per cent between 1906–7 and 1941–42 by another. The highest increases in yield seen in

---

72 See Aditya Mukherjee, "Planned Development in India 1947–65: The Nehruvian Legacy" in Akita 2000; also in Chandra, Mukherjee and Mukherjee 2008, ch.25. These figures are from an extremely persuasive piece by Kelkar 1980.

73 Blyn 1966, p. 123 and p. 102. See also Goldsmith 1983, p. 68.

74 Blyn 1966, Table 7.1, p. 151, Table 5a, p. 327 and p. 83–85 for an explanation of how Blyn uses ten 'reference decades' for his analysis. See also Sivasubramonian 2000.

75 See my chapters on "Land Reforms and the Green Revolution", in Chandra, Mukherjee and Mukherjee 2008.

76 See Blyn 1966, Table 5.8, p. 119; Raj 1965 for the pre and post-independence figures respectively. See also my chapter on "The Indian Economy, 1947–65: The Nehruvian Legacy", in Chandra, Mukherjee and Mukherjee 2008.

77 See my chapter "Agricultural Growth and the Green Revolution", in Chandra, Mukherjee and Mukherjee 2008.

78 Roy 2000, Ch.3, e.g., p. 51.

Punjab were in non-food crops of an average of 1 per cent per annum between 1891–1951[79]. In contrast the value productivity of eleven major crops in Punjab increased between 1950–51 and 1969–70 by 255 per cent, i.e., an average annual increase of more than 12.5 per cent[80]. The huge productivity difference certainly signifies a *structural* break.

Table 3: *Gross Domestic Capital Formation (GDCF) as percentage of GDP, Public Expenditure at Current Prices and Public Expenditure as Percentage of GDP 1901–2006 (All figures are annual averages)*[81]

	GDCF as % of GDP	Public Expenditure in Million Rupees (current prices)	Share of Public Expenditure in Gross Domestic Capital Formation (GDCF) as % of GDP
1901–1913	06.92*	754 (1925–30)#	
1914–1946	06.75*	417 (1930–38)#	
1950–1955	09.04	3,318	3.14
1955–1960	13.3	7,696	5.62
1960–1970	14.66	1,9121	6.96
1970–1980	17.63	80,034	8.19
1980–1990	21.23	264,169	9.98
2004–2006	32.65		

The rate of capital formation, the key to economic development, occurred at a very slow pace during the colonial period. India was in fact losing to Britain as drain or tribute an equal proportion, if not more, of what was invested in India. The drain has been variously calculated to be between 5 to 10 per cent of her national income[82]. The average annual rate of capital formation between 1901

---

79 See Mukherjee 2006, p. 157–161, the first estimate is computed from Blyn and the second is of John Lindauer and Sarjit Singh.

80 Mukherjee 2006, p. 162.

81 Source: Computed from *Economic Survey 2006–07*, Government of India, New Delhi, 2007, Tables 1.4 and 1.5, S-6 to S-9. *: Goldsmith 1983, Table 1–10, p. 20 and Table 2–9, p. 80. #: Computed from Ray 1979, Table 40, p. 257.

82 See for example Irfan Habib, "Colonization of the Indian Economy 1757–1900", in Habib 1995 pp. 304–5 and Bipan Chandra, chapter on "The Colonial Legacy", in Chandra, Mukherjee and Mukherjee 2008, p. 10. See also f. n. 19 above for other estimates of the drain.

to 1913 was 6.92 per cent of GDP, falling to 6.75 per cent between 1914–46
(see Table 3). Public expenditure, an important engine of capital formation
in backward countries, declined sharply from Rs. 75.4 crores annually during
1925–1930 to Rs. 41.7 crores during the Depression years 1930–38, when the
opposite needed to be done. The massive cut in government expenditure along
with other deflationary fiscal and monetary policies greatly exacerbated the
negative effects of the Depression on the Indian economy.

The contrast between the colonial and the post-independence scenario is
evident. While public expenditure was low and *declining* during the last decades of colonial rule[83] the initial forty years of independence (1950–1990) saw
it rise by more than three times (see Table 3, column 2 and 3). Similarly, while
the last fifty years or so of colonial rule (1901–1946) saw the gross capital formation in the economy hover around 6 to 7 per cent of GDP annually, the first
fifty years after independence saw the rate of capital formation rise consistently
and sharply, ending up at a rate of 33.8 per cent in 2005–06 about *five times* the
colonial rate[84].

There was also a rapid *per capita* increase in the availability of some of the in-
frastructural and social benefits as they grew several times faster than the population immediately after independence. In 1965–66, as compared to 1950–51,
installed capacity of electricity was 4.5 times higher, number of town and villages electrified was 14 times higher, hospital beds 2.5 times higher, enrollment
in schools was a little less than 3 times higher and very importantly admission
capacity in technical education (engineering and technology) at the degree and
diploma levels was higher by 6 and 8.5 times, respectively. This when population
increased only by 37.3 per cent over the period[85].

Also, Jawaharlal Nehru and the early Indian planners were acutely aware of
India's backwardness in science and technology (an area left consciously bar-
ren in the colonial period) and therefore made massive efforts to overcome this
shortcoming. An unprecedented increase occurred in the educational opportunities in science and technology in the universities and institutes. National
expenditure on scientific research and development kept growing rapidly with
each plan. For example, it increased from Rs. 10 million in 1949 to Rs. 4.5 billion
in 1977. Over roughly the same period the stock of India's scientific and technical manpower increased more than 12 times from 190 thousand to 2.32 million.

---

83 Increase in expenditure during the Second World War was due to British War needs
    and not capital expenditure promoting development in India.
84 See Table3, column 1 and *Economic Survey 2006–0, op.cit.,*I Table 1.5, S-9.
85 Calculated from Bhagwati and Desai 1970, p. 74.

A spectacular growth by any standards, a growth whose benefits India reaps today as the world moves towards a 'knowledge' society[86].

The quantum jump in investments, growth rates, improvements in health, education etc., listed above did not occur because of any dramatic change in India's "climatic risks," "resource endowments," "hunger for gold," or tendency to "have sumptuous marriage feasts," some of the causes listed by Tirthankar Roy for the Indian economy stagnating in the colonial period[87]. They occurred because of the concerted effort to break away from the disabilities created by the colonial structure.

However despite the paradigmatic change since independence India is still faced with intolerable levels of poverty and backwardness[88]. Undoing the ravages of nearly two hundred years of colonialism was never going to be an easy task. What is certain, however, is that the answers to the future challenges would not lie in building on the continuities with colonialism but on the breaks.

---

86 See Aditya Mukherjee, "Indian Economy, 1947–65: The Nehruvian Legacy", in Chandra, Mukherjee and Mukherjee 2008, p. 349.

87 Roy 2000.

88 See Aditya Mukherjee, "Indian Economy in the New Millennium", in Chandra, Mukherjee and Mukherjee 2008 where I have highlighted the spectacular growth along with the immense human development challenges.

Agnès Maillot
Dublin City University

Arthur Griffith's *Sinn Féin* and Non-Violent Resistance in India

When Arthur Griffith, founder of the *Sinn Féin* (SF) movement, died in August 1921, Mahatma Gandhi sent a letter expressing his sorrow and his regret upon hearing the news. Yet, whereas he praised the Irish nationalist for his visions on passive resistance, he was quite critical of what he saw as the mistaken path taken by the Irish independence movement, having moved away from the non-violence that its founder had advocated. As early as 1920, he made the following appraisal of the events unfolding in Ireland:

> "The Sinn Féiners resort to violence in every shape or form. [...] We may pardon it because we sympathise with their cause. But it does not on that account differ from General O'Dwyer's violence. [...] Our success depends on our ability to control all the violent and fanatical forces in our movement."[1]

Indeed, the party that had once advocated passive resistance was long gone by 1920, replaced by one that was closely associated to armed struggle and whose name had been used, or rather misused, as early as 1916 by the British authorities, in relation to the 1916 Rising, a rebellion with which, ironically, *Sinn Féin* had had little if anything to do.

Nevertheless, the *Sinn Féin* movement, founded in 1905, was quite visionary both in terms of policy and orientation, as it defined a strategy that was quite novel. But Griffith's ground-breaking electoral strategy, summarised in the policy of abstentionism, and his approach to passive resistance, which could be said to have led to the tactic of hunger strikes so characteristic of subsequent generations of *Irish Republican Army* (IRA) prisoners, are rarely acknowledged. Indeed, scholarly works on passive, or non-violent, resistance, rarely if ever mention Griffith's name, in spite of the fact that there is no doubt that he had a major influence on his contemporaries, not only within the island of Ireland, but further afield. This article seeks to bridge the connection that existed between the early Indian independence movement and the *Sinn Féin* policy as advocated by Griffith. In order to investigate this, it will first look at the political legacy

---

1   Gandhi 1958, p. 219–220.

which Griffith inherited, and how this impacted on his policy choices. Providing some attention to the strategy itself and its specific characteristics, this paper will then assess how these theories were received by the early Indian independence movement.

The founding of Griffith's non-violent strategy: Irish influences and beyond

Griffith was, first and foremost, a scholar, a journalist, a writer and a great intellectual. His knowledge of and interest in history were extensive, and the strategy of passive resistance that he articulated owed in great part to his analysis of the tactics used by some of the leaders of nineteenth century nationalist Ireland. The *Land League*[2], for instance, could be considered a precursor of the tactic of civil disobedience, not only putting together a novel approach to resisting landowners, but giving the English language a new word: "boycott". This strategy was summarised in a speech delivered by Charles Stuart Parnell, then president of the *Land League*, in Ennis, on 19 September 1880:

> "When a man takes a farm from which another had been evicted you must shun him on the roadside when you meet him, you must shun him in the streets of the town, you must shun him in the shop, you must shun him in the fairgreen and in the marketplace and even in the place of worship, by leaving him alone, by putting him in a moral Coventry, by isolating him from the rest of his country as if he were the leper of old, you must show your detestation of the crime he has committed."[3]

But Griffith was also immersed in a culture of armed rebellion that had been a feature of Irish nationalism since the late eighteenth century and the passing of the Act of Union, which he saw as the core evil of the Irish situation, considering it "illegal and unconstitutional. Acceptance of seats in the British parliament by Irishmen cannot render this illegal enactment legal."[4]

Griffith was also quite critical of the Irish Parliamentary Party, especially since the downfall of Parnell. In his eyes, the tactic used by Irish nationalist MPs in Westminster, that of obstructionism, consisting in impeding or delaying the workings of the House of Commons as a form of protest, did not go far enough. In some way, Gandhi came to a similar conclusion some years after,

---

2   The *Irish National Land League* was founded in Castlebar, County Mayo in 1879, with Charles Stewart Parnell as its first President. The aims were to reduce the back rent payments due to landlords, and to facilitate the buying of soils by Irish peasants.
3   Quoted in McCaffrey 1995, p. 93.
4   Griffith 1904, p. 91.

when he stated that "Ireland gained absolutely nothing through the policy of harassment and obstruction, and remember, it had an able leader like Parnell to fight for it".[5]

Interestingly, however, Griffith was not opposed to armed strategy per se, which distinguishes him quite markedly from Gandhi and subsequent non-violent movements. In fact, he was, for a time, a member of the *Irish Republican Brotherhood* (IRB)[6]. But his practical spirit led him to conclude that no Irish military organisation would ever be a match for British imperial might and he eventually left the secret movement. As the paper that he co-founded with William Rooney in 1899, *United Irishman*, stated:

> "The United Irishman has never advocated armed resistance because – and only because – it knows that Ireland is unable at the present time to physically wage war against England. But it has maintained, and always shall maintain, the right of the Irish nation to assert and defend its independence by force of arms."[7]

Therefore, Griffith's passive resistance was not conceived in opposition to armed resistance. His biographers are keen to emphasise that he was an admirer of previous Irish revolutionaries Tone, Emmet and the *Young Irelanders*. What he sought was a third way, which would take Ireland down the path of neither parliamentarism nor militarism.

Griffith's main source of inspiration came from Hungary, which was where his most original, and probably most efficient and long-lasting proposal, came from. He did not so much invent a strategy as make use of another historical experience, that of the 1848 Hungarian revolution, adapting it to the Irish situation. His 1902 pamphlet, *The Resurrection of Hungary*, outlined the tactic used by the Hungarians to free themselves from the Austrian empire in the following terms: "The Hungarians rejected that policy (parliamentarism) and refused to permit their representatives to appear in the imperial Parliament. Six years of persistence in this attitude reduced the imperial parliament to impotence"[8].

The lesson to be learnt from the Hungarian experience was obvious: if it were to be translated to the Irish situation, the Irish nationalists would stand a better chance of achieving their objective:

---

5 Gandhi 1958, p. 56.
6 The IRB, considered the ancestor of the Irish Republican Army (IRA), was a secret organisation founded in 1858 with the aim of establishing in Ireland an independent democratic Republic.
7 McCartney 1973, p. 8.
8 Griffith 1904, p. 85.

"The parliamentary policy no longer attracts support. Its abandonment and substitution by the wise and self-respecting policy followed by the Hungarians in like circumstances will find no intelligent opponent save among those who place their personal interests above their country's welfare."[9]

Therefore, at the third annual convention of *Cumman na hGaedhal*[10], Griffith outlined his Hungarian policy and the following resolution was passed:

"That we call upon our countrymen abroad to withhold any assistance from the promoters of a useless, degrading and demoralising policy until such times as the members of the Irish Parliamentary Party substitute it for the policy of the Hungarian deputies and refuse to attend the British Parliament or to recognise its right to legislate for Ireland, remain at home to help in promoting Ireland's interests and to aid in guarding its national rights."[11]

Griffith's proposed withdrawal of all Irish MPs from Westminster to constitute their own assembly in Ireland presented, in his view, two main advantages. Firstly, it would put Ireland on a level playing field with Britain, giving her the status of nation as opposed to province which Griffith felt was downgrading. Secondly, it would give the Irish people the opportunity to be directly represented and therefore would offer the best possible form of resistance to British imperialism. This policy, called abstentionism, was to become a pillar of the independence process.

In the years that followed the setting up of the National Council, or *Sinn Féin* movement, some other nationalist movements followed suit and adopted the strategy. One such movement was the Dungannon Clubs, founded by Bulmer Hobson, who saw this as opening up the possibility of having "A representative council of the whole people of Ireland can be brought into existence, a Council which would have the full sanction and approval of the governed, and which would solely work in their interests"[12].

After the 1916 Rising, and in spite of the seeming change of mood within the nationalist movement, Griffith continued to insist on the importance of that strategy. Abstentionism was used in the 1918 General elections, when all *Sinn Féin* candidates campaigned for the right to form their own assembly were they to be elected. It then led to the establishment of *Dáil Éireann* in 1919, and

---

9   Griffith 1904, p. 96.
10 *Cumman na nGaedhael* was founded in 1900 by Griffith to protest against the visit of King Edward VII to Ireland.
11 Henry 1920, p. 66.
12 Hobson 1905, p. 4.

to some extent, to the creation of the *Sinn Féin* courts during the war of independence. So essentially, what Griffith had advocated became a truly revolutionary weapon insofar as it meant that the Irish put in place a comprehensive, alternative system of government in a country still under the authority of the British Empire.

Abstentionism was to become the cornerstone of resistance to the British presence in Ireland, the starting point of an analysis which deemed the institutions created by the 1921 partition illegitimate and therefore not to be recognised or worked with. It was, possibly, the most fundamental aspect of the passive resistance strategy advocated by Griffith and his followers.

Economic resistance

Griffith second main idea was based on the premise that political independence would mean nothing if it wasn't assorted with economic independence. Whereas he might have, as Lyons argues, overestimated the resources of his own country,[13] he placed a lot of emphasis on self-sufficiency: "Our policy, in one word, is to lead our people to Reliance in themselves"[14]. He thus put forward a policy of economic resistance which would not only impact directly on the British economy, but also give the Irish population a tangible role to play. His reasoning was simple:

> "The taxation of Ireland is 3/4th indirect – a method of taxation morally and politically the worst for a free country, but the method of oppression most easily used against a country enslaved (5)... Since two thirds of the taxation of Ireland is raised out of duties on articles of consumption which may be dispensed with, I have suggested that the people of Ireland should reduce their consumption of these articles by 1/3 to 1/2, a proceeding which, without involving a single person in the necessity of going to jail, would cost England between 2 and 3 million pounds a year."[15]

Economic resistance was to be pursued on three levels: individual, with the boycotting of English goods; local, by encouraging local government bodies to award contracts to Irish firms; and national, with the creation of a general council of Ireland County Councils as the national authority for the protection of Irish industry. This was to be accompanied by more symbolic gestures, all in the spirit of resistance, all aimed at weakening the image and the influence

---

13 Lyons 1983, p. 254: "*It can be made an objection against him that, like many others, he fell into the trap of overestimating Ireland's resources*".
14 Griffith 1905, p. 29.
15 Griffith 1905, p. 29.

of the British in Ireland. One such measure was the boycotting, or shunning, of its representatives. To this end, a National Council was set up as an ad-hoc group in 1903 to prevent a loyal address to Edward VII being presented by Dublin Corporation on his visit to Ireland. This then developed into a political movement:

> "The National council was established four years since. In the first year of its existence, by inducing the representative body of the Irish capital to decline recognition to the head of the British government on the occasion of his official visit to our country, it raised the Irish question to the level of International politics from the provincialised position to which a mistaken and degrading policy had caused it to be reduced."[16]

The passive resistance strategy was summarised in a pamphlet published in 1907[17] and it contained the following elements: boycott of British army and parliament, by preventing enlistment and through abstentionism; cultivation of the Irish language and nationalisation of education; refusal to welcome British monarchs visiting Ireland; withholding of taxes and opening up of trading with foreign countries; formation of arbitration courts for the settlement of industrial and other disputes among Irish people. If followed, this policy would make Ireland "irresistible", concluded the pamphlet.

This was actually the conclusion that Jawaharlal Nehru came to, after his visit to Ireland in the summer of 1907, while a student in Trinity College, Cambridge. In a letter to his father, he described this new strategy as follows:

> "Have you heard of the Sinn Féin in Ireland? It is a most interesting movement and resembles very closely the so-called extremist movement in India. Their policy is not to beg for favours but to wrest them. They do not want to fight England by arms but to ignore her, boycott her, and quietly assume the administration of Irish affairs". Among people who ought to know, this is causing consternation. They say that if this policy is adopted by the bulk of the country, English rule will be a thing of the past."[18]

However, although the quote is indeed interesting as a measure of the enthusiasm that the policy generated in the future Indian nationalist leader, Nehru didn't really dedicate much time, in his subsequent writings, to the Irish situation. On the other hand, a movement that was most influenced by *Sinn Féin* was undoubtedly Swadeshi. As early as 1906, there is mention, in Indian newspapers, of the *Sinn Féin* policy:

---

16 Sinn Féin [ed.] 1907, p. 2.
17 Lynd 1907.
18 Nehru 1965, p. 12.

"What is good for Ireland ought to be good for India in many respects [...] Mr Griffith was asked to think out a practical scheme for the amelioration of their condition. And he suggested the SF policy, which shows that he deserved the trust reposed in him by his country,. What we have to do now is to keep this scheme before us as our model, and utilise so much of it for our regeneration as is possible for us to do."[19]

Indeed, one of the tactics mentioned by the President of the Barisal Conference was reminiscent of Griffith's own strategy: "The word boycott may be offensive to some ears, but the success of the Swadeshi movement means the abstention from or boycotting of foreign goods [...] Surely in our own houses at least we are our own masters and can choose what articles to buy and what to reject"[20].

The Swadeshi movement, in line with the *Sinn Féin* ideals, promoted the use of the vernacular language and the creation of a national university. Similarly, their analysis of the Home Rule prospect for India held striking similarities with that of the Irish: "Have not the Irish for a number of decades been crying for Home Rule and have they not been crying in wilderness? What has so long been denied to the Irish cannot surely be granted in a hurry to the Bengalese"[21].

Both Indian and Irish were looking at each other's situations and making parallels. Even the vocabulary used by the Swadeshi movement had echoes with that of *Sinn Féin*:

"Heaven, itself, seems to have pointed out to us in the year of Swadeshi the real way, the way of Swadeshi: of the boycott of British goods, of national education, intellectual, moral, physical and technical, of the assumption of the people's work into the hands of the people. It order to follow that path we demand a strong organisation. We propose a **National Council [my emphasis]**."[22]

Sinn Féin saw obvious parallels between the situation of Ireland and that of India, and identified similar tactics used by the British to rule its empire, one of which was religious sectarianism. Indeed, the antagonisms that the British did not hesitate to exploit in Ireland, those between Protestants and Catholics, had their equivalent in India, between what the SF paper labelled "Mahommetans and Hindus":

"The rapid progress of the Indian Sinn Féin movement is testified by the open approval given by the English press to the formation of an association for the promotion of sectarian hatred amongst the Indians. England has ruled in India as she rules in Ireland, by setting the rival sects at each others' throats. Hindu and Mahommetans answer to

---

19 *Sinn Féin*, 4 August 1906.
20 *Sinn Féin*, 4 August 1906.
21 *Sinn Féin*, 1 December 1906.
22 *Sinn Féin*, 1 December 1906.

Catholics and Protestants in Ireland so far as English imperial policy is concerned. The Swadeshi movement has broken through that policy and combined, for the first time in history, the two seats in the common bond of Indian nationalism."[23]

Conclusion

Griffith's non-violence as advocated by the early *Sinn Féin* was essentially pragmatic. He did not preach it from a moral or spiritual viewpoint, but because it worked, because he saw it as the best possible alternative. It was the weapon of the weaker party faced with the colossal power of the empire. However, the Irish independence leaders, even those who had enthusiastically embraced passive resistance at an early stage, did not reject violence. The two were not seen as being incompatible, but rather as different stages of the independence process and in some way, complementary. As Bulmer Hobson, an early follower of Griffith, pointed out,

"As the government is weakened by passive resistance, the strength of the nation is built up. As they weaken, stronger methods can be applied until, ultimately, the relative strength of aggressive resistance and defendant people has to altered that even the attitude of devende can gradually be abandoned."[24]

It is perhaps this blurring of the boundaries between passive resistance and violence that explains why so little attention has been paid to *Sinn Féin*'s earlier vision, as it is the anti-thesis of Gandhi's preaching:

"Indeed, violence is the negation of this great spiritual force, which can only be cultivated or wielded by those who will entirely eschew violence. It is a force that may be used by individuals as well as by communities. It may be used as well in political and domestic affairs. Its universal applicability is a demonstration of its permanence and invincibility."[25]

Nevertheless, it is undeniable that Griffith's *Sinn Féin* policy left its mark in the Indian context, and possibly further afield. As noted by one of Griffith's biographers,

"The political situation in one part of the UK at the very core of the Empire had been deeply affected by Griffith's reading of history and the propagandist use he made of it. And the tremors that emanated from Griffith's historical views were eventually felt, however faintly, in the British Empire beyond."[26]

---

23 *Sinn Féin*, 9 March 1907.
24 Davis 1959, p. 29–44.
25 Geetha 2004, p. 66.
26 McCartney 1973, p. 19.

Ingrid C. Sankey
Université Catholique de Lille

Les princes et le Raj britannique ou les aléas du système d'administration indirecte dans l' Empire des Indes

Introduction

Après la Révolte de 1857, la politique d'appui sur les élites naturelles grâce à un système d'administration indirect (*Indirect Rule*) avait permis aux Britanniques de contrôler plus ou moins directement le tiers du sous-continent qui leur échappait encore, et ce, sans heurts majeurs, ni coût excessif, jusqu'en 1947[1]. Soutenir l'ordre ancien permettait de prévenir un ordre nouveau d'émerger trop rapidement.

De leur côté, les princes purent maintenir une certaine illusion de pouvoir dans les derniers jours du *Raj*[2]. Cependant, lorsque les Britanniques n'eurent plus besoin d'eux, ils furent abandonnés à leur sort. Accusés de collaboration avec les Britanniques après l'Indépendance, ils virent leurs privilèges graduellement réduits, puis confisqués par le jeune gouvernement indien.

Or, pour conserver l'appui des princes dans les derniers jours du *Raj*, la politique britannique envers ces derniers s'était considérablement assouplie. Il n'était plus question de s'immiscer dans les affaires privées des souverains (*Darbar*[3]), ni de leur donner des conseils de bonne gouvernance. Les discours

---

1   Pour un bilan historiographique sur cette question de l'*Indirect Rule*, voir Hira Singh dans Ernst and Pati 2007, p. 26 : « A model for the study of the princely states during colonial rule has to be premised on resistance by the landed aristocracy, the ruling class in the princely states, to the colonial state's attempt to encroach upon its traditional economic, political rights and symbols of authority resulting in compromise and accommodation. »

2   Ikegame 2012 permettra de mieux comprendre l'adaptation à la modernité des princes indiens au pouvoir dans l'état de Mysore, ce qui donnera un aperçu loin des clichés courants sur la question. Voir aussi les deux études de Copland 2005 sur les bonnes relations qu'entretenaient hindous et musulmans dans ces états, contrairement au reste de l'Inde britannique, ainsi que Copland 1997 sur la rapide disparition de ces mêmes états princiers.

3   *Darbar* ou *Durbar* (selon les transcriptions) : terme d'origine persane désignant l'audience générale donnée aux dignitaires de l'empire par l'empereur moghol ; à

de l'époque et la création d'une Chambre des princes dans l'entre-deux-guerres, sont révélateurs d'un changement de cap qui montre bien la fragilité croissante du gouvernement colonial. Dès lors, l'orientation que choisirent les Britanniques fut le *laisser-faire*. Les résidents et les agents politiques du régime colonial se contentèrent alors d'un rôle de représentation, chassant le tigre avec les *rajahs* et les *nababs*.

En retraçant les grandes lignes de cette histoire mouvementée dans les dernières années du *Raj*, on montrera comment l'évolution de la politique coloniale envers les États princiers permet de mesurer la fragilité croissante du pouvoir britannique dans le sous-continent entre 1914 et 1930. Puis on abordera les évolutions majeures de la politique d'*Indirect Rule* suite à la Première Guerre mondiale jusqu'à la création d'une Chambre des princes en 1921, en passant par les évolutions doctrinales au sein du *Political Service*.

La Première Guerre mondiale : le révélateur d'une tendance plus ancienne

L'Inde participa à l'effort de guerre sous la forme de contributions financières et de l'envoi de troupes importantes (le plus important contingent de troupes volontaires au monde)[4]. Ces dernières furent déployées en France, en Égypte (protection du Canal de Suez), au Moyen-Orient et surtout en Mésopotamie où l'essentiel des troupes était originaire des Indes britanniques, à tel point que le sous-continent se trouva à un moment presque dépourvu de présence militaire. De leur côté, les princes n'étaient pas en reste et participèrent activement à l'effort général, certains allant jusqu'à se battre en personne sur les champs de bataille européens, tels le Maharajah Ganga Singh de Bikaner (1880–1943), qui mit ses ressources personnelles au service du *Government of India* et servit en France et en Égypte ou le Maharajah Bhupinder Singh de Patiala (1891–1938) qui servit, entre autres, en France et en Palestine.

---

l'époque du Raj, réunion solennelle de l'aristocratie princière autour du souverain (ou de son représentant). Il s'agissait le plus souvent de fastueuses cérémonies au cours desquelles les représentants britanniques récompensaient les princes les plus loyaux et les plus méritants par l'octroi de terres et de titres honorifiques. Dans certains royaumes rajputs et dans les documents britanniques, ce terme désigne également la personne du prince et par la même occasion de son gouvernement.

4   Voir Sehrawat 2007.

Or, cette poussée de loyalisme ne devait pas durer car la défaite des Britanniques à Gallipoli en 1915 puis, en 1916, la prise de Kut[5], en Mésopotamie, par les Ottomans, après une retraite désastreuse et un long siège de la ville où s'étaient retranchées les troupes anglo-indiennes, remettaient en question l'invincibilité supposée de la puissance coloniale. Il devenait urgent de réagir même si le gouvernement britannique aurait préféré attendre la fin du conflit.

Ainsi, dès février 1916, sous la vice-royauté de Lord Hardinge[6] entre 1910 et 1916, une commission composée, entre autres, des maharajahs de Bikaner et de Gwalior, de la *Begum* de Bhopal, du Secrétaire du *Foreign and Political Department*, John Wood (nommé en 1914) et de deux agents politiques, se réunit à Delhi afin de discuter de la politique impériale dans les cas, souvent controversés, des *minority administrations*[7], c'est-à-dire l'administration d'un État princier par un agent du gouvernement colonial lorsque l'héritier du trône se trouvait être mineur. Cette rencontre faisait suite à une plainte, en 1915, du maharajah Scindia de Gwalior, qui regrettait que cette pratique éloignait le peuple des États concernés de leurs dirigeants légitimes et que cela contribuait à remettre en cause l'adhésion du peuple à ses coutumes et traditions séculaires. À l'issue de cette rencontre, il fut décidé que toute mesure prise par les agents britanniques au cours d'une telle administration serait révocable après l'accession de l'héritier du trône. Cette nouvelle concession est bien révélatrice du changement de cap

---

5   C'est en partie suite au désastre de Kut que le Secrétaire d'État à l'Inde, le conservateur Austen Chamberlain démissionna, cédant sa place au libéral Edwin Montagu en 1917.

6   Vice-roi de 1910 à 1916.

7   Le terme *minority administration* désignait la période de régence exercée par un agent colonial dans un État princier lorsque le prince héritier était mineur au moment de son accession au trône. C'était l'occasion pour le gouvernement de l'Inde d'exercer un maximum d'ingérence dans les affaires des États princiers. Durant toute la période pendant laquelle le jeune prince était mineur, le gouvernement de l'État était alors entre les mains d'un agent politique, parfois aidé dans sa tâche par un conseil de régence nommé par les Britanniques. En effet, le gouvernement de l'Inde se considérait dès lors comme le gardien légitime des intérêts du futur héritier, garant de ses droits et des traditions de son État. Ainsi, les Britanniques devenaient alors les maîtres tout-puissants de l'État et en profitaient bien souvent pour y introduire de nombreuses réformes. Cependant, dans les années précédant la Première Guerre mondiale, il fut de plus en plus demandé aux agents politiques de respecter les anciennes traditions et coutumes des États dont ces derniers avaient la charge. Dès lors, le point le plus délicat d'une *minority administration* fut de jongler avec les traditions de l'État tout en profitant de l'occasion pour y introduire les réformes souhaitées par le gouvernement colonial.

de la politique impériale et de la position, fragilisée par la guerre, de la puissance coloniale.

En avril 1916, Chelmsford remplaça Hardinge comme vice-roi de 1916 à 1921 et, en 1917, le libéral Edwin Montagu (1879–1924) remplaça le conservateur Austen Chamberlain (1863–1937) en tant que Secrétaire d'État à l'Inde jusqu'en 1922. Montagu avait déjà une bonne expérience des princes et des États princiers de l'Inde puisqu'il avait effectué un tour de ces États au cours de l'hiver 1912–1913. Il effectua un second tour de ces États de novembre 1917 à avril 1918, afin d'avoir une vue d'ensemble des aspirations des princes avant de rédiger son célèbre rapport conjoint avec Lord Chelmsford (1868–1933). Au cours de ces deux visites, il garda un excellent souvenir des princes occidentalisés qu'il qualifia de personnalités parmi les plus distinguées de l'Inde et, par contraste, condamna l'attitude pompeuse et autoritaire des agents du *Political Service*. D'après lui, ces derniers étaient les principaux responsables des plaintes et des revendications des princes[8].

Chelmsford demanda alors à un comité de se réunir afin de rédiger un rapport rassemblant les doléances des princes. Ce comité, composé des *maharajahs* de Bikaner, d'Alwar, de Patiala et de Nawanagar, rendit son rapport au vice-roi quelque temps plus tard. L'essentiel des demandes visait à protéger les princes contre un usage abusif de la politique de *Paramountcy* (ou suzeraineté britannique sur leurs États)[9], et, pour ce faire, les princes recommandaient l'établissement d'une Chambre des princes régnants (*Chamber of Ruling Princes*). Une rencontre entre Montagu, Chelmsford et les princes se tint à Delhi en février 1918 pour discuter de ce rapport. Cette nouvelle réunion rassemblait les *maharajahs* de Jaipur, Jodhpur, et Kolhapur, le *Maharao* de Cutch, et la *Begum* de Bhopal.

C'est donc avant la fin de la Première Guerre mondiale que le rapport de recommandations issu de ces rencontres avec les princes, nommé *Montagu-Chelmsford Reform Proposals*[10], redéfinit complètement la politique du gouvernement britannique dans l'Inde coloniale, mais aussi la stratégie qui guidait les relations de ce dernier avec les États princiers. Une partie de ce rapport était ainsi consacré à ce sujet. L'action du *Political Department*, spécialement sous la vice-royauté de Lord Curzon (1859–1925), y était vivement critiquée. En effet,

---

8   Ashton 1982, p. 53.

9   Concept imprécis inventé par Charles Metcalfe (1785–1846), agent de l'*East India Company* utilisé sans valeur légale, mais qui fait référence au devoir des Britanniques d'assurer la bonne transmission du pouvoir à une aristocratie locale vassale des Britanniques en Inde, même après la conquête.

10   Wheeler 1918.

la tentative de ce dernier d'uniformiser le système des relations du pouvoir suzerain avec les États princiers avait abouti à des injustices car les grands États, qui étaient normalement dotés d'une plus grande autonomie du fait de la respectabilité de leur statut, étaient traités à la manière des petits États, qui jouissaient d'une moindre autonomie dans leurs affaires internes et étaient parfois même administrés comme des districts britanniques :

> « It was freely recognised in the Montagu-Chelmsford Report that the position of the States as it had evolved during the preceding few decades required reconsideration. The authors of the joint report recognised the injustice which had been done by the attempt of the Political Department to attain uniformity of practice. »[11]

Désormais, chaque État serait traité comme une entité particulière et unique. Ce procès fait au *Political Department* et à Curzon semble néanmoins un peu simpliste. Le *Political Department* semble avoir toujours agi au cas par cas et, même sous Curzon, n'était jamais parvenu à rendre ses rapports avec les États princiers homogènes. Le simple fait que certains États dépendaient de gouvernements provinciaux était une raison suffisante pour justifier différentes approches dans différents contextes.

Dans une section du rapport intitulée *Effects of the wars*, Montagu et Chelmsford rappelaient l'importance de l'effort de guerre réalisé par les États princiers et en profitaient pour souligner la communauté d'intérêts qui unissait les États princiers au gouvernement colonial :

> « No words of ours are needed to make known the services to the Empire which the States have rendered. They were a profound surprise and a disappointment to the enemy; and a cause of delight and pride to those who knew beforehand the Princes devotion to the Crown. With one accord, the Rulers of the Native States in India rallied to fight for the Empire when war was declared; [...]. They have shown that our quarrel is their quarrel; and they have both learned and taught the lesson of their own indissoluble connection with the Empire, and their immense value as part of the polity in India. »[12]

Ainsi, les principaux développements du rapport portaient sur la reconnaissance d'une communauté d'intérêts entre les princes et la puissance coloniale. Il y était spécifié que les changements qui affectaient l'Inde affectaient également les États princiers :

> « Our immediate purpose is to point out how changes in British India may react upon the States. [...] There is a strong(er) reason why the present stir in British India cannot be a matter of indifference to the princes. Hopes and aspirations may overleap frontier

---

11 Directorate of the Chamber's Special Organization 1929, p. 96.
12 Wheeler 1918, p. 82, par. 298.

lines like sparks across a street. There are in the Native States men of like minds to those who have been active in spreading new ideas in India. It is not our task to prophesy: but no one would be surprised if constitutional changes in British India quickened the pace in the Native States as well. We know that the States cannot be unaffected by constitutional developments in adjoining provinces. […]. All that we need or can do is to open the door to the natural developments of the future. […]. With these indications of the position to be occupied by the Native States in future, we may rest content. We believe that the trend of events must draw them still closer into the orbit of the Empire; we think that the process need give rise to no alarm lest their internal autonomy be threatened. »[13]

Aux princes, qui réclamaient une réaffirmation de leurs droits et prérogatives, tels qu'ils étaient consignés dans les traités conclus avec l'*East India Company*, puis, réaffirmés et consolidés après la Révolte de 1857, le rapport rappelait la contrepartie de non-ingérence dans les affaires du gouvernement colonial.

« The independence of the States in matters of internal administration carries with it the counter-obligation of non-interference in British Indian affairs. […]. The obligation of mutual abstention must be always borne in mind in estimating the future position of the Native States in a changing Indian Empire. »[14]

Ces obligations mutuelles constituaient la base de discussion préalable de l'alliance des autorités coloniales avec les princes indiens. C'est justement le non-respect de ces droits par les agents du *Political Department* qui constituait, d'après les princes, la principale source de revendications. En effet, le degré d'ingérence autorisé dans les affaires des princes n'était pas spécifié dans les traités et dépendait de l'appréciation personnelle des agents concernés.

Ainsi, après un rappel historique des relations de l'Angleterre avec les États princiers, un rappel de l'effort de guerre consenti par les princes pour aider la puissance suzeraine lors de la Première Guerre mondiale et des nouvelles conditions politiques dans le sous-continent (modern influences), puis un rappel des droits et des obligations mutuelles des deux parties, le rapport Montagu-Chelmsford reconnaissait la nécessité d'une réinterprétation des traités préexistants dans le but de rassurer les princes quant à la protection que leur offrait la puissance suzeraine en échange de leur non-ingérence dans les affaires de l'Inde coloniale et de leur soutien inconditionnel à la cause impériale.

Par conséquent, si l'ingérence dans les affaires des princes avait été un mal nécessaire par le passé, elle n'était, au regard des nouvelles conditions politiques en Inde, plus du tout indispensable. Le *Political Department* se trouvait ainsi

---

13 Wheeler 1918, p. XLV et 84 à 91.
14 Wheeler 1918, p. 82.

complètement dépossédé de sa seule raison d'être. Quant aux droits et aux prérogatives des princes, ils furent constamment réaffirmés dans les discours des
souverains britanniques qui multiplièrent les proclamations en ce sens d'Edward
VII, en 1875–1876, à George V en 1911, en 1919 et en 1921. Ces proclamations
royales successives figurent en première page de l'édition de 1924 du manuel
d'instructions aux résidents et aux agents politiques.

Les différentes propositions émises par Chelmsford et Montagu dans le rapport, qui, rappelons-le, servit de préalable à l'*India Act* de 1919, concernant les
États princiers de l'Inde furent : l'établissement d'un Conseil des princes où seraient discutés les sujets relatifs aux États princiers, d'un Comité consultatif rela-
tif aux affaires des princes afin de conseiller le *Political Department* en la matière
et d'une Commission d'enquête, dite impartiale, en cas de litiges entre États, mais
aussi entre un État et l'Inde coloniale. Dans les cas de mauvaise gouvernance,
un Comité composé d'un haut juge et d'au moins deux princes statuerait et ren-
drait ses délibérations publiques. Les États seraient désormais en relation directe
avec le gouvernement colonial sans avoir besoin de passer par l'intermédiaire
des gouvernements provinciaux. Enfin, le rapport préconisait des délibérations
conjointes dans les litiges d'intérêts communs au gouvernement colonial et aux
États princiers.

Toutes ces mesures allaient dans le sens général d'un relâchement de la tutelle
coloniale et du développement d'une plus grande autonomie dans les processus
de décision, tant au sein du *Government of India* que dans les États princiers.
C'était le but avoué de l'ensemble des propositions de réforme qui allaient aboutir à l'*India Act* de 1919 comme le souligne d'ailleurs le grand défenseur et historien de l'Empire qu'était Vincent Arthur Smith (1843–1920) :

> « The principles of the Montagu-Chelmsford proposals, usually now known as the
> Montford reforms, were the recognition of self-government as the goal of British policy
> in India, the realization of that principle by instalments and judgement of the moment
> and manner of taking each step as a result of the co-operation received and responsi-
> bility shown. »[15]

Cependant, la Première Guerre mondiale allait avoir une autre conséquence, une
mesure difficile, hautement symbolique et révélatrice de l'évolution de la politique britannique en Inde dans les dernières années du *Raj*. Cette mesure, qui
avait été suggérée dès 1907 à l'époque du vice-roi Lord Minto (1845–1914), ne
verrait le jour qu'en 1921, après bien des difficultés qui n'émanaient pas nécessairement des Britanniques, contrairement à ce que l'on pourrait penser.

---

15 Smith 1970, p. 786–787.

À l'issue du conflit, la participation des troupes des États princiers à l'effort de guerre fit prendre conscience de l'importance de ces derniers dans la stabilité de l'édifice colonial, notamment à un moment où le mouvement anticolonialiste en Inde britannique commençait à prendre une certaine ampleur. Pour remercier les États princiers une Chambre des princes fut créée en 1921. Dès lors, les résidents perdirent l'un de leurs rôles essentiels, celui d'intermédiaire entre les princes et le pouvoir suzerain[16].

La création d'une Chambre des princes : étapes et difficultés

L'idée d'associer les princes à la politique impériale n'était pas nouvelle en Inde, mais souffrait d'un manque de volonté générale de la part du gouvernement colonial et du manque d'unité des princes eux-mêmes. En effet, jusqu'à la Première Guerre mondiale, les propositions en ce sens émanaient plus d'individus comme les vice-rois Lord Lytton (1831–1891) et, plus tard, Minto, que d'une réelle volonté politique du gouvernement britannique dans son ensemble. Là encore, le conflit mondial et la montée des revendications indépendantistes allaient changer quelque peu la donne. Ainsi, si Lytton avait évoqué l'idée d'une réunion informelle des princes une vingtaine d'années seulement après la Révolte des cipayes, c'est Minto qui tentera le premier projet concret en la matière, en 1907. Notons que même Curzon avait envisagé, puis abandonné, un projet similaire.

Face à la montée du terrorisme après la partition du Bengale par Curzon, et celle d'une frange extrémiste au sein du parti du Congrès, initialement modéré, le Secrétaire d'État à l'Inde, Lord Morley, demanda à Minto, dès 1906, d'envisager une rencontre informelle, une sorte de Conseil privé, qui réunirait, une fois par an, pendant une semaine ou deux, les princes mais aussi les membres les plus modérés du parti du Congrès. Contrairement à Morley, Minto ne pensait pas que le Congrès deviendrait assez puissant pour constituer une menace pour l'Inde coloniale[17]. Néanmoins, il s'exécuta, d'autant que le projet fut fortement soutenu par le prince de Galles.

---

16 Le changement fut vite perceptible et les premières mesures virent le jour rapidement. Ainsi, en 1916, le vice-roi, Lord Chelmsford, proposait au Secrétaire d'État à l'Inde, Austen Chamberlain, l'abolition du poste de Résident à Indore, à la demande du maharadjah Tukoji Rao Holkar, dans IOR/R/1/1/558, Government of India, Foreign and Political Department, Secret-I, June 1916, Proceedings Nos. 48–57, « Proposed abolition of the appointment of the Resident at Indore ».

17 Ashton 1982, p. 40.

Cependant, de même que Lytton, Minto dut abandonner son projet. En effet, réunir les princes supposait faire face à d'insolubles problèmes de protocole et de préséance. Pour les princes, divisés et jaloux de leurs prérogatives et de leurs statuts respectifs, il paraissait difficile de s'asseoir à la même table et de négocier et de voter sur un pied d'égalité.

Le *Government of India* considéra, sans doute, que la menace que représentait alors le parti du Congrès ne justifiait pas de pousser plus avant la réalisation de ce projet. Face à la complexité de cette ambition, et au regard des bénéfices supposés de l'entreprise, il décida de reporter ce projet à une date ultérieure et indéterminée. Il fallut attendre encore une dizaine d'années pour que cette idée soit remise au goût du jour. La Première Guerre mondiale allait lui donner un nouvel élan.

Néanmoins, les premières rencontres informelles entre une assemblée de princes et le *Government of India* eurent lieu bien avant la fin de la guerre. Ainsi, une rencontre au sujet des *minority administrations* fut organisée en février 1916[18] et une réunion se tint à Delhi en février 1918 afin de discuter du futur rapport Montagu-Chelmsford[19].

Au début du mois de décembre 1916, le vice-roi Chelmsford annonça que le gouvernement britannique avait décidé d'inviter deux représentants de l'Inde à participer à l'*Imperial War Conference* qui se tiendrait à Londres en mars 1917. Cet honneur devait concerner deux personnalités, l'une britannique et l'autre indienne, et venait en remerciement de l'effort de guerre consenti par l'Inde. Austen Chamberlain, le Secrétaire d'État à l'Inde penchait pour le prince Ganga Singh de Bikaner, qui avait combattu en Europe. Il fut suivi en ce sens par le *Government of India*, même si le Maharajah Bhupinder Singh de Patiala, qui avait, lui aussi, combattu en Europe, n'avait pas caché son désir d'être désigné pour représenter les États princiers à ce grand événement.

Or, comme le souligne Barbara Ramusack[20], si des princes indiens avaient déjà assisté à de grandes cérémonies européennes, comme le couronnement d'Edward VII, c'était la première fois qu'un prince était invité à représenter les États princiers aux côtés des dirigeants politiques européens et dans le cadre d'une rencontre destinée à déterminer la nouvelle politique impériale. Cette nomination révéla à la fois l'implication politique des princes, mais également les problèmes inédits que soulevait cette situation sans précédent[21]. Ainsi, la

---

18 Cf. *supra.*
19 Cf. *supra.*
20 Ramusack 2004, p. 115.
21 Ramusack 1978, p. 31.

politique qui consistait à isoler les princes physiquement et politiquement qui avait prévalu jusque-là semblait révolue :

> « By emphasizing the irrelevance of this policy to current political conditions, World War I delivered a death blow to this anachronism as it had done to the other policies and institutions appropriate only in a vanished era of world politics. Princely support of the British war effort demanded suitable recognition and compensation by the imperial recipient. »[22]

Elle ajoute que le fait que cette invitation émane d'un Secrétaire d'État conservateur prouve bien le changement majeur d'orientation de la politique britannique et que la Première Guerre mondiale ne fut finalement que le révélateur d'un changement déjà préparé depuis quelques années.

Les princes étaient donc devenus une partie intégrante de l'édifice impérial britannique et se trouvaient, par la même occasion, étroitement associés à la politique impériale. Cependant, les difficultés survinrent bientôt, essentiellement liées à des jalousies et à des rivalités entre les princes eux-mêmes. En effet, lorsque le prince de Bikaner déclina une invitation à se rendre à la seconde *War Conference* en 1918, il suggéra au *Government of India* de choisir le prince de Nawanagar pour le remplacer. Or, après avoir porté son choix sur le prince de Gwalior, qui déclina pour raison familiale, le *Government of India* choisit finalement le prince de Patiala, contre l'avis du Secrétaire d'État Montagu, qui préférait suivre le conseil du prince de Bikaner de choisir le prince de Nawanagar. Furieux que son avis ne soit pas considéré, Ganga Singh de Bikaner refusa de se rendre à la soirée offerte par Bhupinder Singh de Patiala en l'honneur de son départ à Londres, ce qui, pour les princes, s'apparentait à un affront.

Il semble donc bien que les désaccords des princes, leurs rivalités et leurs jalousies qui s'étaient jusque-là exprimés dans des « guerres » de protocole et de préséance[23] dont le régime ne s'était pas privé de tirer parti, devaient rendre la création d'une Chambre des princes plus compliquée qu'il n'y paraissait au premier abord.

> « Any new British favour, consequently, provoked an eruption of personal rivalries and jealousies among the princes. They furthermore were not prepared for participation in activities in which they would have to recognize any Indians, whether princes or commoners, as equals. Their paternalistic and autocratic methods within their states did not encourage the formation of political relationships on the basis of equality. »[24]

---

22 Ramusack 1978, p. 31.
23 Voir le dernier chapitre du livre de Keen sur la hiérarchie et les rituels de cette élite aristocratique indienne n'ayant pas encore totalement disparu encore de nos jours.
24 Ramusack 1978, p. 32.

Cette hiérarchie des princes, que les Britanniques avaient contribué à perpétuer, allait grandement nuire à l'établissement, puis au bon fonctionnement d'une Chambre des princes. Les Britanniques aussi avaient leur propre agenda politique et favorisaient souvent un prince plutôt qu'un autre, quand le *Government of India* à Delhi ne s'opposait pas tout simplement au Secrétariat d'État à l'Inde à Londres dès lors qu'il s'agissait de promouvoir un prince plutôt qu'un autre.

« The preference for Bikaner and aversion to Patiala is indicative of priorities at the India Office in their employment of the princes. Their twin objective were to parade a convincing example of Indianization before English and imperial political leaders and to stimulate the war effort. Although they shared these goals with the British hierarchy in Delhi, the London officials placed more emphasis on the first one. »[25]

Malgré ces difficultés, une Chambre des princes fut finalement inaugurée par proclamation royale le 8 février 1921. Elle était constituée de 108 princes membres permanents, et de douze membres représentatifs des plus petits États[26]. Or, les dissensions ne tardèrent pas à apparaître et la Chambre prit très rapidement des allures d'arène où les luttes de pouvoir finirent par avoir raison de certaines bonnes volontés. Ainsi, le prince Scindia, qui dirigeait Gwalior, l'un des États les plus importants de l'Inde en termes de richesse et d'étendue, finit par démissionner en 1924 pour ne jamais revenir et le *Nizam* d'Hyderabad, le plus grand État de l'Inde, refusa même de faire partie de la Chambre, considérant que les princes de petits États sans importance n'avaient pas à discuter des problèmes de son État. Les princes de Baroda, Indore, Mysore[27], Jaipur et Udaipur, des États pourtant très importants, suivirent l'exemple d'Hyderabad. Par conséquent, la Chambre fut vite dominée par un consortium de princes Sikhs et Rajputs dirigeant des États de taille moyenne au Punjab, au Rajpoutana et en Inde de l'Ouest et devint peu représentative de l'ensemble des États princiers.

Enfin, un autre problème, plus grave, se posait pour Londres. En effet, les princes réclamaient une définition claire et une codification de la pratique de la *Paramountcy*. En effet, la reconnaissance de la permanence des traités signés avec l'East India Company impliquait, *ipso facto*, une reconnaissance certaine de l'autonomie des princes dans leurs affaires intérieures, si ces derniers ne s'immisçaient pas dans les affaires des Britanniques. Cependant, afin de donner à ces

25 Ramusack 1978, p. 34.
26 Il y avait plus de 650 États princiers dont certains ne dépassaient pas la taille d'une petite ville. Le nombre exact de ces États ne semble jamais avoir fait consensus.
27 Sur cet État particulièrement intéressant, voir l'étude de Nair sur la modernisation du système légal et la protection des mineures contre le mariage précoce.

derniers une plus grande marge de manœuvre, la *Paramountcy* n'avait jamais été clairement définie, puisqu'elle s'adaptait aux circonstances du moment, ni codifiée, puisqu'à chaque État correspondait une situation particulière.

Or, une définition précise de la *Paramountcy* impliquait nécessairement d'en indiquer les limites et de définir précisément les droits et prérogatives des princes mais aussi de la Couronne à leur égard. Cela aurait forcé les Britanniques à reconnaître bien des excès d'ingérence et aurait considérablement diminué la crédibilité du *Government of India* ainsi que sa marge de manœuvre. Définir la *Paramountcy*, outre la difficulté, et même l'impossibilité de la tâche, revenait à reconnaître et à garantir l'indépendance interne des États princiers au sein de l'édifice impérial. C'est ce que réclamèrent les princes et que l'Angleterre ne leur donna jamais, comme le souligne V.P. Menon « *the paramount power continued to be paramount, and Paramountcy remained as vague as ever.* »[28]

Qui plus est, une codification de la *Paramountcy* n'était pas du goût de tous les princes car les traités garantissaient à chacun des droits et des prérogatives particuliers qu'une homogénéisation aurait, sans conteste, contribué à niveler. La promesse d'une autonomie croissante du gouvernement dans l'Inde coloniale, mais aussi dans les États princiers, contenue dans l'*India Act* de 1919, semblait aux princes encore bien lointaine en 1929, malgré les avancées indéniables des deux côtés, quand ces derniers rédigèrent les paragraphes suivants après l'une de leurs réunions :

> « The present generation of Ruling Princes in India differs from the last more than any generation in the past has differed from its immediate predecessors. In particular the attitude of the Princes towards the doctrine of Paramountcy has undergone a radical change[29]. The growth of the nationalist movement in British India caused him [Minto] alarm and he saw in the Princes a strong bulwark against subversive movements[30]. During the decade 1908–18, the isolation of one state from another was a rule of policy to some extent modified by the action of different Viceroys who consulted the Princes on various particular matters and especially so during the war-consulting them as a class, if not as a political body. […]. It was freely recognised in the Montagu-Chelmsford Report that the position of the states as it had evolved during the preceding few decades required reconsideration. The authors of the joint report recognised the injustice which had been done by the attempt of the Political Department to attain uniformity of practice. […]. It may, with some justice, be said that with the inauguration of the Chamber of Princes a new era has dawned in the relations between the Government of India and the States; that with the frank recognition of the Government that mistaken policies

---

28 Ashton 1982, p. 58.
29 Directorate of the Chamber's Special Organization 1929, p. 95–97.
30 Directorate of the Chamber's Special Organization 1929, Introduction, p. xix.

have been pursued in the past and that treaties though declared inviolable and inviolate have often been treated as non-existent or obsolete, the rights of the Princes stand better chance of recognition. The Government of India of to-day has no doubt modified in favour of the States' contentions certain of the autocratic views it once held. »[31]

Ainsi, même si l'inauguration de la Chambre des princes, malgré ses nombreuses difficultés et son manque de représentativité, entendait montrer clairement que le temps de l'isolement des princes était révolu, ces derniers n'en étaient pas moins conscients que les Britanniques ne leur concédaient que ce qui ne leur coûtait pas trop, et que le chemin vers plus d'indépendance était encore bien long, comme les princes le reconnaissaient eux-mêmes en 1929 :

« The anomaly of the position is recognized now by the Government of India, but it is doubtful whether they yet realise how vicious the present system is and how radical an alteration is required in their attitude towards Indian States if common justice is to be meted out to them. »[32]

Une fois de plus, les Britanniques déçurent les princes, coincés entre les vagues promesses du *Government of India* et l'hostilité croissante des dirigeants nationalistes indiens à leur égard.

Un nouveau manuel pour les résidents et les agents

Un texte extrait des mémoires de Sir Francis Younghusband (1863–1942), dans lequel il évoque son affectation comme résident au Cachemire de 1906 à 1910, exprime bien le dilemme auquel les résidents et les agents politiques étaient sans cesse confrontés dans l'exercice de leurs fonctions. En effet, ces derniers, investis de pouvoirs considérables, devaient sans cesse refréner leur fougue réformatrice, tantôt selon les souhaits du prince, ou selon ceux du *Government of India* dont les politiques en la matière varièrent mais ne se ressemblèrent pas.

« In performing his duties a Resident is torn in two directions. All the energetic efficiency-loving part of him urges him to make use of his influential position to develop the natural resources of Kashmir and improve the lot of the people ; to get a railway constructed into the country, have good roads everywhere, open up the mineral wealth, double the yield per acre by improving the methods of agriculture, increase the culture of fruit and of silk, turn the water-power into electric power, develop the timber, do everything to attract visitors and bring their money into the country as it is brought into switzerland. But then comes the pull in the other direction. The Maharajah is the responsible ruler. Why interfere with him ? If he does not want to have railways built and

---

31 Directorate of the Chamber's Special Organization 1929, p. 94.
32 Directorate of the Chamber's Special Organization 1929, p. 96.

mines sunk and oil extracted and factories set up, why bother him? And after all, isn't Kashmir much more delightful undevelopped. »[33]

En 1908, la nomination de Spencer Harcourt Butler (1869–1938), comme Secrétaire des affaires étrangères du *Government of India*, sonna officiellement le glas de l'ère Curzon au sein du *Political Service* et déplut profondément au corps des résidents et des agents politiques[34]. En effet, issu du *Civil Service*, Butler n'avait aucune connaissance des États princiers et suivait scrupuleusement la politique prônée par Minto, une politique qui était en contradiction croissante avec les intérêts du *Political Department*. Harcourt Butler était, en effet, chargé de mettre en place une toute nouvelle politique de non-ingérence. Dans une note datée du 11 mars 1909, Butler résumait la nouvelle politique du *Government of India* : « *We are only, I take it, at the beginning of an anti-British movement which is a permanent factor now in Indian politics. Surely, it is beyond measure important to strengthen the position of the chiefs and attach them to our side.* »[35] De nombreux résidents et agents politiques envoyèrent des lettres de protestation au Secrétariat de Minto, et certains membres du *Political Service* n'hésitèrent pas à qualifier la nomination de Butler d'insulte à la profession [« *a slur on us all* »] tandis que d'autres la décrivaient comme un coup porté au *Political Service* dont ce dernier aurait beaucoup de mal à se remettre[36].

Fidèle à sa mission et à la nouvelle orientation de la politique du *Government of India* en matière de relation avec les États princiers, Butler élabora un manuel d'instruction à l'attention des résidents et des agents politiques. Publié en 1909, ce manuel[37] servit de base au discours prononcé à Udaipur par Minto la même année et qui instituait la nouvelle orientation politique de *laisser-faire* déjà mentionnée plus haut.

En effet, si la rédaction d'un tel ouvrage fut longtemps considérée comme nécessaire – la question avait déjà été abordée à l'époque de l'East India Company- il fallut attendre Charles Lewis Tupper (1848–1910) et son *Indian Political Practices* publié en 1895 pour avoir une idée plus précise des charges et responsabilités des résidents et des agents politiques. Cependant, le Manuel politique reprenait, d'une manière plus synthétique, ces différentes fonctions,

---

33 Younghusband 1927, p. 180.

34 Cf. *supra*.

35 Butler's note, 11 March 1911, GOI (Government of India), FPD, Confidential B, Internal Branch A, 1911, No. 3, in Ashton 1982, p. 40.

36 Ashton 1982, p. 42.

37 *Manual of Instructions to Officers of the Political Department of the Government of India*, 1909, Minto Collection, No. 12629, *Ibid.*, p. 53.

puisqu'il s'agissait de rappels généraux sur la nouvelle politique en vigueur, de conseils et de procédures à suivre à l'usage des agents du gouvernement, et non, comme c'était le cas dans *Indian Political Practices*, de précédents juridiques à partir desquels les agents politiques étaient amenés à se faire leur propre opinion, adaptée aux problèmes spécifiques de leurs États respectifs.

Une réédition de ce même manuel en 1924[38] donne une idée plus précise de l'évolution du rôle et des responsabilités des membres du *Political Service* à partir de 1909. L'introduction de ce manuel donnait aux résidents et aux agents politiques un résumé des conseils élémentaires à l'accomplissement de leurs fonctions, on pouvait ainsi y lire les grandes lignes de l'évolution de la politique impériale en matière de relations avec les États princiers. Ainsi, le préambule rappelle que le tout premier rôle d'un Officier politique est celui d'intermédiaire entre le gouvernement et les princes. Mais il insiste également sur la dualité de la fonction :

> « The first duty of a Political Officer is to cultivate direct, friendly, personal relations with the Ruling Princes and Chiefs with whom he works. [...] A Political Officer as the representative of the Imperial Government has a dual function; he is the mouthpiece of Government and the custodian of Imperial policy; but he is also the interpreter of the sentiments of the Darbar. In the exercise of this dual function, he will gradually acquire an experience and attitude of mind which will lead him instinctively to right and sound courses of action. »[39]

Le résident ou l'agent politique était donc avant tout un médiateur qui devait s'identifier au mieux aux intérêts des deux parties qu'il représentait. Il était recommandé à ce dernier d'avoir de fréquentes discussions, sur un mode informel, avec les princes : « *He should assume an identity of interest between the Imperial Government and the Darbar and discuss questions freely in oral conversation.* »[40]

Il était également recommandé de réduire au maximum la correspondance écrite avec les princes, et de préférer les entretiens en face-à-face, le passage à l'écrit administratif ne devant se limiter qu'à la confirmation par écrit des propositions et engagements finals : « *while the ordinary principles of public business require that there should be a written record of the proposals, [...] written correspondence with Darbars should be reduced as far as possible.* » Il était aussi rappelé aux résidents et aux agents politiques d'éviter d'employer des intermédiaires qui

---

38 L/PS/20, H113, *Manual of Instructions to Officers of the* Political Department *of the Government of India* (1924).

39 L/PS/20, H113, *Manual of Instructions to Officers of the* Political Department *of the Government of India, op. cit.*, Introduction, p. xii.

40 *Ibidem*, p. xii.

ne pourraient très certainement qu'ajouter à la confusion ambiante : « *He should avoid employing intermediaries* ».

De plus, les résidents et les agents politiques devaient non seulement s'identifier aux intérêts des États dans lesquels ils officiaient, mais il leur était également demandé de se mettre à la place des princes et d'imaginer quel pourrait être leur point de vue sur les sujets abordés : « *He should always endeavour to place himself in the position of the Darbar and endeavour to realise the Darbar's point of view* »[41].

En conséquence, ils ne devaient prodiguer leurs conseils que lorsque le prince le demandait : « *He should ordinarily refrain from offering advice unless it is sought* ». De plus, il était essentiel de ne pas nuire au prestige ou à la dignité dont ces princes jouissaient auprès de leur peuple afin de ne pas encourager la création d'un contre-pouvoir au sein du même État, ce qui ne pourrait conduire qu'à l'anarchie : « *He should be careful to uphold the dignity of the Darbar ; he should not interfere between a Darbar and its subjects, nor encourage petitions from the latter against the former* »[42].

Enfin, la dernière recommandation du manuel, et pas des moindres, était finalement assez surprenante : « *He should leave well alone ; the best work of a Political Officer is very often what he has left undone* ». En effet, ces injonctions visant à la passivité, étaient en totale contradiction avec la mission dont se sentaient investis les membres du *Political Service*. Nul doute que de nombreux agents se demandèrent alors à quoi ils pouvaient bien encore servir, si ce n'était à symboliser physiquement la présence du pouvoir suzerain. Le manuel expliquait également qu'ils ne pouvaient en aucun cas inspecter les institutions de leur État, à moins d'y avoir été invités par le prince lui-même.

C'est pourquoi le manuel énumérait comme qualités essentielles des résidents et des agents politiques le tact, la patience, la franchise, l'attention portée aux affaires qui pouvaient sembler de peu d'intérêt mais qui, pour les princes, étaient primordiales, comme les détails des protocoles des cérémonies[43]. L'agent du gouvernement britannique était mis en garde contre toute critique intempestive : « *He will ordinarily find his relations with Darbars made easy if he cultivates frankness, courtesy, patience, tact, care in matters of ceremonials, and above all, readiness to see the good in things, and slowness to criticise* ».

---

41 *Ibid.*, p. xii.
42 *Ibid.*, p. xiii.
43 Voir l'ouvrage récent de Jhala, sur l'importance de l'architecture, la décoration intérieure, la mode et la haute cuisine et des plaisirs de luxe chez les princes de l'Inde coloniale.

La mainmise du gouvernement britannique se relâchait de plus en plus, au point que l'intervention de ce dernier ne se justifiait plus que lorsque la mauvaise administration (*misrule*) y avait atteint un seuil qui violait les lois élémentaires de la civilisation : « *It may be stated generally that, unless misrule reaches a pitch which violates the elementary laws of civilisation, the Imperial Government will usually prefer to take no overt measures for enforcing reform : and in any case the attempt to reform should, so long as is possible, be confined to personal suasion* ».

Il était également rappelé que le gouverneur général était opposé à la moindre pression pour imposer aux princes la mise en œuvre de méthodes d'administration britanniques dans leurs États, et que l'efficacité administrative n'était pas le but recherché, si cela entrait en contradiction avec les coutumes et les traditions séculaires des États : « *The Governor-General in Council is opposed to anything like pressure on Darbars to introduce British methods of administration. He prefers that reforms should emanate from the Darbar, and grow up in harmony with the traditions of the State. Administrative efficiency is at no time the only or indeed the chief object to be kept in view* »[44].

Ces termes sont ceux du discours du vice-roi Minto à Udaipur le 3 novembre 1909. Le but du gouvernement britannique était désormais de préserver les États princiers en l'état, afin d'en garantir la stabilité. Des réformes trop radicales auraient fait courir le risque de déstabiliser un système qui était alors essentiel à la pérennité du contrôle britannique dans le sous-continent. C'est pourquoi, en conclusion, il est rappelé que la solidité des bases du système reposait sur un respect des traditions séculaires qui en avaient fait le succès :

> « Abuses and corruption should be corrected as far as possible; but the general system of administration to which the Prince and the people have been accustomed should be unchanged in all essentials. The methods sanctioned by tradition in States are generally well adapted to the needs and relations of the ruler and people. The loyalty of the latter to the former is generally a personal loyalty, which administrative efficiency, if carried out on lines unsuited to local conditions, would lessen or impair. »[45]

Ce manuel montre bien le changement radical qui s'était opéré depuis le départ de Curzon. Ainsi, si les Britanniques croyaient encore dur comme fer à la stratégie du soutien aux élites naturelles, ils entendaient plus que jamais s'assurer du soutien de ces dernières grâce à une attitude faite de compromis et de conciliation en totale contradiction avec les idéaux d'un vice-roi interventionniste comme Curzon quelques années auparavant.

---

44 *Ibid.*, p. xiv.
45 *Ibid.* (d'après le discours de Lord Minto à Udaipur le 3 novembre 1909).

Cependant, ils ne semblaient pas encore mesurer le poids d'une nouvelle élite, la nouvelle classe moyenne indienne qui, elle, avait su s'adapter aux exigences de la modernité occidentale, ce qui lui avait permis de s'émanciper peu à peu de la tutelle coloniale. Ayant sans doute pris conscience de ce danger, le gouvernement colonial souhaitait ainsi ralentir un processus de « civilisation » qui aurait à terme fatalement amené l'Inde à prendre sa place dans le concert des nations.

Conclusion

La réaction qui suivit le départ de Curzon en 1905 fut de mettre un frein à l'interventionnisme qui avait marqué la période afin de se concilier le soutien des princes. C'est Minto qui donna le coup d'envoi définitif de cette nouvelle politique lorsque, dans un célèbre discours prononcé à Udaipur en 1909, il annonça la nouvelle politique britannique envers les États princiers : une politique de non-intervention et de *laisser-faire*. Ce discours sonna le glas de la mission des résidents et des agents politiques. La Première Guerre mondiale eut pour effet de renforcer la coopération militaire entre les princes et l'Angleterre, ces derniers participant activement à l'effort de guerre et conservant un rôle prépondérant dans la protection des intérêts britanniques en Inde, pendant que l'Angleterre était occupée sur d'autres fronts. Les princes étaient les garants de l'ordre ancien et leurs intérêts étaient alors associés à ceux du pouvoir colonial, ce qui leur fut d'ailleurs vivement reproché après l'Indépendance. Le manuel rédigé à l'intention des résidents et des agents politiques porte la trace de cette lente évolution initiée par Lytton, plus ou moins négligée sous Curzon et finalement confirmée par Minto.

Ainsi, après l'âge d'or de l'ingérence avec Curzon, vice-roi interventionniste, l'augmentation des tensions en Europe et l'intensification des velléités indépendantistes avec l'arrivée sur le sol indien en 1914 du jeune Mohandas Karamchand Gandhi (1869–1948), puis la désillusion générale et la montée des revendications à l'issue de la Première Guerre mondiale, le besoin du soutien des classes aristocratiques indiennes se fit à nouveau plus pressant. Cependant, toute éducation réussie visant à l'émancipation et à l'autonomisation, les princes demandèrent à l'Angleterre des garanties plus importantes en échange de leur soutien, réalisant désormais combien leur appui était nécessaire à la perpétuation du *Raj*[46]. Par conséquent, le rapport Montagu-Chelmsford de 1918, préalable à l'*India Act* de 1919, fut augmenté d'un volet qui redéfinissait les relations entre le

---

46 Bhagavan 2003, p. 84–121 à propos des universités princières de Baroda et Mysore, novatrices dans le contexte de l'Inde coloniale.

gouvernement colonial et les États princiers en des termes nettement plus avantageux pour ces derniers. De plus, suite à la participation des princes à l'effort de guerre, le *Government of India* annonça la création d'une Chambre des princes en 1921. Le *laisser-faire* était désormais de rigueur[47].

Les résidents et les agents politiques perdirent dès lors leur principale raison d'être et durent se contenter de n'être plus que de simples représentants diplomatiques aux pouvoirs désormais quasiment inexistants. L'heure de gloire était passée et les derniers survivants de l'âge d'or de l'impérialisme britannique durent se contenter des chasses au tigre, des matchs de polo et des réceptions fastueuses qui aidaient à faire oublier la perte de leur pouvoir et une certaine vacuité de leur fonction. Profitant des derniers feux d'un empire sur le déclin, ceux qui s'étaient parfois mués en explorateurs de régions reculées ou de passes himalayennes stratégiques, qui avaient négocié avec les tribus fières et indomptables de l'Hindou-Kouch, ou avec des maharajahs capricieux dont la richesse dépassait parfois celle de la cour d'Angleterre, ces aventuriers de la politique indigène étaient désormais relégués au rang de simples observateurs passifs et impuissants, de la fin d'une époque.

Cette nouvelle orientation générale de la politique britannique en Inde ne changea plus jusqu'en 1947. Avec la crise économique de 1929 et les difficultés croissantes de l'entre-deux-guerres, le *Raj* semblait avoir atteint son crépuscule. C'est le second conflit mondial qui allait avoir raison de lui et de l'entreprise impériale britannique dans son ensemble.

Ainsi, l'évolution de la politique d'*Indirect Rule* dans les dernières années de l'Empire des Indes permet bel et bien de mesurer la fragilité croissante de la présence coloniale dans le sous-continent, et ce, dès la fin de la vice-royauté de Curzon, considérée, à juste titre, comme l'apogée de l'aventure impériale britannique en Inde. Pour les princes aussi c'était une fin de règne, puisque, en 1947, leurs territoires furent intégrés sans heurts, à quelques notables exceptions près (essentiellement le Cachemire et Hyderabad), à l'Union Indienne et, en 1971, le Premier ministre Indira Gandhi, fille de Jawaharlal Nehru (1889–1964), supprima leurs ultimes privilèges. Si les États princiers accusèrent un certain retard de développement vis-à-vis de l'Inde britannique, ces principautés, souvent qualifiées de despotiques, s'intégrèrent cependant sans trop de mal à l'ensemble qui allait devenir l'une des plus grandes démocraties du monde.

Néanmoins, comme Barbara Ramusack le souligne encore dans *The Princes of India in the Twilight of Empire*, les princes, bien que déçus par l'attitude des

---

47 Ikegame 2012, p. 9.

Britanniques à leur égard, furent généralement présentés, souvent de manière excessive, comme les grands perdants de l'indépendance de l'Inde. Placés dans une position délicate dans les dernières années du *Raj*, entre l'indifférence progressive des Britanniques et l'hostilité croissante à leur égard des dirigeants nationalistes et même, parfois, de leurs propres sujets, les princes durent chercher des alternatives et former de nouvelles alliances afin de continuer à jouer un rôle dans l'édifice politique de l'Inde et de survivre à la disparition de leurs États[48].

« They are generally characterized as losers in the battle for power between the British Empire and Indian nationalist leaders, which came to a dramatic resolution in 1947 with the creation of India and Pakistan. Still many members of former princely families continue to be active in Indian and Pakistani politics, and events since 1971 indicate that the political configuration of South Asia was not set in cement in 1947. »[49]

Il semblait important, pour conclure cette étude, de rappeler que certains princes parvinrent, parfois même brillamment, à dépasser ce lourd passé colonial, contredisant ainsi tout l'héritage fantasmatique que la politique impériale britannique avait contribué à façonner autour d'eux, et que l'historiographie indienne ne tenta que tardivement et timidement de questionner.

---

48 Ramusack 1978, p. 28.
49 Ramusack 1978, p. xv.

Julia A. B. Hegewald

University of Bonn

Images of Empire: Re-Use in the Architecture and City Planning of British India

Introduction

The political instability in Bengal and the general fragility of the British presence in India at the start of the twentieth century led, amongst other reasons, to the decision to move the imperial capital from Calcutta to Delhi. This article will examine the design of the governmental headquarters and the layout of the newly-planned capital city as well as the surrounding debates and the underlying political reasons.

Announced by King George V during the coronation *darbar* in 1911, the development process of this new imperial centre sparked intense debates amongst British architects in India and politicians at home in England. The main question was the style of architecture to be chosen to visually represent the British Empire in its colony. Should a purely Western style be chosen to indicate a perceived superiority of the British or should local architectural elements be integrated to indicate the significance and acceptance of the local culture? This was a deeply political question, signalling different approaches in dealing with the political crisis and insecurity facing the colonial power at the time. In the end, a hybrid style, combining aspect of Western architectural traditions and local motifs and building conventions was chosen.

The colonial administration was given pristine buildings at the centre of a newly-founded city as were the representatives of the Indian princely states. This chapter shows that the city plan of New Delhi also draws on Western settlement traditions as well as on Indian concepts of space and religious symbolism. In this area too, the aim was to start afresh at a time of political tensions, to strengthen the empire and to provide the Indian aristocracy with an acceptable place in a new imperial spatial setting.

Inaugurated in 1931, the modern colonial capital and its integrative architecture appeared to appease local sentiments and reinvigorate the strength and spirit of the empire. Nevertheless, the transfer of power was inevitable. With Independence, the recently constructed capital was handed over to the independent nation of India in 1947. However, due to the strong elements of re-use, making direct reference to local styles and traditions[1], the Indian government took over the colonial buildings as they stood and has, till the present day, not replaced them with purely South Asian conceptions.

Government buildings and colonial politics

Public buildings and administrative headquarters, as visual expressions and symbols of state and government, play a crucial part in allowing the public to identify with the ruling elite. This fact was utilised by the British colonial rulers when planning the design of their state headquarters in New Delhi in the early twentieth century. This was a time when the British in India were confronted with the rising popularity of the nationalist movement. At the Coronation Durbar on 12th December 1911, at which Queen Mary was proclaimed Empress of India, King George V announced that the seat of government would be transferred from Calcutta to Delhi.

Although King George did not provide reasons for this relocation, several issues are believed to have played a role. One motivation was to remove the government from the increasingly tense political conditions of Bengal and from the instability of Calcutta. A second aim was to escape the relatively uncomfortable climate of eastern India with its hot and humid summers[2]. Another reason, which will be explored in more detail later in this chapter, is the historical associations of the site of Delhi with great ruling dynasties of the past. Fourthly, the newly-designed capital was located in a strategically more central position within the country. Finally, also the importance of creating a clearly visible sign of British rule over the princely states of India to reconfirm its strength and desired perseverance seem to have played a significant role[3].

---

1   Re-use describes the act of using an item more than once. Particularly interesting is the so-called 'new-life' re-use, where the re-employed item is used for a different purpose than before and fulfils a different function in a new framework. Re-use helps to strengthen tradition and makes cultures adapt and survive periods of change. For a detailed discussion of the concept of re-use, see Hegewald 2012a, especially p. 31–34, and the edited volume Hegewald and Mitra 2012.

2   These issues have been discussed in more detail in Metcalf 1989, p. 211; Tillotson 1989, p. 103 and Volwahsen 2004, p. 11.

3   Volwahsen 2004, p. 18, p. 78.

Debates about the design of public buildings

The relocation of the state capital demanded the construction of novel governmental buildings and a conscious decision about their architectural style. King George and the Viceroy, Lord Hardinge of Penhurst[4], favoured the application of the then popular Indo-Saracenic style of architecture to the governmental buildings. They regarded this hybrid style an appropriate representation in stone of the empire and its cultural diversity. The Indo-Saracenic style typically combines elements from Mughal architecture with the characteristic elements of the Gothic revival, which was fashionable in the Victorian Britain of the late nineteenth century. At the same time, the term 'Indo-Saracenic style' can refer to a combination of Classical and Mughal architecture, which was the combination to be used in the case of Delhi's new public architecture. The Indo-Saracenic style appealed especially to British politicians as it was seen to make an appropriate political gesture towards India[5]. The Viceroy wanted the public buildings of the modern capital to appear Indian to reflect the position of Indians in the colonial government. However, in order not to offend the British in India and at home, a compromise in the form of a blended style, which would integrate Indian features and motifs, was selected. All involved in the process were aware that the choice of style would send political messages to the people of India, to those in Britain and in the wider world. Due to this reason and as a result of the enormous expense associated with raising an entirely new government headquarters on the flat ground of the Delhi plains, the issue of the style of architecture to be chosen was extensively debated in the House of Commons in London[6].

Appointed with the task of planning this innovative capital and its major buildings were the two British architects Sir Edwin Lutyens (1869–1944) and Sir Herbert Baker (1862–1946). They were advised by a group of architects, which amongst others included Sir Samuel Swinton Jacob (1841–1917), responsible for the Indian architectural details[7]. Yet his involvement did not prove very influential, as he had recently retired and retuned to live in England.

---

4   Lord Hardinge (1858–1944) was Viceroy of India from 1910 to 1915.
5   Tillotson 1989, p. 105.
6   For further information on these discussions, Tillotson 1989, p. 105 and British Parliamentary Debates 1912–1913, p. 1910–1919, on which he bases his analysis.
7   Jacob 1890–1913. Jacob had risen to prominence through the publication of this *Jeypore Portfolio*, a twelve volume work on architectural details, including 713 plates, prepared under the patronage of His Highness Maharaja Sawai Madhu Singh of Jeypore (Jaipur).

The application of the Indo-Saracenic style was a political gesture, which created much controversy at the time. Back in England, some felt that Britain should set a clear example and build a city which showed the greatness of the empire and was distinctly British in nature and design. There were clear voices in Parliament and in the British press at the time, who warned that an integration of Indian motifs and anything less than a confident and purely Western style would threaten the survival of the empire[8]. Others, such as the architects John Begg, F. O. Oertel and E. B. Havell, rejected the application of a Western style of architecture and favoured a purely Indian architecture to reflect the present and future of the country and the significance of erecting buildings at a historically important site in India[9].

Interestingly, for these planners, Indian architecture was largely Mughal architecture, exemplified by Akbar's strongly Hindu-influenced palace buildings at Fatehpur Sikri (1571–1585 CE) in Uttar Pradesh[10]. Baker and Lutyens, taking the side of those favouring a Western style were initially strongly opposed to the assimilation of Indian details[11]. Baker argued that "it is the spirit of British sovereignty which must be imprisoned in its stone and bronze" which led him to conclude that it is the style of public buildings in Britain which should be reproduced in India[12]. Because of their reluctance to engage with Indian architecture, the Viceroy sent Lutyens and his assistants on a study tour of Agra and Jaipur to view Mughal and Rajput buildings in the spring of 1912, and to Dhar and Mandu to examine early sultanate architecture in the following December[13]. Lutyens commented after his return that "there is lots of, but no real architecture and nothing is built to last not even the Taj. ... Personally I do not believe there is *any* real Indian architecture or any great tradition"[14].

---

8   Followers of this counter-movement favoured the Classical style of buildings designed by Inigo Jones (1573–1652), Sir Christopher Wren (1632–1723) and their supporters in the eighteenth century, whom they considered desirable models for representing the might of the British homeland in the colonies (Tillotson 1989, p. 106).

9   Metcalf 1989, p. 215–216.

10 Oertel argued that the merging of Hindu and Muslim styles in the palace at Fatehpur Sikri had created a "really national Indian style" (Metcalf 1989, p. 216).

11 Quotes indicating how outspoken the two British Architects were against the fusion of styles have been provided in Tillotson 1989, (p. 106–107). It is surprising that following their initial hesitation they produced such balanced hybrid constructions.

12 Baker 1912, p. 8.

13 Tillotson 1989, p. 106 and Volwahsen 2004, p. 179, provide further details on these educational tours.

14 Lutyens 1991, p. 123. It is noteworthy that when the government commissioned one of the members of the Archaeological Survey of India, Gordon Sanderson, to make a

However, the decision had been made at a higher level and the fact that the architect understood and accepted the political implications of the chosen style of architecture is clear from an article in *The Times*, in which Baker argued that he hoped that the interweaving of elements from different traditions would "symbolize a 'happy marriage' of political ideas"[15]. E. B. Havell, who strongly supported local crafts and building traditions, hoped that the cooperation of Indian builders and British architects "would prove that Indian and British Imperial interests were not antagonistic, but really and truly identical" and lead to a "reconciliation between Eastern and Western ideals"[16]. The combination of styles was a clear attempt by the British to win over the Westernised English-educated Indian elite, whose active engagement in the areas of law and politics was becoming increasingly risky to the rule of the British Raj in India[17].

Combining Indian and western styles

Lutyens was responsible for the design of the Viceroy's House, the official residence of the Viceroy[18], which was given a prominent position in the overall arrangement of the government buildings and the surrounding city. Baker was in charge of planning the Secretariats, divided into the north and the south blocks. Together, these public buildings were grouped on a low hill known as Raisina[19]. Slightly later, Baker was put in charge of the design of the Council House, which served as the central legislative assembly[20]. Lutyens was in control of formulating the

---

survey of contemporary Indian architecture in 1913, he concluded that some of the structures he saw were weak in design. Interestingly, Sanderson attributed this deficiency to Western influence and not to the mixing of styles or to the weakness of the indigenous architecture (Tillotson 1989, p. 110–111 and p. 125).

15 Tillotson 1989, p. 118.

16 Metcalf 1989, p. 214.

17 For a more detailed discussion of these issues, see Metcalf 1989, p. 218.

18 Nowadays, the Viceroy's House is the official residence of the President of India, and known as Rashtrapati Bhavan, commonly translated as President House or the Presidential Palace.

19 The fact that Baker's two Secretariats were also constructed on Raisina Hill, which was not initially intended, upset Lutyens' original design and led to a design fault, whereby the Secretariats obscure the view towards the Viceroy's House due to the steep gradient of the approach road leading up the hill. Amongst others, this issue has been explored by Irving, in his chapter "Quarrel at Rasina" (Irving 1981, p. 142–165) and by (Tillotson 1989, p. 123–124).

20 Today known as Parliament House, the circular Legislative Building was planned and constructed between 1919 and 1928.

layout of the streets around the governmental headquarters and the All India War Memorial arch, nowadays better known as India Gate. After a long planning and construction process, delayed by financial problems and World War I, New Delhi and its public buildings were formally opened and inaugurated in February 1931.

As architects, Lutyens and Baker accomplished similar results in the design of their eclectic buildings. However, Lutyens has generally been credited with achieving more of a fusion of East and West[21]. Both of them started off with classicism as the basic style of their buildings. The importance of the Classical tradition at this time derives from the fact that it was seen as an embodiment of order and rationalism and was regarded as a suitable style to symbolise the empire, which regarded itself as an embodiment of these precise qualities. For Baker, the Classical style symbolised the "conception of orderly government"[22]. This was what the British government hoped to regain and hold on to as India, 'the Jewel in the Crown', remained economically and strategically more vital than ever in the general architecture of the British Empire at the end of World War I.

Taking a Classical design as its main architectural core, Lutyens and Baker set out to apply various Indian architectural elements and to fuse the two traditions in the fashion of re-use. The newly-planned edifices were furnished with the characteristic Indian dripstones, locally referred to as *chajja*s. These allow the run off of rainwater, provide a certain amount of shade and play a central role in structuring the facades of indigenous historic buildings. In the architecture of New Delhi, they take the place of friezes in Classical architecture. There are regular occurrences of domed pavilions, *chattri*s, and of protruding balconies, *jharoka*s. These are supported on elaborate brackets and often integrate pierced stone work, called *jali*s. Following the local Hindu and Jaina technique of construction, openings, such as doorways and windows, are commonly bridged by corbelled arches[23]. Elsewhere, we find arches, reflecting the Mughal architectural tradition. Also the colour scheme of the new government buildings, combining locally available red and buff-coloured sand-stones, alludes directly to the prominent use of this striking colour combination in the local Mughal architecture[24].

---

21 This becomes clear in the design of their buildings and in their writings on the archi-
    tecture of Delhi. This has been discussed in Tillotson 1989, (p. 118–122).
22 Tillotson 1989, p. 121.
23 These are not true arches made of a van of voussoirs, which are wedge-shaped build-
    ing blocks, held together by a coping stone at the top, but are based on a post and lintel
    system, which is horizontal in construction.
24 The prominent colour combination of red and white was already used in earlier Is-
    lamic architecture in India, such as the Alai Darwaza, constructed in 1311, in the

There is even more direct re-use of Indian motifs, for instance, in Lutyens' Viceroy's Court. The pillars are adorned with bell and chain motifs, known from indigenous temple architecture. There are sculpted elephants, which in a local context, are regularly found at the entrance to temples and palace buildings. There are fountainheads in the shape of snakes, in South Asia venerated as sacred *nagas*, and many references to lotus designs. Snake and lotus are both significant elements of Indian architectural decorations. A clear reference to Islamic structuring of space is found in the water gardens surrounding the stately residence. The formal gardens with water basins and fountains lining King's Way at the front and those lying behind Viceroy's House directly reflect the tradition of formal Mughal water gardens. Another remarkable reference to indigenous architectural traditions, this time to the Buddhist legacy, is to be found in the towering element above the roof of the Viceroy's House. The central dome or tambour makes direct reference to early Buddhist stupa architecture at Sanchi in Madhya Pradesh, dating from the third century BCE. This becomes particularly clear with regards to the hemispherical dome and the railings associated with Stupa number 3 at the site[25]. Typical of re-use, the visual references to Sanchi are not simply aesthetic but bear a strong political message as well[26]. The pilgrimage centre was founded by Emperor Ashoka, who succeeded for the first time in Indian history to unite almost all of the territory of the modern state of India under his rule. To have such a clear symbol of a unified Indian empire, raised above the seat of the representative of the British Crown in India, would have been understood as a clear visualisation of the union of the Indian colony and of Britain under one united British rule.

Though not only Indian models of architecture were taken into account when planning the government headquarters in Delhi. It is fascinating to observe that

---

complex of the Quwwatul Islam Masjid in Delhi. However, during the later Mughal period, and especially in the buildings raised under the patronage of Shah Jahan, this colour scheme gained an iconic significance. Jainas too frequently combine these two contrasting colours in the outer design of their temple structures. In Hinduism red is linked to blood and white to milk, two essential substances used in Hindu ritual. To mark the sacredness of temple precincts, their walls have often been painted in red and white stripes.

25 Furthermore, parallels can be drawn between the shape of the dome towering above Viceroy's House and the domed towers of the fort at Gwalior, located in central India too. The reference to the architecture of Sanchi, however, is more immediate.

26 The study by Hegewald 2012a discusses the political dimension of re-use and analyses examples where re-use is seen to serve a number of different agendas.

the edifices on Raisina Hill can be directly related to certain architectural models in the West as well. The government buildings at Washington D.C. in the United States of America are similarly raised on a low mound and there are undeniable parallels in the design of the central rotunda of Viceroy's House and the Capitol in Washington. Additionally, these relate to the Pantheon in Rome and to a number of churches copying it. Amongst the latter are St. Paul's Cathedral in London and St. Nicholas Church in Potsdam[27]. The re-use of gigantic sculptural representations of urns bearing pine cones and avenues lined by rows of seated guarding lions also establish direct references to the architecture of Classical Rome and antiquity more generally.

Making direct reference to the Classical orders of architecture, the style of the new governmental buildings by Lutyens were called the 'Delhi Order'[28]. This describes the pillars, combining elements of a Classical column with the design of hanging bell chains and their capitals, reminiscent of Ashokan examples. One might argue that because the Indian contribution to the governmental buildings in New Delhi largely consists of inserted details, it is questionable whether we are dealing with a real 'combination,' with a 'fusion' or even a 'synthesis' of styles, or whether it simply is an 'interpolation' of elements. For the local people, however, the style of the latest government buildings appears to have worked. When in 1947 the British departed, Indians generally had no problems with accepting these buildings as representative symbols of the new independent India. Today, the colonial style of British India has been adopted by Indians as an 'almost' indigenous style, leading to endless re-castings in architecture and reproductions in furniture, produced by the flourishing local heritage industry[29].

The discussion in this paragraph has illustrated that the architects of New Delhi, the Viceroy Lord Hardinge and British politicians knew how mutually dependent architectural style and political power are[30]. The debates surrounding the design choices of the novel colonial headquarters in Delhi have communicated the central function which symbols, decorative motifs and architectural styles play in the conception of public buildings as reflections of the state, the

---

27 Also the interior decorations below the rotunda, inside the so-called Darbar Hall, make reference to the cassetted ceiling of the Pantheon. On these connections and for photographic illustrations, see Volwahsen 2004, p. 78 and p. 120–121.

28 Tillotson 1989, p. 122.

29 This reflects one specific form or a sub-form of re-use, known as nostalgia, which particularly in the context of furnishings can come close to retro-branding. On this, see Hegewald 2012a, p. 42.

30 Volwahsen 2004, p. 7.

state's claim to power and the diversity of its governed citizens. The integration of local Indian elements into the architecture of government served as a conscious statement and an integrative step towards the Indians who were meant to feel like full citizens of the British crown and who were equally represented in the new design. Although the architecture aimed to impress, to represent order and Western philosophical ideals of the Enlightenment, it is Indian and local at the same time. The architects involved in this important venture might initially have considered this as a concession, but few would disagree that a certain strength and potency lies in this form of architectural re-use. The aim of the public buildings at the centre of power in New Delhi was to serve as symbols of a British world empire and India's place within it.

The new Imperial capital city

The government buildings were not incorporated into an already existing old city structure but formed the core area of an entirely freshly-designed capital, New Delhi. The following paragraphs will examine the importance of urban planning in the context of re-establishing order and solidifying one's power as a colonial presence. India has a long tradition of sacred pilgrimage cities, commercial trading centres and royal urban seats of power. The analysis will illustrate that historic, strategic and socio-religious reasons played a significant role in the shaping of India's latest colonial city foundation. As will be shown, the consciously structured layout of the settlement was designed to transform the local subjects into committed and integrated citizens of the British Empire, by portraying itself as a British and Indian capital as well as an international world metropolis.

In New Delhi, as in many other planned or transformed centres of power, there is a close relationship between seats of government and the fabric of the cities. The urban configuration provides a stage for and an approach to the public buildings. Volwahsen reminds us that "Both the temple and the palace require an urban environment, not only during periods of construction, but also in order to function"[31]. The poignant statement published in *The Builder*, that "having conquered the world, Alexander the Great controlled it not by the marshalling of troops, but by the founding and establishing of cities of Greek design"[32], illustrates that the city planners of New Delhi were probably very aware of the political implications and the impact their creation would have on the empire and its people.

---

31 Volwahsen 2004, p. 7.
32 This quote has been taken from the 1912 edition of *The Builder*. Tillotson 1989, p. 106.

The Moghul model

Long before the British, the Mughal emperor Shah Jahan (1592–1666) had created a poignant political symbol in the form of a new city structure at Delhi. Between 1639 and 1649, Shah Jahan built a palace, known as the Lal Qila (Red Fort), and adjacent to it founded the city of Shahjahanabad (Old Delhi). The structuring of space inside his palace and the adjoining city strictly followed Islamic principles of layout. The buildings and streets were formally laid out and based on geometric and axial arrangements. The principal axis of the city, the main commercial thoroughfare known as the Chandni Chowk, still connects the city and the palace fort, located at the eastern end of the bazaar street. The approach towards and into the palace complex symbolised a movement from the public and common to the private and royal areas of the city. The approach from the town towards the palace, and towards the meeting with the sovereign at the end of this prominent axis, was carefully and psychologically planned. The aim was to impress and to intimidate the visitor, with the emperor as the final climax in the long approach[33].

The site for Shah Jahan's capital city had been consciously chosen and was loaded with historic and political meaning. The emperor chose a location, well-known for previous royal cities, both Hindu and Muslim. By doing so, the Mughal emperor placed himself, his rule and his subjects into a long line of powerful dynasties, who had all governed from Delhi. Shah Jahan's settlement represented the seventh city foundation at Delhi.

The British admired the Mogul might and were aware of the important political connotations of the site. In the light of the continuity of settlements, King George V's announcement of the transfer of the capital of British India from Calcutta to Delhi, takes on a specific significance. On the plains outside Shahjahanabad, the seventh city of Delhi, the British raised the eighth capital city at a deeply historic location. Contrasting with the earlier 'Purana Dilli' or 'Old Delhi', they named their latest foundation 'New Delhi'.

The structure and layout of the city were shaped by Lutyens and Baker. The city as a whole and the streets surrounding the centre of government in particular, were designed on a hierarchical plan. This aimed at emphasising the strength

---

33 The movement along this axis involved visitors dismounting from their elephants or horses and proceeding further into the palace on foot. The first confrontation and meeting with the ruler occurred across a large open courtyard. At the end of this, the monarch would appear seated in the Diwan-i-Am, high above the visitors, on a raised and roofed ceremonial platform.

of the Raj, and is in many ways similar to the carefully designed Mughal approach towards the emperor in the Red Fort along Chandni Chowk. The axial arrangement of New Delhi, focussing on the linear layout of the dominating central avenue of King's Way, now known as Rajpath, was devised to celebrate the authority and implied supremacy of the Viceroy as the representative of the British crown in India, ruling from his throne in the Durbar Hall of Viceroy's House.

At the end of Rajpath, at an appropriate distance from the colonial headquarters, the Indian princes were provided with splendid new residences[34]. This allowed the *maharajas* to partake in the grandeur of the novel imperial capital and to remain allies of the British. However, it was a spatial conception, which displayed unity and closeness as well as a clear separation[35]. In the same way as the government buildings, the residences followed the British imperial style of Delhi, the Indo-Saracenic style of architecture, and many were planned by Lutyens himself.

New Delhi was designed to symbolise the power and enduring supremacy of the British Raj in India. George V's decision was clearly motivated by strategic incentives. He wished to stabilise India by uniting the different princely chiefdoms and territories under his rule and to calm the agitated situation by making a vigorous statement of authority, control and superiority through the establishment of this mighty modern urban centre of power. His plan has generally been judged as a success. The Raj are believed to have developed a new national identity, and the *maharajas* of India, who had lobbied for a transfer of power to northern India, largely regarded it as an honour to have their residences in novel imperial Delhi[36].

Western archetypes

In addition to the Mughal influences outlined above, the strictly planned and geometrically designed layout of New Delhi reveals multiple references to a number of Western city models. Lutyens admired the Classical tradition and specifically the monuments of ancient Rome and the Italian Renaissance. Typical of his time, he had largely worked in the British Georgian style when designing architecture in Britain. This incorporates elements from Palladianism and from

---

34 The Montagu-Chelmsford-Reform of 1919 provided a settlement, which secured the needs of the *maharajas*. Volwahsen 2004, p. 250.

35 The British needed the Indian princes, who were regarded as symbols of an unchanging 'traditional' India, as a source of legitimacy for their rule. Metcalf 1989, p. 105.

36 Volwahsen 2004, p. 11.

the Classicism of continental Europe. This formal canon, with an emphasis on clarity, symmetry and frontality, in which Lutyens had been trained, was believed to agree well with the colonial objectives of contemporary international British foreign policy[37]. From a background of perceived unlimited military strength and a belief in the cultural supremacy of the colonial presence in India, a number of Western monumental city models were considered by the British architects and urban planners and clearly influenced the spatial conception of Delhi.

One of the most significant archetypal historic city models, employed as inspirations for the new imperial capital of British India, was Georges-Eugène Haussmann's plan of Paris. The radical transformation of the capital city of France by Napoleon III under the guidance of Haussmann had largely been implemented between 1852 and 1870. There are direct parallels between the Arc de Triomphe in Paris, with its twelve radiating avenues, and the layout of the All India War Memorial in Delhi, standing like the hub of a wheel at the centre of a star-shaped arrangement of streets[38]. The hexagonal street pattern surrounding the Champs Elysées in Paris appears to have acted as a model for the street pattern around King's Way in Delhi. Particularly pronounced is the axial sequence of the Louvre palace, followed by the obelisk in the Place de la Concorde and the triumphal arch of the Arc de Triomphe, which were directly reproduced in the latest capital of India. In New Delhi, the three consecutive architectural elements are the Viceroy's House, the Jaipur column and the All India Memorial[39].

There are a number of earlier but related capital cities, which also seem to have impacted on the design of New Delhi, even though Paris appears to have been most influential. For example, Sir Christopher Wren's unrealised plan for the rebuilding of central London after the Great Fire of 1666 shows similar frameworks of radial street patterns, which were further developed in the layout of Paris. It is likely that both were based on an even earlier version of axial road patterns found in the urban arrangement of ancient Rome. This can, for instance, be observed in the road configurations surrounding the Piazza del

---

37 Volwahsen 2004, p. 33.
38 After Independence, the All India War Memorial was renamed India Gate and this colonial triumphal arch – and New Delhi as a whole – were not destroyed or torn down as the disliked symbols of unpopular colonial rulers. This expresses the strength of the concept of re-use, which offers the opportunity for some elements to survive but to be provided with a different position or meaning in a new context. On the concept of re-use, see the introduction to Hegewald and Mitra 2012.
39 Volwahsen 2004, p. 34–37, has written in much detail on the Parisian model and its reflection in the urban plan of New Delhi.

Popolo (Volwahsen 2004: 38). The plan of imperial Delhi includes other allusions to Classical architecture and to urban elements of the Italian Renaissance. A sketch drawing by Lutyens, dated 14th June 1912, indicates that he studied the space shaped by Bernini's colonnades, which creates St. Peter's Square in Rome, when investigating various forms for the design of the ceremonial entrance area at the front of Viceroy's House[40].

Closely connected to the centre of political power, the palace of the Viceroy and its representational parade streets, is the commercial centre of New Delhi, conceived at the same time. Connaught Circus forms the centre of this trading nucleus. Between 1928 and 1931 it was designed on a strictly circular plan by R. T. Russell, the Chief Architect to the Government of India. At the centre lies a large public garden, Connaught Place. Based on ideas raised in the last paragraph, which connect the architecture of New Delhi with Classical models, the circular layout of this market area has been linked to the architecture of the Coliseum in Rome, however in Delhi, with the outer facade turned inwards[41].

Besides, the formal plan of Connaught Circus is directly related to similar round and oval-shaped plazas in England with some of the best known illustrations in Bath in the west country. These are John Wood's circular arrangement of town houses known as the Circus, realised between 1754 and 1768, and the semi-circular Royal Crescent, designed by his son John Wood the Younger, dating from 1767 to 1774. Similar in design is the early nineteenth-century semi-circular terraced crescent created by John Nash at the foot of Regent's Park in London, called Park Crescent. As symbols of fashionable living for the bourgeoisie these urban layouts were replicated throughout the country, for instance, in Pittville Circus Road in Cheltenham and in Park Town in Oxford[42]. From there, the fashion quickly spread throughout the empire. Contrasting with the commercial use of this design in India is the strictly residential nature of the earlier architectural models in Britain. Furthermore, the architectural arrangement in Delhi is much lager than any of the British examples, and Connaught Circus consists of two concentric rings of buildings.

The application of this striking geometric town-planning concept in India represents the transfer of a popular fashionable design, however, it also appears to carry deeper symbolic meanings. John Wood Snr (senior) was a Freemason

---

40 A reproduction of Lutyens' drawing has been published in Volwahsen 2004, p. 83.
41 Volwahsen 2004, p. 41–42.
42 These crescent-shaped streets provided the upward-moving groups of society at the time with affordable terraced housing associated with a distinct quality of appearance and appeal.

himself. We know that both his son and large sections of British society and royalty at the time were fascinated by Masonic concepts of geometry. The street layouts in Bath reflect on a gigantic scale the stellar bodies of the sun and moon[43], and many of the buildings in the Circus at Bath, bear decorations of Masonic symbols in the form of the square, the compass and other architect's tools which are employed in Masonic ceremonies[44].

The urban plan of the novel imperial city, which is characterised by a hexagonal arrangement of wide streets and the positioning of key monuments at important junctions, which are often roundabouts, can be related to the layout of Pierre Charles L'Enfant's design of Washington D.C. in North America too. President Washington established the city of Washington D.C. in 1790 as the capital of the new 'United States of America'. It is not surprising that when in 1911, Britain's King George V in his capacity as Emperor of India, founded a new capital which he hoped to act as a unifying agent for his shaken empire, he turned to and took inspiration from this famous centre of power. By relating his latest foundation to the prosperous capital of the United States of America, he struck a significant symbolic connection[45]. Herbert Baker and Lord Hardinge clearly expressed their appreciation of the design of the city and the Viceroy ordered maps of Washington D.C. for the Delhi city development team before work commenced[46]. There are clear connections in the layout of the Capitol and its radiating avenues in Washington D.C., specifically in the Mall leading to the Triumphal Arch, and the government buildings on Raisina Hill in Delhi. Both reflect an earlier Parisian archetype. Interestingly, the plan of the new capital of the United States combines other elements from prominent European city models[47] and illustrates that eclectic town planning, as emphasised in the case of Delhi,

---

43 Curl 1991, p. 91.

44 Volwahsen 2004, p. 40, 42. Other elements in the town plan too, indicate that the culture of the Freemasons had a pronounced influence on the design of New Delhi. These will be explored later in this chapter.

45 We know that Washington D.C. also served as a model for other foundations at the time. For instance, it acted as model for the newly-founded city of Rabat in Morocco. This was designed and realised by Henri Prost between 1910 and 1920. Rabat is typified by a similar radial street network and is known as the 'Washington D.C. of Marocco'. Çelik 1999, p. 197. Ten years later, the same system served as a planning paradigm for Ernst Hébrard's urban extension of Hanoi in French-Indochina.

46 They had ordered maps of the city of Paris too, to be used in the designing of New Delhi. On both, see Volwahsen 2004, p. 44.

47 There are further references to urban elements taken from the plans of Madrid, Amsterdam, Naples, Venice and Florence (Volwahsen 2004, p. 43).

was not unique but almost generally practiced in the process of designing capital cities which were meant to signal important cultural and imperial continuities and connections.

The city plan of Washington D.C., displays even stronger connections with symbols and concepts of the Freemasons than are obvious in the plazas designed in England. Washington D.C. has been based on a strict grid pattern in its street layout, which is punctuated by diagonal roads creating hexagonal and triangular shapes. The triangle and the hexagram are established Masonic symbols[48]. Even more than in Paris and Washington D.C., these provide the basic pattern of imperial Delhi's town plan. Since the eighteenth century, members of the Royal Arch of English Freemasons have worn the hexagram in a circle as their emblem and many members of the Royal Family and of British high society in the early part of the twentieth century are supposed to have been Freemasons. Therefore, the triangle and the hexagram as prime planning principles in the urban design of Delhi seem not to have been an unintentional choice[49].

Indigenous motifs

In addition to Western Masonic connections, the geometric motifs outlined in the plan of Delhi, can be related to indigenous Indian traditions of Islamic, Hindu and Jaina architecture. The presence of triangular and hexagonal shapes in the street pattern of Delhi appears to make direct reference to traditional indigenous Indian architecture. Especially in abstract architectural decorations, dating from the Mughal period, the combination of hexagrams and hexagons figure prominently[50]. The use of these designs in Lutyens' town layout can therefore be argued to demonstrate a further link between the British crown and the past splendour of the Mughal empire, which has already been noted in the choice of the site.

---

48 The geometric shape of a hexagram is produced by superimposing two triangles of equal size, one pointing up (towards heaven) and one pointing down (towards the earth). In Freemasonry, the hexagram is the symbol of 'The Great Architect of the Universe' (The Almighty).

49 Tillotson 1989, p. 124, judges the plan of Delhi as "not successful" as "It is a confusing web of triangles stacked in hexagons with a roundabout at each junction". However, the previous analysis explains one side of the double symbolic significance of this basic layout based on the symbolic forms of triangle and hexagram.

50 Hexagrams are, as outlined above, star-like shapes formed out of two equilateral triangles. In Mughal architectural decorations, hexagons are frequently created at their centres and often as an outer shape surrounding them.

The same symbolic shapes are encountered in sacred diagrams of Hindus, Buddhists and Jainas, such as *yantras* and *mandalas*. These have generally been used for visualisations and meditation, but at the same time as underlying principles for structuring sacred space[51]. In particular, from a Hindu background, clear evidence is available, which illustrates the use of symbolic shapes in the planning of temple complexes and cities[52]. We know that through his wife, Lady Emily, who was a member of the Theosophical Society, Edwin Lutyens was familiar with sacred Hindu symbolism and with symbolic shapes[53]. These indigenous motifs appear to have played a crucial role in shaping the urban environment of New Delhi as well.

Conclusion

The discussion above has shown that New Delhi, its governmental headquarters and economic centre were built in order to remove the British administration from the politically increasingly unstable Calcutta and to reaffirm the strength and splendour of the British Empire in stone. In this context, it is interesting to note that not a purely alien style of architecture was chosen but that by re-using elements from the Western and the Indian traditions, a hybrid architecture, acceptable to both cultures, was born. In this, British India differentiates itself clearly from other colonial nations and their approach to public edifices[54].

A similar approach was applied when developing the urban setting. The newly-founded imperial capital of the British Raj aimed to combine the fame and

---

51 In examples of Hindu *yantras* in the shape of a hexagram, the two triangles represent the union of the male (*purusha*) and the female (*prakriti*) principles. In Shiva *yantras*, they symbolise Shiva and Shakti. It is intriguing that the same shape of the hexagram plays a central role in Judaism in the form of the Star of David and in the Chinese I Ching. For a detailed study of *yantras*, see Khanna 1994.

52 For drawings illustrating the underlying *yantra* and *mandala* shapes below temples and city plans in India, see Khanna 1994, p. 147–148; Stierlin 2002, p. 65 and Fischer, Jansen und Pieper 1987, p. 13.

53 Volwahsen 2004, p. 64.

54 Sir Herbert Baker also designed public and government buildings in South Africa before starting his work in India. Planned by him, the Union Buildings in Pretoria, completed in 1913, make, for instance, no reference to local traditions. Similarly, the new colonial capital of Canberra in Australia appears not to establish any obvious links to indigenous spatial planning concepts. For further details and other comparative architectural or urban examples of the time, which do not make reference to local elements, see Hegewald 2012b, p. 291–337.

splendour of the great European capitals, such as Paris and London, and that of the United States of America. The political connotations of the choice of powerful city models as inspiration for Delhi has been brought to the point by Volwahsen who writes: "It was a matter of which motif, perspectives and spatial orders most effectively illustrated the British Crown's claim to leadership"[55]. However, these foreign imperial ideas of spatial planning were applied to an ancient Indian site, associated with great Hindu and Muslim ruling dynasties, and combined with Indian symbols, prominently figuring in the street layouts of this new imperial capital. This created a process of town planning, which was neither English nor Indian and transformed New Delhi into one of the great international and cosmopolitan cities of the world.

The imperial capital was of significance in the establishment and development of an emerging national consciousness in India. This is clearly expressed by the fact that after Independence the importance of the capital did not decline. In June 1948, when the last Viceroy Lord Mountbatten, who had also served for another ten months as governor general, left Delhi, the President of the Republic of India moved into the palace of the British Viceroy, a democratically elected parliament took up its seat in the Legislative Building and the former imperial city of the Raj functioned instantly as the capital of an independent India.

---

55 Volwahsen 2004, p. 33.

Guillaume Ducœur

Université de Strasbourg

Histoire comparée des religions et construction identitaire nationaliste dans le processus d'indépendance de l'Inde

> "The Hindoo proper has long and thin feet. The sandal-wearing Mohammedan has the great toe well separated from the others, because the thong is commonly passed between."
>
> Arthur Conan Doyle, *The Sign of the Four*, 1890.

L'indianiste français Alfred Foucher (1865–1952), qui vécut, de loin ou de plus près sur le sol indien lui-même, les évènements qui marquèrent la progressive indépendance de l'Inde, avançait en 1922 que « c'est la loi de son histoire que la périodique reconstruction et désintégration de ses empires, et il n'est pas encore d'exemple qu'aucun d'eux ait duré plus de trois cents ans. »[1] Si l'année 1947 marque symboliquement l'indépendance de l'Inde face à l'Empire colonial britannique, il faut remonter au dernier quart du XIXᵉ siècle pour voir s'organiser, dans l'ensemble du sous-continent, de multiples partis politiques de confessions hindoue et islamique qui œuvrèrent, dans un face à face concurrentiel, à la construction d'une identité singulière qui ne pouvait passer que par la déconstruction du paysage religieux de l'Inde d'alors et la reconstruction d'un nouveau. Or, bien que le modèle occidental eût permis aux différents leaders politiques indiens, occidentalisés ou non, de mieux asseoir leurs partis et d'assurer une plus large diffusion à leur propagande d'indépendance, un autre facteur aida, notamment les partis politiques hindous, à la reconstruction d'une identité nationale commune : la restitution de l'histoire préislamique de l'Inde par les indianistes européens. De fait, les savants occidentaux britanniques, allemands et français, apportèrent aux indiens, politiquement engagés dans la revendication de décolonisation de leur pays, les matériaux nécessaires à la construction de leur identité nationale et participèrent, indirectement, à l'édification d'une nouvelle histoire de l'Inde, celle que les leaders politiques hindous érigèrent et revendiquèrent dans leur lutte contre l'implantation de l'islam, qui remonte à la fin du XIIᵉ siècle,

---

[1]   Foucher 1922, p. 576.

et l'occupation britannique qui fut véritablement effective à partir du XVIIIe siècle. Que l'indianiste britannique Vincent Arthur Smith (1843–1920), retraité de l'*Imperial Civil Service*, écrivît en 1920 sans aucune approche historique critique qu'au temps d'Aśoka, la population bouddhiste, et seulement bouddhiste, devait être moins illettrée que sous la gouvernance du British Raj[2], et voici que l'historien indien Radha Kumud Mookerji affirmait en 1924 que les foules pouvaient lire les édits aśokéens et que la population indienne dans son ensemble, sous le règne d'Aśoka, était moins illettrée que sous la domination coloniale britannique :

> « Lastly, we may note the considerable extent of literacy in the country, where the masses could read the edicts of Asoka written in their own dialects and scripts. Vincent Smith thinks that the percentage of literacy in Asokan India must have been higher than it is now in many provinces of British India »[3]

Cette révision de l'histoire indienne relève du fantasme et de l'utopie lorsque l'on sait que les deux écritures, la karoṣṭhī pour transcrire les langues indo-ārya du Nord-Ouest indien et la brāhmī pour les parlers indo-ārya de l'Inde du Nord et Centrale, furent créées à partir de l'écriture araméenne, elle-même utilisée par l'administration achéménide, et que seuls les intendants de la chancellerie Maurya en avaient l'apanage. Si les inscriptions sur pilier et sur rocher étaient, pour certaines, suffisamment à hauteur d'homme pour pouvoir être déchiffrées, rares devaient être ceux à même de les lire. Comme dans l'empire achéménide, ces inscriptions témoignaient avant tout aux yeux des hommes et surtout auprès des dieux, combien le roi Aśoka s'évertuait à faire le bien dans son royaume, après les massacres du Kaliṅga, afin de racheter sa dette dans l'espoir d'atteindre le Ciel (svarga). Quant au peuple, il était directement informé de la loi (dharma) royale par des officiers (mahāmāttā) qui avaient à charge de la lui rappeler régulièrement par proclamation orale[4]. Du reste, les moines bouddhistes (bhikṣu) durent assez rapidement utiliser ces deux graphies pour consigner leur doctrine (dharma) et leurs règles disciplinaires (vinaya)[5] et être à l'origine de la diffusion de l'écriture indienne. Mais là encore, il ne devait s'agir sous le règne des rois Maurya que de quelques spécialistes de l'écriture dans les monastères (saṃghārāma).

---

2 « I think it likely that the percentage of literacy among the Buddhist population in Asoka's time was higher than it is now in many provinces of British India. », Smith 1920, p. 139.
3 Mookerji 1996, p. 131.
4 Voir par exemple les édits du Kaliṅga retrouvés à Dhauli et à Jaugada.
5 Voir l'édit de Bhabra.

Les śramanes dans leur ensemble, qui devaient accomplir leurs pérégrinations en dehors de la saison des pluies, et combien plus encore les brāhmanes, qui avaient développé tant de moyens mnémotechniques pour assurer la transmission orale de leur savoir (veda), ainsi que le reste de la population, n'avaient certainement accès ni à l'écriture, ni à la lecture.

Ce genre de reconstruction de l'histoire de l'Inde hindoue demeure encore aujourd'hui d'actualité puisque les archéologues nationalistes indiens et les militants du Bharatiya Janata Party soutiennent toujours l'autochtonie indienne des Ārya qui auraient fondé la civilisation dite Indus-Sarasvatī, du nom de deux fleuves, le premier le long duquel s'implantèrent de grands ensembles urbains (Harappa et Mohenjo-Daro) de 2500 à 1800 av. J.-C., le second connu depuis le *Rgveda* comme rivière mythique et dont le lit ancien, et aujourd'hui asséché, aurait été localisé dans le Nord de l'Inde[6]. Ces différentes théories sur l'origine des Indo-ārya, pénétration en Inde du Nord ou autochtonie, opposent irrémédiablement encore aujourd'hui les savants de toutes nationalités :

> « La seconde série de discussions oppose une poignée de savants indiens, souvent âgés, formés à l'occidentale et considérés par leurs collègues occidentaux comme étant au moins leurs égaux, à ce qui est en passe de devenir l'*opinio communis* d'une majorité d'Indiens hindous résidant en Inde ou travaillant aux États-Unis. Elle se déroule dans la presse et l'édition populaire indiennes ainsi que dans les forums sur l'internet. Elle est, pour les « révisionnistes », d'inspiration nettement religieuse, nationaliste et même raciste. Elle va trouver son expression dans les manuels scolaires, dont l'actuel gouvernement nationaliste indien a ordonné la révision. Les hindous nationalistes qui ont relancé la controverse ces dernières années partent de l'idée que le sanskrit n'a pas été apporté en Inde par des populations d'origine indo-européenne, qu'il y est autochtone et, pour certains, d'essence éternelle ; qu'on le parlait dans les villes de l'Indus et que la quasi-totalité des langues indiennes contemporaines en dérivent ; que la vue contraire n'est qu'une fiction des colonialistes occidentaux. La documentation utilisée par ces « révisionnistes » est l'interprétation indienne traditionnelle du *Rig-Veda*, différente sur beaucoup de points des interprétations occidentales, et l'analyse des fouilles, souvent peu ou mal publiées, des cites de l'Indus. La littérature occidentale récente est en général ignorée et considérée comme ne pouvant et ne valant pas la peine d'être consultée dès qu'elle est écrite dans une langue autre que l'anglais. »[7]

Cette revendication territoriale et d'autochtonie n'est pas nouvelle et, si l'on considère les propos d'Alfred Foucher, à savoir l'histoire des nombreuses invasions du territoire indien et l'émiettement répété des Empires qui se sont succédé au profit de petites principautés sur lesquelles régnaient des rājan, il faut admettre que

---

6   Cette théorie nationaliste a été relancée par Feuerstein, Kak et Frawley 1995.
7   Fussman 2003, p. 784.

Pañtajali (IIe s. av. J.-C.) dans son *Mahābhāṣya* 2.4.10[8] et l'auteur (IIe s. ap. J.-C.) du *Mānavadharmaśāstra* 2.17.22[9] avaient déjà en leur temps, essayé de définir les limites du territoire proprement ārya. Durant ces quatre siècles qui séparent ces deux auteurs et qui furent riches en évènements politiques et en conquêtes militaires, les frontières de l'Āryavarta avaient fluctué en fonction de l'hégémonie brāhmanique au sein des différentes chancelleries royales. Quant à la remise en question du fonctionnement de la société ārya par des Ārya eux-mêmes, celle-ci remonte encore plus loin dans l'Antiquité. Dans le *Veda*, apparaît déjà une redéfinition du statut socio-religieux du brāhmane par la bouche même d'Indra, kṣatriya par excellence, le brāhmane n'étant plus alors celui qui est né de parents appartenant à la classe sacerdotale (varṇa brāhmanique) mais toute personne reconnue pour son savoir (veda), sa science[10]. En dehors de cette revendication du savoir, parfois par des kṣatriya engagés dans des joutes oratoires contre des brāhmanes comme celle opposant Janaka, roi de Videha, et Yājñavalkya, narrée dans la *Bṛhadāraṇyakopaniṣad*, les écoles śramaniques critiquèrent vivement les pratiques sacrificielles brāhmaniques et les brāhmanes qui, sans jamais avoir ni étudié le *Veda*, ni pratiqué les observances, faisaient valoir leur rang social par leurs seuls varṇa héréditaire et accoutrement. Pour ces śramanes, souvent des brāhmanes convertis[11], le glissement sémantique du terme « brāhmaṇa » était inévitable comme en témoignent, par exemple, les stances bouddhiques du *Dhammapada* (IIIe s. av. J.-C.) : « Ce n'est ni par les tresses, ni par le clan, ni par

---

8 « Quel est le pays des Ārya ? [C'est la région] à l'est du lieu où la Sarasvatī disparaît, à l'ouest de la forêt Kālaka, au sud de l'Himālaya et au nord des montagnes Pāriyātra. » (kaḥ punaḥ āryāvartaḥ | prāg ādarśāt pratyak kālakavanāt dakṣiṇena himavantam uttareṇa pāriyātram ||).

9 « Depuis la mer orientale jusqu'à la mer occidentale, l'espace compris entre ces deux montagnes [Himālaya et Vindhya] est considéré par les sages comme le pays des Ārya. » (ā samudrāt tu vai pūrvād ā samudrāc ca paścimāt | tayor evāntaraṃ giryor āryāvartaṃ vidur budhāḥ ||).

10 « Se faisant passer pour brāhmane, Indra s'en vint à Manu et lui dit : 'N'es-tu pas un sacrificateur dont la seule divinité est la foi ?' Manu l'interrompit : 'Qui es-tu donc ?' '[Je suis] brāhmane ! Pourquoi s'enquérir du père ou de la mère d'un brāhmane ? Si on trouve de la science en lui : voilà son père, voilà son aïeul ! » (tam indro brāhmaṇo bruvāṇa upait so'bravīn mano yajvā vai śraddhādevo'si yājayāni tvā katamas tvam asi brāhmaṇaḥ kiṃ brāhmaṇasya pitaraṃ kimu pṛcchasi mātaram śrutaṃ ced asmin vedyaṃ sa pitā sa pitāmahaḥ) *Maitrāyaṇī Saṃhitā* 4.8.1.

11 Le Jina et le Buddha appartenaient tous deux, selon leur biographie traditionnelle respective, à la classe des kṣatriya. Néanmoins la communauté bouddhique (saṃgha) ne comptait pas moins pour moitié de brāhmanes. Schumann 1989, p. 214.

la naissance que l'on est brāhmane. Celui en qui existe la vérité et la doctrine, celui-là est heureux, il est brāhmane », ou encore : « Je ne l'appelle pas brāhmane celui qui, né de caste [brāhmanique] par [sa] mère, n'est en fait qu'un nanti interpellant [autrui] par 'Bho !'. Celui qui n'a rien, qui ne s'attache à rien, celui-là je l'appelle brāhmane »[12]. Cette dénonciation du statut du brāhmane revint régulièrement tout au long de l'histoire de la société indienne et, au XIXe siècle, par exemple, Dayānanda Sarasvatī (1824–1883) s'insurgea vivement encore et toujours contre la primauté sociale des brāhmanes sur les autres castes hindoues[13].

En Europe, le XIXe siècle fut une période importante dans la lente définition de l'État-nation et dans la construction d'une identité nationale qui ne pouvait exister sans l'invention d'une histoire nationale. Les grammairiens comparatistes des langues indo-européennes, les historiens des religions et les mythologues ont contribué par leurs travaux à fournir autant de pièces historiques éparses, en fonction des différentes approches des vestiges archéologiques et textuelles des peuples, qu'exigeait la restitution d'un nouveau puzzle d'historicité orientée. Parmi ces données historiques passées au crible de la critique et réutilisées ensuite dans la construction identitaire des nations européennes, les sources sanskrites offrirent jusqu'au milieu du XIXe siècle un double avantage, celui de remettre en question l'histoire construite judéo-chrétienne en redonnant aux peuples européens un semblant d'histoire protohistorique commune et celui de jeter un pont entre Europe et Asie, une Asie en grande partie colonisée par les pays européens eux-mêmes[14]. Or, ce fut durant les guerres européennes des XIXe et XXe siècles, qui

---

12 *Dhammapada* 393 (na jaṭāhi na gottena na jaccā hoti brāhmaṇo | yamhi saccañ ca dhammo ca so sukhī so ca brāhmaṇo ||) et 396 (na cāhaṃ brāhmaṇaṃ brūmi yonijaṃ mattisambhavaṃ | bhovādī nāma so hoti sa ve hoti sakiñcano | akiñcanam anādānaṃ tam ahaṃ brūmi brāhmaṇaṃ ||).

13 Lajpat Rai 1915 ; Jordens 1997.

14 En 1924, l'historien Radha Kumud Mookerji affirmait que « the discovery of Samskrit by the West has led the way to a far more important discovery of the proper place of Hindu thought in the culture history of the world. Vague and conflicting notions about the mere external accidents and superficial aspects of Hindu life have now yielded their place to a genuine, systematic, and scientific appreciation of Hindu philosophical and religious systems, and a due recognition is at last made of the immense value of the special contributions made to the progress of humanity as a whole by the Hindu people. It is, in a word, to her philosophy that India at present owes the respect of the world. » (Mookerji 1921, p. 1–2). Pourtant, dès la fin du XIXe siècle, en France tout au moins, la philosophie indienne n'avait déjà plus l'intérêt qu'on lui avait porté en Europe cinquante ans plus tôt. Jules Barthélémy-Saint-Hilaire (1805–1895), professeur de philosophie grecque au Collège de France, ancien ministre des Affaires

marquèrent profondément les esprits des Occidentaux et qui modifièrent la délimitation des territoires et des appartenances nationales, que les savants fouillèrent
les archives de l'Inde en quête d'un comparatisme heuristique pouvant leur apporter des éléments de réflexion nécessaire à la construction de leur propre identité en
devenir. De même que la tradition judéo-chrétienne maintenait que le berceau de
l'humanité avait été le Proche-Orient, de même les opposants à cette théorie religieuse des origines, qui touchait de près l'autochtonie des Européens, affirmaient
que le sanskrit avait été la langue mère de toutes les langues indo-européennes et
que le berceau des peuples européens devait donc être recherché en Inde même.
Néanmoins, ces derniers durent réviser leur propre théorie en considérant que le
« peuple » indo-européen d'avant la séparation avait dû émigrer dans toutes les
directions, tant vers le ponant que vers le levant, le nord que le sud, à partir d'une
région qu'ils situaient alors quelque part en Russie[15]. Sous domination britannique,
l'Inde entreprit également de travailler, dès la fin du XIXe siècle, et plus encore
après la Grande Guerre, à la construction de sa propre identité nationale afin de se
faire reconnaître comme nation à part entière. Pour ce faire, les leaders politiques
hindous eurent pour objectifs de restituer et de diffuser une histoire de l'Inde ancienne, préislamique et préchrétienne. Pour les nationalistes hindous, revendiquer
l'indépendance avait un double objectif : se libérer de l'occupation britannique et
se soustraire à son passé islamique. Les bouleversements géopolitiques, les grandes
découvertes archéologiques et philologiques européennes du XIXe siècle et du début du XXe siècle allaient les y aider et leur apporter des arguments pour étayer
leur revendication nationaliste à l'exemple de celle de Vināyak Dāmodar Sāvarkar
(1883–1966). Après son voyage en Europe et son arrestation à Marseille, celui-ci
développa, durant sa détention à la prison d'Andaman and Nicobar Islands, sa
doctrine de l'hindouité (hindutva[16]) :

étrangères de Jules Ferry, qui avait publié des ouvrages, en 1854, sur le *Veda* et, en
1855, sur le bouddhisme, déclarait en 1887 que « la sagesse indienne se réduit […] à
un génie poétique et religieux qui doit tenir une assez grande place dans les annales
de l'esprit humain, sans être l'égale du génie grec, ni surtout l'égale du judaïsme »
(Barthélémy-Saint-Hilaire 1887, p. 321). N'a-t-on jamais vu dans les programmes
scolaires de philosophie en Europe une partie consacrée aux philosophies indiennes
anciennes ? Dès la mise en place de l'instruction publique et laïque, la philosophie ne
pouvait qu'être grecque. Sur cette dénégation européocentrique consciente et affirmée
de la philosophie indienne voir Droit 2004.

15 Schrader 1890.

16 Bien que Savarkar ait prôné le sanskrit comme langue commune, il forgea néanmoins
son néologisme hindutva non à partir de la forme sanskrite Síndhu (*sindhutva) mais
à partir du persan Hindu (< vieux-perse Hi(n)duš) auquel il ajouta l'affixe –tva servant

« Are they (Italy, Germany, France, America) still a people, a nation and do they possess a common history? If they do, the Hindus do. If the Hindus do not possess a common history, then none in the world does.

As our history tells the story of the action of our race, so does our literature taken in its fullest sense tell the story of the thought of our race. Thought, they say is inseparable from our common tongue, Sanskrit. Verily it is our mother-tongue – the tongue in which the mothers of our race spoke and which has given birth to all our present tongues. Our gods spoke in Sanskrit, our sages thought in Sanskrit, our poets wrote in Sanskrit. All that is the best in us – the best thoughts, the best ideas, the best lines – seeks instinctively to clothe itself in Sanskrit. »[17]

Si la notion de nation désigne, depuis le XVIᵉ siècle en Europe, une communauté d'origine, de langue et de culture, les politiques indiens avaient pour difficulté de définir ce que serait l'Inde-nation. Jusqu'en 1914, les sécularistes hindous qui prônaient comme nation la délimitation du territoire indien, mettant ainsi à égalité les religions confessées sur le sol de l'Inde, et les nationalistes hindous qui ne reconnaissaient comme nation indienne que la seule nation ethnico-religieuse hindoue, s'opposèrent vivement et *a fortiori* aux partis indiens islamiques. Or, le plus grand obstacle à une telle « naissance » était de pouvoir écrire une histoire nationale de l'Inde avec des évènements historiques antérieurs à la naissance même, à l'existence constitutionnelle d'une Inde-nation indépendante qui n'existait pas encore. Cette écriture ne pouvait donc être qu'une réécriture arbitraire de l'histoire de l'Inde par une sélection de périodes historiques qui eurent pour fonction de renforcer le projet nationaliste hindou. En faisant la propagande de cette histoire reconstruite et sélective, les leaders politiques apportaient au « peuple hindou » les référents nécessaires pour légitimer la fondation d'une civilisation hindoue postislamique et postchrétienne entièrement renouvelée. Réinscrire l'Inde et son histoire dans la chronologie générale des peuples était donc indispensable. Or, ceci aurait été impossible sans le travail des indianistes européens qui, dans leur manie de tout historiciser, dans leur historiomania, avaient redonné une chronologie historique à l'Inde. Comment, en effet, les Indiens eux-mêmes auraient-ils pu établir une telle chronologie de l'Inde ancienne à partir de sources sanskrites et prakrites dont les auteurs étaient dits être pour la plupart soit des dieux soit des êtres mythiques et dont les indications temporelles des règnes, par exemple, renvoyaient le lecteur,

---

à former en sanskrit les abstraits. C'est donc un barbarisme mais un barbarisme qui avait l'avantage certain de s'opposer au néologisme anglais hinduism créé vers la fin du XVIIIᵉ siècle et calquant celui déjà forgé par les islamistes quelques siècles auparavant.

17 Savarkar 1969, p. 95.

certes, à une chronologie, mais entièrement indigène et sans aucune référence
à celle de ses voisins proches ou lointains ? Un texte tardif comme le *Bha-*
viṣyapurāṇa, souvent cité par Vināyak Dāmodar Sāvarkar (1883–1966) dans
son *Hindutva*, relate bien quelques faits historiques et mentionne des noms de
peuples ayant envahi successivement l'Inde mais l'auteur, qui employa le genre
littéraire prophétique pour attribuer à son écrit une ancienneté et ainsi asseoir
son autorité, annonça ces événements non comme des faits passés mais futurs.
D'où le titre de son ouvrage *[Récit] antique sur les temps à venir* et l'affirmation
de Sarvepalli Radhakrishnan (1888–1975) : « Les Purāṇas avec leur fantasque
chronologie et leur prévision de la destinée, forment une littérature surtout ima-
ginative, mais passèrent pour faire partie de la tradition sacrée pour cette simple
raison que des gens y prenaient intérêt »[18]. Ce qui posait donc problème n'était
pas la représentation indienne ancienne du temps, sur laquelle les brāhmanes
et les śramanes de l'Inde ancienne avaient déjà longuement discouru et à partir
de laquelle ils avaient établi des calendriers solaire, lunaire ou luni-solaire, mais
la manière indienne d'être dans le temps. Il est un fait que pour pouvoir revendiquer une autochtonie face aux autres nations voire aux allogènes présents sur
un territoire, tout indigène doit déterminer l'histoire de sa propre « origine ».
Or, cette démarche, somme toute alors inévitable, demandait aux nationalistes
hindous d'être dans le temps à la manière des Occidentaux. S'il ne peut y avoir
d'histoire des origines sans archives[19], démontrer l'ancienneté de la civilisation
indienne obligeait donc à considérer non seulement les sources textuelles, notamment le *Ṛgveda*, mais aussi et surtout les vestiges archéologiques, en particulier ceux des grandes cités indusiennes de Mohenjo Daro et Harappa[20] et de
l'empire Maurya (IVᵉ-IIIᵉ s. av. J.-C.). Encore fallait-il pour obtenir une reconnaissance internationale les inscrire dans le temps, celui que les Occidentaux
utilisaient pour restituer la chronologie du passé des peuples.

L'histoire de l'Inde moderne reste d'une très grande complexité tant les facteurs religieux, sociaux, politiques et économiques indiens, européens et plus
largement encore mondiaux s'imbriquent et interagissent les uns sur les autres.
Il n'est possible ici que de rappeler quelques faits qui ont contribué à côté de
bien d'autres à conduire l'Inde vers l'indépendance et la naissance d'une nation

---

18 Radhakrishnan 1935, p. 11.
19 Voir sur ce point Goody 1979 et 2007.
20 Les premiers sceaux en stéatite furent publiés par Alexander Cunningham (1814–
    1893) de 1872 à 1875. Les fouilles archéologiques systématiques d'Harappa et de
    Mohenjo Daro débutèrent dès les années 1920 sous la direction de John Marshall
    (1876–1958).

reconnue et pour lesquelles tant d'humains, qu'ils se fussent eux-mêmes considérés comme indigènes ou qu'ils fussent montrés du doigt comme allogènes, furent déplacés dans des conditions atroces et, irrémédiablement pires, furent massacrés. Sans revenir sur les liens tissés au XIXe siècle entre les membres du Brahmo Samaj[21] et les indianistes européens, il semble donc important de revenir sur les avancées de ces derniers, plus précisément sur celles de James Prinsep (1799–1840) et Max Müller (1823–1900), et sur la réutilisation de leurs travaux par des historiens, intellectuels et politiques hindous tels Bal Gangadhar Tilak (1856–1920) et surtout, dans la continuité de ce dernier, Sarvepalli Radhakrishnan (1888–1975).

La plupart des leaders politiques hindous prirent en exemple l'empire Maurya (322–185 av. J.-C.), dont les frontières s'étendaient de l'Afghanistan actuel à l'Inde du sud (Mysore), non seulement pour l'étendue de son territoire, plus vaste que celui du British Raj d'alors, et sa prétendue cohésion sociale, malgré son paysage pluriethnique et plurireligieux, mais aussi pour les relations commerciales et diplomatiques tissées avec les chancelleries hellénistiques (yavana), séleucide et ptolémaïque, que ses rois successifs surent entretenir. Parmi la dynastie Maurya, Aśoka fut assurément pour les nationalistes hindous l'exemple même du dirigeant politique qu'ils érigèrent en modèle car, sous son règne, affirmaient-ils, « many a small state or people in the remaining parts of India was spared its independence. India became a happy family of nations under an international system of Liberty, Equality and Fraternity for all, great or small. States unequal in size and strength were deemed equal as regards their status or sovereignty »[22]. Mais que connaissait l'Inde, d'avant 1837, du roi Aśoka et de son règne ? Une vie légendaire construite par les Écoles bouddhiques connue sous le titre d'*Aśokāvadāna*. Il restait de cette geste du roi Aśoka des extraits dans le *Divyāvadāna* sanskrit, dans les Chroniques singhalaises palies (*Dīpavaṃsa*, *Mahāvaṃsa* et *Samantapāsādikā*) ainsi que des allusions dans des textes jaina ou dans des généalogies royales brāhmaniques consignées dans les *Purāṇa*. Quant à l'*Aśokāvadāna* lui-même, il n'était plus accessible que par deux traductions chinoises, l'*Āyùwáng zhuàn* (阿育王傳, T 2042) et l'*Āyùwáng jīng* (阿育王經, T 2043) datant respectivement du IVe siècle et du VIe siècle ap. J.-C. À la différence de son grand père Candragupta dont le patronyme avait été transcrit par les Grecs par Sandrakottos (Σανδράκοττος), et dont le règne était contemporain

---

21 Notamment Ram Mohan Roy (1772–1833), Debendranath Tagore (1817–1905), Keshab Chandra Sen (1838–1884), Vivekananda (1863–1902). Voir Müller 1884.
22 Mookerji 1924, p. 119. Sur le réemploi de la devise républicaine française, voir Radhakrishnan ci-dessous.

de celui de Séleucos Ier Nicator, Aśoka ne fut sujet d'aucun commentaire ou allusion dans les textes grecs et latins. Seuls les sources bouddhiques et les *Purāṇa* affirmaient qu'il avait été le petit-fils de Candragupta. De fait, rien ne permettait d'inscrire précisément son règne dans une chronologie en dehors de celle de l'ère bouddhique qui avait pour date inaugurale le parinirvāṇa du Buddha, mais que les savants européens ne pouvaient néanmoins aucunement situer sur leur propre échelle temporelle fondée par convention sur l'ère chrétienne. Rien ne permettait de restituer le programme politique et sa mise en place sur l'ensemble du territoire maurya par Aśoka. Ne demeurait plus alors, dans les textes, qu'une figure construite par le saṃgha bouddhique qui s'enorgueillissait de montrer que la vraie doctrine (saddharma), celle du Buddha, avait eu raison de la cruauté du petit-fils de Candragupta.

Pourtant, l'Inde avait conservé des piliers antiques sur lesquels figuraient des inscriptions. Mais encore fallut-il que les intellectuels indiens pussent les déchiffrer. L'historien arabe Shams-i Siráj 'Afíf (XIVe siècle) raconte dans le neuvième *Mukaddama* de son *Táríkh-i Fíroz Shahí* comment le sultan Firuz Shah (1309–1388) fit transporter de Tobra l'une de ces colonnes de quatorze mètres de haut, sur un chariot à quarante-deux roues tiré par 8 400 hommes, en lui faisant franchir la Yamunā pour l'aller ériger en la ville de Delhi. Les islamistes l'appelèrent *minaret en or* (menāra-ye zarrin), les hindous *bâton de marche de Bhīmasena* (Bhím), du nom de l'un des cinq frères Pāṇḍava, héros de la grande épopée indienne, le *Mahābhārata*. Les inscriptions ne manquèrent pas d'attirer l'attention et d'être l'occasion de toutes les imaginations comme en témoigne Shams-i Siráj : « On ne savait pas qui avait planté (ce minaret) à Tobra et qui l'avait préservé. Quelques lignes, reconnues comme étant d'une écriture hindoue, avaient été gravées en bas du minaret. Le sultan Firuz Shah fit appel à de nombreux Porteurs de cordon[23] (zennār-Dārān) et Sivažgān[24] mais personne ne parvint à les déchiffrer. On dit que certains mécréants lurent cette écriture hindoue et qu'il était écrit : 'Ce minaret, personne ne peut de toutes ses forces le bouger de cet endroit, ni aucun parmi les sultans musulmans ni aucun parmi les rois tyrans, sauf dans les derniers temps, lorsqu'arrivera un roi somptueux dont le nom sera Firuz. C'est lui qui décidera et c'est (encore) lui qui extirpera ce minaret de cet endroit.' »[25]. Aux dires de Muhammed Arim dans son *Haftaklím*, ni islamistes ni hindous n'avaient pu comprendre l'inscription qui l'entourait : « Round it have been

---

23 Brāhmane.
24 Sevaka, c'est-à-dire dévots hindous.
25 Shams-i Siráj 1891, p. 312 ; Elliot 1871, p. 352.

engraved literal characters which the most intelligent of all religions have been unable to explain. »[26]. Dès 1801, un fac-similé de l'inscription fut publié dans les *Asiatic Researches*, mais il fallut attendre 1837 pour qu'un administrateur britannique, James Prinsep (1799–1840), parvint, après plusieurs années de travail épigraphique acharné sur des inscriptions kuṣāṇa et gupta, d'études numismatiques et grâce à une géniale intuition[27], à percer le mystère de cette inscription[28] puis de celles d'Allahabad, de Girnar et de Dhauli. Son déchiffrement exceptionnel des alphabets anciens, nommés brāhmī et kharoṣṭhī, lui permit de restituer un dialecte ancien qu'il situait entre le sanskrit et le pali et dont il parvint à découvrir le sens par tâtonnements et grâce à l'aide de pandits indiens :

> « The difficulties with which I have had to contend are of a very different nature from those presented by more modern inscriptions, where the sense has to be extracted from a mass of hyperbolical eulogy and extravagant exaggeration embodied still in very legible and classical Sanskrit. Here the case is opposite: – the sentiments and the phraseology are perfectly simple and straightforward – but the orthography is sadly vitiated – and the language differs essentially from every existing written idiom: it is as it were intermediate between the Sanskrit and the Pálí; and a degree of licence is therefore requisite in selecting the Sanskrit equivalent of each word, upon which to base the interpretation – a licence dangerous in the use unless restrained within wholesome rules; for a skilful pandit will easily find a word to answer any purpose if allowed to insert a letter or alter a vowel *ad libitum*. »[29]

---

26 Prinsep 1837b, p. 566.

27 Considérant que les constructions de Sānchī avaient été des commandes de donateurs zélés, il supposa que le terme qui se répétait systématiquement en finale de chacune des inscriptions des piliers devait être dānam (don). Ceci lui permit d'identifier deux caractères et lui fournit une clé d'entrée dans cet alphabet ancien.

28 « I am already nearly prepared to render to the Society an account of the writing on Sultan Firoz's lát at Delhi, with no little satisfaction that, as I was the first to analyze those unknown symbols and shew their accordance with the system of the Sanskrit alphabets in the application of the vowel-marks, and in other points, so I should be now rewarded with the completion of a discovery I then despaired of accomplishing for want of a competent knowledge of the Sanskrit language. », Prinsep 1837a, p. 452.

29 Prinsep 1837b, p. 567. Lorsqu'il dut rentrer en Angleterre à cause de son état de santé alarmant, James Prinsep savait qu'il n'aurait plus l'occasion de poursuivre ses travaux de déchiffrement et surtout de traduction en consultant les savants indiens : « C'est une immense interruption de mes recherches, car je ne serai pas assez longtemps en Europe pour augmenter la somme de mes connaissances, et, faute d'un Pandit à côté de moi, je serai incapable d'y poursuivre mon projet de lire les inscriptions, dont j'ai encore un si grand nombre entre les mains ! », Lettre de James Prinsep à Eugène Burnouf datée 24 octobre 1838 de Calcutta. Lisle 1891, p. 533.

Cette découverte et cette avancée prodigieuses enthousiasmèrent les indianistes européens tel Eugène Burnouf (1801–1852), fondateur de la Société asiatique de Paris, professeur au Collège de France et initiateur de la bouddhologie
en Europe. Le 27 décembre 1837, il écrivait à James Prinsep :

> « Le jour où je l'ai reçu[30], j'allais à l'Académie. Quoique ce savant corps ne prête son
> attention en ce moment qu'au grec et à l'arabe, j'ai demandé la parole, et j'ai trouvé de
> la verve pour exposer tout ce que vous veniez de faire de beau et de grand par votre
> découverte. J'ai été écouté avec une religieuse attention, et je sais que la communication
> a fait quelque effet.
>
> Chose singulière ! J'avais déjà fait des essais infructueux sur les copies du VIIᵉ volume
> des *Asiatic Researches*. J'avais huit lettres, mais m'étant lourdement trompé sur l'une et
> ne sachant que faire d'une autre, je n'avais pu passer outre… Votre *N* est un véritable
> trait de vive lumière, qui a rendu à ce caractère le même service que le *n* des inscriptions
> cunéiformes de Rask. »[31]

En déchiffrant le nom Devānaṃpiya (« Ami des dieux ») et en prenant également en compte les renseignements de l'anglais George Turnour (1799–1843),
traducteur du *Mahāvaṃsa* (Chronique bouddhique singhalaise), James Prinsep identifia ce dernier à Tissa, roi de Ceylan et allié d'Aśoka. Puis, découvrant
qu'une inscription de la grotte de Nagarjuni attribuait aussi devānaṃpiya au roi
Dasalatha, petit-fils d'Aśoka, J. Prinsep comprit que devānaṃpiya n'était qu'une
titulature royale et que le nom propre du roi devait alors être Piyadassi (« Au
regard amical »). Or, dans le *Mahāvaṃsa*, Piyadassi était associé au roi Aśoka.
Celui qui avait fait graver ces inscriptions sur des piliers et des rochers et qui
commençait ses proclamations royales par devānaṃpiye piyadassi lāja hevaṃ
āhā (« Le roi ami des dieux au regard amical parle ainsi ») devait donc avoir été le
roi Aśoka, petit-fils de Candragupta. Néanmoins, il fallut attendre la découverte
de l'inscription de Maski, en 1915, pour confirmer cette conjecture. En effet, ce
texte est le seul à mentionner le nom du roi, devānaṃpiyassa asokassa (« de l'ami
des dieux Asoka »).

Mais, outre cette identification précieuse, l'intérêt pour ces inscriptions aśokéennes devint inestimable lorsque James Prinsep déchiffra les deuxième et trei-
zième édits sur rocher de Girnar dans lesquels Aśoka fit citer le nom de rois
grecs (Aṃtiyako/Antiochos II de Syrie, Turamāyo/Ptolémée II Philadelphe
d'Égypte, Aṃtekin/Antigone Gonatas de Macédoine, Magā/Magas de Cyrène)
qui, tous, vivaient encore vers 260 av. J.-C. Ces identifications et ce synchro-
nisme entre ces rois grecs, auxquels il convient d'ajouter Alikasudaro/Alexandre

---

30 Le cahier de juin 1837 du *The Journal of the Asiatic Society of Bengal*.
31 Lisle 1891, p. 312–313.

d'Épire, donnèrent enfin la clé de la chronologie de l'Inde ancienne. Dès lors, puisqu'Aśoka déclarait, huit ans après son sacre, avoir fait promulguer par ses émissaires sa loi socio-politique (dharma) jusque chez les rois grecs (yonarājā), son sacre avait dû avoir lieu en 268 av. J.-C. À partir de cette date plausible, il était devenu possible de calculer approximativement le parinirvāṇa du Buddha en fonction des indications temporelles de la tradition bouddhique conservée dans le *Mahāvaṃsa* (218 ans avant le sacre d'Aśoka), 268+218, soit en l'année 486 av. J.-C. La tradition bouddhique rapportant également que le Buddha aurait vécu 80 ans, il était alors aisé de calculer pareillement son année de naissance, 486+80, soit 566 av. J.-C.[32] Mais cette datation de la vie du fondateur du bouddhisme, qui pouvait dorénavant faire son entrée dans la chronologie historique générale de l'humanité restituée par les savants européens du XIXe siècle, car attestée par des vestiges archéologiques, ouvrait d'autres perspectives nouvelles, celles de la datation possible du *Veda*.

Après les tentatives de Henry Thomas Colebrooke (1765–1837) visant à déterminer les périodes de composition du *Veda*, l'indianiste Max Müller (1823–1900)[33], qui, à l'instigation d'Eugène Burnouf, s'employa avec ténacité durant vingt-neuf ans à l'édition du *Ṛg veda* et de son commentaire médiéval de Sāyaṇa[34], tenta à son tour d'établir une chronologie des textes védiques[35]. Aidé par la découverte de J. Prinsep, les datations possibles du règne d'Aśoka et de la

---

32 Les chiffres avancés par la tradition bouddhique sont probablement eux-mêmes construits (218 = 100 + 100 + 18). Les traditions sanskrite et tibétaine donne 100 et 110 ans entre le parinirvāṇa du Buddha et le sacre d'Aśoka et non 218. La durée de vie du Buddha, 80 ans, est elle aussi sujette à caution. Elle signifie que le fondateur de ce mouvement śramanique aurait vécu assez longtemps. D'après les dernières recherches archéologiques, les indianistes datent aujourd'hui la mort du Buddha entre 400 et 380 av. J.-C. Voir Bechert 1991.

33 Sur la vie de M. Müller voir George Harris, *Notice sur la vie et les ouvrages de M. Max Müller, professeur à l'Université d'Oxford, membre correspondant de l'Institut de France*, Paris, A. Durand et Pedone Lauriel, 1867 ; Max Müller, *My autobiography, a Fragment*, New York, Charles Scribner's Sons, 1901 ; Georgina Adelaide Müller, *The Life and Letters of the Right Honourable Friedrich Max Müller*, 2 vol., London, Longmans, Green and Co, 1902 ; Nirad Chandra Chaudhuri, *Scholar extraordinary: the life of professor the Rt. Hon. Max Müller*, London, Chatto and Windus, 1974 ; Lourens Van Den Bosch, *Friedrich Müller: a Life Devoted to the Humanities*, Leiden, Brill, 2002 ; Jon Stone, *The Essential Müller on Language, Mythology and Religion*, New York, Palgrave Macmillan, 2002.

34 Ducœur 2013.

35 Müller 1859.

datation de la vie du Buddha, il admit que les textes védiques étaient assurément antérieurs à ce dernier. Il remonta le temps en répertoriant les sources védiques selon quatre grandes périodes : les *Sūtra*, entre 200 et 600 av. J.-C., les *Brāhmaṇa*, entre 600 et 800 av. J.-C., les *Mantra*, entre 800 et 1000 av. J.-C.) et enfin les *Chandas* supposés avoir été composés entre 1000 et 1200 av. J.-C. Cette chronologie hypothétique, qui avait le seul tort de voir dans toutes ces productions religieuses des périodes successives distinctes, fut largement acceptée durant tout le XIXe siècle et une grande partie du XXe siècle comme le rappelait l'indianiste français Louis Renou (1896–1966) : « Il a donné partout des directives avec une si déconcertante intuition que si, à sa mort, toute son œuvre semblait ruinée, on ne peut dire qu'aujourd'hui aucun de ses résultats soit gravement compromis. »[36]. Ainsi, selon l'hypothèse émise par Max Müller, la composition des hymnes (sūkta) r̥gvédiques remontait vers la fin du IIe millénaire avant notre ère[37]. Ces sūkta étaient, de ce fait, bien plus anciens que tous les textes grecs et latins jusque-là connus[38]. N'ayant aucunement subi une quelconque influence judéo-chrétienne, Max Müller qui avait grandement orienté ses recherches dans le domaine de la grammaire et de la mythologie comparées indo-européennes, pouvait alors déclarer : « In so far as we are Aryans in speech, that is, in thought, so far the R̥g Veda is our own oldest book »[39]. Ceci ne laissa pas indifférents les intellectuels et politiques indiens comme Sarvepalli Radhakrishnan qui, citant cette phrase de Max Müller en 1939, ne pouvait qu'en conclure à son tour que « Thus in the R̥g veda the European will find memorials of his own racial inheritance. »[40]. Au vu des correspondances linguistiques entre les langues grecque, latine, celtiques, iraniennes, germaniques, slaves et le sanskrit védique, les rapprochements possibles entre les mythes appartenant à tous ces anciens peuples dont les langues dérivaient toutes d'une langue commune, Max Müller supposa que les compositeurs

---

36 Renou 1928, p. 20.
37 Aujourd'hui, grâce à des études dialectologiques plus minutieuses et à l'appui de découvertes archéologiques, les spécialistes s'accordent pour donner une datation encore plus haute. Les hymnes auraient été composés durant la période chalcolithique et l'âge du Bronze de 1700 av. J.-C. à 1200 av. J.-C., date de l'apparition du fer dans les régions du Nord-Ouest indien. Voir Witzel 1989.
38 Les tablettes comportant des inscriptions dites Linéaire B ne seront découvertes par Arthur John Evans (1851–1941) qu'en 1900 et le Linéaire B déchiffré par Michael Ventris (1922–1956) qu'en 1952. Et encore, ces quelques inscriptions n'ont rien de comparable avec la richesse poétique des 1017 hymnes du R̥g Veda. Quant au hittite, il ne sera déchiffré qu'à partir de 1914 par Bedřich Hrozný (1879–1952).
39 Kaegi 1886, p. 25.
40 Radhakrishnan 1959, p. 119.

des sūkta, qui se déclaraient eux-mêmes ārya, avait dû investir les territoires du Nord-Ouest indiens puis s'installer au Panjab au cours du IIe millénaire av. J.-C. Mais en aucune manière, Max Müller ne voyait dans ces peuples anciens, qui avaient parlé des langues dérivées d'une langue commune et dont il essayait de restituer les racines nominales et verbales, une quelconque race āryenne :

« I have declared again and again that if I say Aryas, I mean neither blood nor bones, nor hair nor skull; I mean simply those who speak an Aryan language. The same applies to Hindus, Greeks, Romans, Germans, Celts, and Slaves. When I speak of them I commit myself to no anatomical characteristics. The blue-eyed and fair-haired Scandinavians may have been conquerors or conquered, they may have adopted the language of their darker lords or their subjects, or vice versa. I assert nothing beyond their language when I call them Hindus, Greeks, Romans, Germans, Celts, and Slaves; and in that sense, and in that sense only, do I say that even the blackest Hindus represent an earlier stage of Aryan speech and thought than the fairest Scandinavians. This may seem strong language, but in matters of such importance we cannot be too decided in our language. To me an ethnologist who speaks of Aryan race, Aryan blood, Aryan eyes and hair, is as great a sinner as a linguist who speaks of a dolichocephalic dictionary or a brachycephalic grammar. »[41]

Les travaux de Max Müller eurent un accueil non négligeable en Inde et le savant allemand, qui enseigna sa vie durant à Oxford, sut entretenir des liens importants avec les intellectuels indiens, notamment du Brahmo Samaj[42]. L'édition en six volumes du *Ṛg Veda* fut bien accueillie en Inde par des brāhmanes de Bénarès[43]

---

41 Müller 1888, p. 120.

42 En 1845, Max Müller fit la connaissance à Paris, par l'intermédiaire d'Eugène Burnouf, de Dvārkānāth Tagore (1794–1846) avec qui il partagea d'agréables moments et fut encore à ses côtés lors de son entrevue avec Louis Philippe (Müller (G. A.) 1902, vol. 1, p. 38). Il correspondit avec son petit-fils Satyendranath Tagore (1817–1905) et rencontra Keshub Chandra Sen (1838–1884), en 1870, lors d'un dîner avec le prince Léopold (1853–1884), et avec lequel il échangea une longue correspondance jusqu'à sa mort en 1884 (Müller (G. A.) 1902, vol. 1, p. 374). M. Müller fut aussi un proche de Protap Chunder Mozoomdar (1840–1905). Bien qu'il n'agréât aucunement la chronologie védique développée par Bal Gangadhar Tilak (1856–1920), sa clémence envers ce nationaliste indien lui valut quelques griefs de la part des Britanniques (Müller (G. A.) 1902, vol. 2, p. 370). En août 1896, Vivekānanda (1863–1902) et Anāgarika Dharmapāla (1864–1933) vinrent s'entretenir avec lui à Oxford (Müller (G. A.) 1902, vol. 2, p. 350). En août 1900, ce fut le yogin Agamya Yogindra, venu de Bombay, qui lui rendit visite (Müller (G. A.) 1902, vol. 2, p. 413).

43 « Wilson received a letter from Benares the other day, which says that the learned Brahmans there shook their heads mightily at first, but now, after having received and read a specimen of 200 pages, they are highly pleased with the edition of the *Veda*. », (Müller (G. A.) 1902, vol. 1, p. 116.).

dès 1850, puis par ceux de Poona en 1862[44] et lui valut la reconnaissance éternelle des dirigeants de l'Adi Brahmo Samaj en 1875 :

> « Sir, Allow me to convey to you the best and most sincere thanks of the Committee of the Adi Brahmo Somâj for your very kind present of your edition of the *Rig-veda*, the sixth volume of which they received the other day. They cannot express to you their sense of the value of your magnificent present.
>
> The Committee further beg to offer you their hearty congratulations on the completion of the gigantic task which has occupied you for the last quarter of a century. By publishing the *Rig-veda* at a time when Vedic learning has, by some sad fatality, become almost extinct in the land of its birth, you have conferred a boon upon us Hindus, for which we cannot but be eternally grateful. »[45]

Dès lors que ces recherches historiques furent publiées à partir du milieu du XIXᵉ siècle puis reprises et complétées par les savants européens, les nationalistes hindous eurent matière à revendiquer un passé tout aussi ancien, si ce n'est plus ancien, que celui de la civilisation européenne qui se réclamait d'une double tradition, judéo-chrétienne et gréco-romaine, et ô combien plus antique que la civilisation islamique qui n'était née qu'au cours du VIIᵉ siècle ap. J.-C. Diplômé du Decan College de Poona en 1877, Bal Gangadhar Tilak (1856–1920) fut à même de compulser les ouvrages des indianistes européens et de proposer sa propre hypothèse chronologique du *Veda*. En 1893, il publia son *The Orion or Researches into the Antiquity of the Vedas* dans lequel il avançait une datation éminemment plus haute que celle proposée par Max Müller. Basant ses recherches sur l'astronomie védique et la mythologie comparée entre les mondes védique, iranien et grec, il détermina quatre périodes successives au cours de l'histoire de la civilisation aryenne. La période pré-Orion, de 6000 à 4000 av. J.-C., n'aurait laissé de trace que dans les hymnes ṛgvédiques des Aryens indiens qui, à la différence des Grecs et des Iraniens, « have preserved all the traditions with a super-religious fidelity and scrupulousness »[46]. La deuxième période dite Orion, s'étendant de 4000 à 2500 av. J.-C., aurait été la plus importante de la civilisation aryenne durant laquelle Grecs, Iraniens et Indiens auraient développé une nouvelle

---

44 Les brāhmanes de Poona corrigèrent leurs propres manuscrits à partir des trois premiers volumes. L'indianiste allemand Martin Haug (1827–1876), alors professeur de sanskrit à Poona, rapporta à Max Müller le titre honorifique que ces brāhmanes lui attribuèrent : « Their judgement is to this effect. This edition must be written by a great Pundit versed in the *Vedas* and *Sâstras* (*veda-sâstra sampanum*), the highest title of honour of a learned man in India. », (Müller (G. A.) 1902, vol. 1, p. 267).

45 Lettre du secrétaire de l'Adi Brahmo Samaj de Calcutta datée du 28 mai 1875. Müller (G. A.) 1902, vol. 1, p. 488.

46 Tilak 1893, p. 206.

mythologie à partir de celle de la période précédente et qui demeurerait consignée tout autant dans le *Rgveda* que dans les sources grecques et iraniennes. Durant la troisième période, appelée Krittika (2500 à 1400 av. J.-C.), les brāhmanes, qui n'auraient plus eu les capacités de comprendre le sens des vieux hymnes rgvédiques, auraient alors composé les *Samhitā* et les *Brāhmana*, et se seraient orientés vers la spéculation. Bien qu'ils entrassent en contact avec la Chine, leur système astronomique « was decidedly of Hindu origin and of purely Hindu origin being handed down from the remotest or the pre-Orion period in the Vedic literature »[47]. Enfin, la quatrième et dernière période, dite période prébouddhique de 1400 à 500 av. J.-C., aurait été celle des *Sūtra* et de l'émergence des systèmes philosophiques. Tilak fut assurément l'un des premiers nationalistes hindous à avoir voulu accorder aux Indo-ārya la conservation de la civilisation aryenne depuis la période néolithique. Si sa théorie fut personnelle, les remerciements[48] qu'il formula en ouverture de son ouvrage, montrent assez qu'il fit appel tout autant à des savants indiens pour accéder aux travaux des philologues allemands qu'à Max Müller lui-même. Si le savant d'Oxford était loin de cautionner la chronologie[49] de Tilak, il avait toujours néanmoins encouragé ce dernier dans la poursuite scientifique de ses recherches[50] :

> « I wrote to Prof. Max Müller after my release, I thanked him sincerely for his disinterested kindness, and also gave him a brief summary of my new theory regarding the primitive Aryan home as disclosed by Vedic evidence. It was, of course, not to be expected that a scholar, who had worked all his life on a different line, would accept the new view at once, and that too on reading a bare outline off the evidence in its support. Still it was encouraging to hear from him that though the interpretations of Vedic passages proposed by me were probable, yet my theory appeared to be in conflict with the established geological facts. I wrote in reply that I had already examined the question from that stand-point, and expected soon to place before him the whole evidence in support of my view. But, unfortunately I have been deprived of this pleasure by his deeply mourned death which occurred soon after. »[51]

---

47 Tilak 1893, p. 208.
48 « My special thanks are however due to Dr. Ramkrishna Gopal Bhandarkar, who kindly undertook to explain to me the views of German scholars in regard to certain passages from the *Rigveda*, and to Khan Bahadur Dr. Dastur Hoshang Jamasp for the ready assistance he gave in supplying information contained in the original Parsi sacred books. I am also greatly indebted to Prof. Max Müller for some valuable suggestions and critical comments on the etymological evidence contained in the essay. », Tilak 1893, p. VII.
49 Müller (G. A.) 1902, vol. 2, p. 370.
50 Lorsque Tilak fut emprisonné en 1898, Max Müller demanda à ce qu'on lui remit sa seconde édition du *Rg Veda* afin que le savant indien pût poursuivre ses propres recherches sur la littérature védique durant sa détention. Tilak 1903, p. iii.
51 Tilak 1903, p. iii-iv.

En 1903, Tilak publia un nouvel ouvrage sur les origines de la civilisation aryenne, *The Arctic Home in the Vedas*[52], faisant suite au précédent et précisant sa chronologie des sources védiques. Pour lui, il ne faisait plus aucun doute que, vers 8000 av. J.-C., « the primitive Aryan home was both Arctic and inter-Glacial »[53]. Sa thèse, qui renouait avec la théorie polaire de l'origine des Indo-européens développée en Europe à partir de la fin du XVIIIᵉ siècle, eut quelque succès chez les nationalistes hindous et certains savants européens. Elle est encore aujourd'hui régulièrement citée[54]. Comme le rappelle à juste titre Gérard Fussman, « le livre maintenant ancien de Tilak, qui pourtant est connu surtout comme militant de l'indépendance indienne, était en son temps une merveille de science et de raisonnement »[55]. L'auteur, en effet, avait su investir un champ de recherche très complexe, celui de l'astronomie et des calendriers liturgiques védiques. Mais là encore, cette théorie se heurtait à la complexité des mouvements et des échanges des peuples de la période néolithique. Si Tilak avait remis en cause le découpage chronologique que Max Müller avait opéré sur la productivité des compositions védiques en se basant sur une approche linguistique, il apparaît que, s'étant essentiellement fondé sur des données astronomiques, les mêmes critiques pouvaient lui être faites. En effet, il était, et il est toujours, hasardeux de vouloir prouver l'existence d'un peuple originel dont l'historicité ne repose au final que sur la reconstruction hypothétique d'une protolangue unitaire qui, elle-même, ne reflète en rien ni sa richesse dialectologique ni son histoire. De même en est-il, à partir de cette restitution linguistique, de la reconstruction sans histoire d'une mythologie, voire d'une pensée, et de représentations d'espace et de temps communes et unitaires[56].

Lorsqu'en 1911, Sarvepalli Radhakrishnan (1888–1975), né dans une famille brāhmanique, diplômé du Madras Christian College et professeur de philosophie au Presidency College[57], publia un article sur l'étude comparée de la *Bhagavadgītā* et de la philosophie kantienne, Tilak en prit connaissance puis le cita dans l'introduction de son propre commentaire sur la *Bhagavadgītā* : « The second

---

52 Traduit en français par Claire Rémy et publié aux éditions Archè Milano en 1979 : *Origine polaire de la tradition védique: Nouvelles clés pour l'interprétation de nombreux textes et légendes védiques.*

53 Tilak 1903, p. vi.

54 François 2011.

55 Fussman 2003, p. 812.

56 Sur la théorie polaire des origines des Indo-ārya voir en dernier lieu Bongard-Levin et Grantovskij 1981.

57 Murty and Vohra 1990, p. 11.

thesis is by Mr. S. Radhakrishnan of Madras, which has appeared in the form of a small essay in the *International Ethical Quarterly* (July 1911) published in America. In this work, the similarity between the *Gītā* and Kant on questions of Ethics and Freedom of Will has been shown. »[58], le jeune auteur remercia le savant indien en ces termes : « The recognition of my humble work in the field of Indian philosophy, at the hands of one so very able and learned like yourself has encouraged me a good deal. »[59] Dès lors, Radhakrishnan poursuivit son travail comparatiste entre les religions occidentales et indiennes considérant que « a study of comparative religion has broken down the barriers behind which dogmatits seek to entrench themselves and show that their own religion is unique. »[60] et que dans le conflit qui opposait les religions de son temps, notamment en Inde, « l'étude comparative de la religion développe une attitude favorable envers les autres religions. [...] Nous tendons à regarder les différentes religions non comme incompatibles mais comme complémentaires, donc indispensables l'une à l'autre pour la réalisation de la fin commune. »[61]

La naissance de l'histoire comparée des religions, en tant que discipline historique, vit le jour en Europe au cours du XIXᵉ siècle grâce aux découvertes archéologiques au Proche-Orient et aux travaux philologiques sur les sources textuelles avestiques, védiques et chinoises qui permirent une véritable confrontation entre les religions anciennes et une recontextualisation historique du judaïsme et du christianisme. Des chaires d'histoire des religions furent créées dans les universités, notamment en France dans la seconde moitié du XIXᵉ siècle (Collège de France en 1879, Vᵉ section de l'école Pratique des Hautes Études en 1886) et jusqu'au lendemain de la Première Guerre Mondiale (Strasbourg en 1919). Depuis le XVIIᵉ siècle, la méthode historico-critique, d'abord appliquée par les savants protestants sur les écrits bibliques, fut par la suite prônée par les chercheurs européens sur l'ensemble des sources textuelles relatives aux religions et Radhakrishnan, formé dans une école protestante indienne, témoigne de l'influence de cette méthode sur ses propres travaux historiques :

> « As if the disorganisation were not sufficiently decisive, comparative religion and higher criticism which are relatively recent growths are making their own contributions. Comparative religion enables us to study faiths other than our own without condescension or contempt. It traces the history of our ideas of God from the simple conceptions

---

58 Tilak 1936, p. liv–lv.
59 Murty and Vohra 1990, p. 14.
60 Radhakrishnan 1959, p. 59.
61 Radhakrishnan 1935, p. 55–56.

of our remote ancestors who first formulated the experience of the great environing mystery down to the living faiths. Every mortal thing seems to have deified. Powers of nature, sun, stars, fire, water and earth, generative energies were all made into gods. Hero-worship and human apotheosis added to the number. Our mental pictures of God are as varied as we are. [...] The history of religion is the record of the conflicts of contradictory systems, each of them claiming dogmatic finality and absolute truth, a claim made apparently absurd by the plurality of claimants. If comparative religion tells us anything it is that every religion is moulded by fallible and imperfect human instruments, and so long as it is alive it will be changing. Spirit is growth, and even while we are observing one side of its life, the wheel is turning and the shadow of the past is twining itself into it. »[62]

Cette rigueur méthodologique, qui accompagna Radhakrishnan dans ses recherches historiques, fit de lui un pionnier, en Inde, dans le domaine de l'histoire comparée des religions, si ce n'est le premier indien à privilégier l'approche historico-critique des textes anciens. Néanmoins, dans son ouvrage *Eastern Religions and Western Thought*, publié en 1939, Radhakrishnan, ne connaissant ni le latin, ni le grec, ni l'hébreu, avait conscience de ses propres limites face à des sources qu'il ne pouvait aborder que par le biais de traductions ou d'études historiques secondaires européennes. De ce fait, sa préoccupation principale et constante fut de parvenir à produire une recherche digne d'un historien aux méthodes éprouvées en Occident, et non d'un partisan indien :

« I have a feeling that it is to not quite proper for me to write a book where I have to depend for information at least in part on translations, but I thought that it was no use waiting for a scholar who shall have a proper and critical knowledge of Sanskrit and Hebrew, Greek and Latin, French and German, who alone could get all the sides in proper order, for such a scholar has not yet been born. Even translations could be used with care and judgement. So I felt that it was time that some one with some knowledge got together the main points into order. Again, I wish to lay claim to the task of a historian and not that of a partisan. If I have misrepresented any point of real importance, no one will be more grieved than myself. »[63]

Malgré ces précautions méthodologiques, Radhakrishnan fut tributaire des ouvrages scientifiques européens qu'il utilisa pour restituer l'histoire de l'Inde et de ses contacts antiques avec l'Occident. En effet, dès la fin du XIXe siècle, les exégètes bibliques, qui s'étaient affranchis de l'autorité ecclésiale et de sa tradition, poursuivirent leurs recherches sur l'histoire rédactionnelle des textes bibliques et l'histoire du christianisme primitif par une approche

---

62 Radhakrishnan 1932, p. 36–37.
63 Radhakrishnan 1959, p. ix.

historico-critique, en privilégiant la possibilité de contacts culturels extérieurs qui leur auraient permis d'expliquer la présence d'éléments hétérogènes dans le corpus biblique. L'Inde fut alors désignée comme un milieu d'influence plausible puisque les traditions antiques voulaient que Pythagore, Socrate ou Platon devisassent avec des brāhmanes de l'Inde, ou que Pyrrhon se rendît en Inde même pour en rapporter sa doctrine sceptique. La conquête macédonienne et le commerce maritime entre l'Égypte et l'Inde les invitèrent à voir de possibles échanges d'idées qui auraient influé non seulement sur des groupes comme celui des Esséniens, sur les doctrines philosophiques grecques, notamment sur le néopythagorisme et le néoplatonisme durant la période romaine, mais encore sur le gnosticisme et par conséquent sur les théologiens chrétiens des premiers siècles de notre ère. Si les chercheurs européens voyaient dans ces contacts de nouvelles théories explicatives et, au final, s'inscrivaient plus ou moins dans la démarche schopenhauerienne extirpant le christianisme de ses origines juives[64], Radhakrishnan, quant à lui, y vit l'occasion de montrer que les religions de l'Inde avaient eu quelque influence sur la pensée antique occidentale et que, par conséquent, les civilisations européennes ne s'étaient jamais construites sans la pensée indienne.

Les thèmes de l'exemplarité de la civilisation hindoue et de l'indianisation de la pensée occidentale antique furent abordés par Radhakrishnan dans ses conférences délivrées au Manchester College d'Oxford en 1926 et publiées en 1927 sous le titre *The Hindu View of Life*, et dans son ouvrage historiographique *Eastern Religions and Western Thought* édité en 1939. La période d'entre-deux-guerres lui fut profitable pour exprimer sa conviction que l'Inde et son antique civilisation hindoue pouvaient tout autant apporter aux pays occidentaux monothéistes, meurtris et de nouveau en conflit, une solution pacifique à leurs

---

64 Pour Schopenhauer (1788–1860), le judaïsme s'originait dans le mazdéisme. Yaweh et Satan n'étaient autres qu'Ormazd (Ahura Mazdā) et Ahriman. Le christianisme, quant à lui, dérivait de l'hindouisme : « Le *Nouveau Testament*, au contraire, doit avoir une origine hindoue quelconque ; son éthique, qui transfère la morale dans l'ascétisme, son pessimisme et son avatar en témoignent. Tout cela le met en opposition décidée avec l'*Ancien Testament* : de sorte que l'histoire de la chute de l'homme est le seul point de connexion possible entre les deux. [...] La doctrine chrétienne issue de la sagesse de l'Inde a recouvert le vieux tronc, complètement hétérogène pour elle, du grossier judaïsme. [...] On sent dans le *Nouveau Testament* l'esprit de la sagesse hindoue. [...] Ainsi que le sanscrit, avant tout, nous donne la clé des langues grecque et latine, le brahmanisme et le bouddhisme nous donnent celle du christianisme ». Schopenhauer 1908, p. 102 ; 103 ; 104.

rivalités politiques et culturelles qu'ouvrir pour elle-même une nouvelle ère propre à générer une nouvelle civilisation décolonisée.

Dans *The Hindu View of Life*, Radhakrishnan présenta la civilisation hindoue de son temps comme héritière de la culture védique. Cette culture aryenne de la haute vallée indusienne et de la région du Panjab se répandit, selon lui, dans la vallée du Gange, où elle rencontra des tribus primitives, et dans le Deccan, où elle entra en contact avec la culture dravidienne qu'elle finit par dominer :

> « En s'étendant sur la totalité de l'Inde, la civilisation subit diverses modifications, mais elle resta en continuité avec le vieux type védique qui s'était développé sur les rives de l'Indus. 'Hindou' eut d'abord une signification territoriale, non dogmatique – ce terme impliquait résidence dans une aire géographique bien définie. Les tribus aborigènes, sauvages ou demi-civilisées, les Dravidiens cultivés et les Aryens védiques étaient tous des Hindous, comme étant fils de la même mère. »[65]

En présentant l'histoire de la civilisation hindoue ainsi, le futur président de l'Inde eut à cœur de montrer que les hindous d'aujourd'hui étaient unis par leur passé commun préislamique et précolonial et qu'ils demeuraient « une unité culturelles distincte, avec une histoire commune, une littérature commune, une civilisation commune » (p. 4–5[66]). Cette restitution nationaliste du passé hindou permit à Radhakrishnan de passer outre les divergences de croyances, les inégalités sociales, dues au système des castes, ou encore la diversité ethnique[67]. Né en 1888 à Tirutani, en Inde du Sud, dans une famille brāhmanique orthodoxe Telugu, Radhakrishnan était néovedāntiste et considérait sa propre croyance comme l'aboutissement terminal de l'ensemble des transformations qu'eut à subir l'hindouisme depuis l'époque védique. Pour lui, les Aryens védiques avaient eu la capacité philosophique d'accepter les rites et les dieux des tribus indigènes et des Dravidiens, « même des sauvages, des non-civilisés » (p. 37), pour les hisser au même niveau que les leurs puis pour les fusionner aux leurs en une seule et

---

65　Radhakrishnan 1935, p. 3–4.

66　Afin de ne pas amplifier les notes de bas de pages, après une citation dans le texte, nous mettrons dorénavant entre parenthèses la référence de ou des pages de *The Hindu View of Life*, dans sa version française parue, en 1935, sous le titre *L'hindouisme et la vie*.

67　« Nous constatons que l'Hindou admet un seul esprit suprême, malgré les noms différents qu'il lui donne. Dans son économie sociale il a de multiples castes, mais une société une. Parmi la population se rencontrent maintes races et tribus, mais toutes réunies par un esprit commun. Diverses formes matrimoniales sont licites, mais un seul idéal est visé. Il y a une unité de dessein sous la multiplicité des ramifications. », Radhakrishnan 1935, p. 127.

unique réalité suprême[68]. Ces penseurs aryens avaient donc réfléchi sur l'être et l'Univers bien avant tous les philosophes grecs et occidentaux dont les réflexions ne semblaient être, pour Radhakrishnan, que des commentaires inconscients de l'idéal des *Upaniṣad*[69]. Ces spéculations upaniṣadiques, rappela le savant indien, furent donc à l'origine de la pensée vedāntique et traversèrent les millénaires en transformant à son contact tout autre croyance :

> « L'hindouisme ne se dissout pas en un chaos d'opinions, car il représente un accroissement continuel de lucidité, chacune de ses formes, chaque stage de son développement gardant un rapport à la base commune du Védānta. Quoique la pensée religieuse hindoue ait traversé maintes révolutions et fait de grandes conquêtes, les idées essentielles se maintinrent les mêmes quatre ou cinq millénaires. Les notions génératrices sont renfermées dans l'orthodoxie védantique. »[70]

Ainsi, seuls les *Upaniṣad*, les *Brahma sūtra* et la *Bhagavadgītā* « forment ensemble la règle absolue de la religion hindoue » car « le vedānta n'est pas une religion, mais la religion elle-même dans son sens le plus universel et profond » (p. 14). Et pour convaincre son auditoire ou son lectorat, Radhakrishnan fit mémoire de la formule traditionnelle selon laquelle, malgré les divergences textuelles, le *Veda* est un et qu'il est tout autant unitaire que l'est sa signification[71]. D'un point de vue sociologique, il considérait inévitable que « le plus élevé dans la hiérarchie sociale est le véritable brahmane » (p. 120) et qu'« en chaque communauté existe une élite naturelle qui mieux que tout le reste représente l'âme du peuple entier, ses grands idéaux, ses puissantes émotions et sa tendance essentielle. » (p. 92). Radhakrishnan était alors persuadé qu'il existait une hiérarchie du croire dans laquelle ceux qui rendaient hommage au Brahman – entendu comme Principe absolu – se trouvaient être en tête (upāsānā brahmaṇah prāk, p. 24) et regrettait que ces derniers n'aient pas assez contribué au cours du XIXᵉ siècle et de son siècle à « hausser le niveau mental des masses, et placer la population hindoue, dans son ensemble, à un plan spirituel plus élevé » (p. 25–26) car « la tâche d'élever plus haut les non-civilisés fut négligée tristement » (p. 50). Seule la

---

68 Radhakrishnan 1935, p. 32–33.
69 « What we urge is, the *Upanishads* being the earliest form of speculative idealism in the world, all that is good and great in subsequent philosophy looks like an unconscious commentary on the Upanishadic ideal, showing how free and expansive and how capable of accommodating within itself all forms of truth that ideal is. », Radhakrishnan 1920, p. 451.
70 Radhakrishnan 1935, p. 13.
71 Eka eva dvijā vedo vedārthas caika eva tu |, Radhakrishnan 1935, p. 14. Néanmoins, ce vers épique est absent de l'édition critique du *Mahābhārata* publiée à Poona.

modification de la direction des esprits, par la suggestion et la persuasion (p. 37) pouvait élever, affirmait-il, les masses à un niveau intellectuel et moral plus haut (p. 49). C'est pourquoi, la vraie réforme devait passer, pour Radhakrishnan, par une purification, à l'égal de Jésus qui « arracha la religion juive à ses impuretés » (p. 46), et par l'eugénisme, ou sélection biologique (p. 102), développé par le britannique Francis Galton (1822–1911), l'allemand August Weismann (1834–1914) et le néerlandais Hugo Marie De Vries (1848–1935). Les Grecs, qui étaient souvent pris en modèles par les penseurs européens, n'avaient-ils pas eux-mêmes développé « explicitement une théorie de l'amélioration de la race par l'extermination des types inférieurs et la multiplication des types supérieurs » (p. 101). Les théories de l'hérédité, avancées à la charnière entre le XIXe et le XXe siècle par les chercheurs en Europe, lui donnèrent l'occasion de justifier l'endogamie indienne[72] pratiquée au sein des différentes castes et d'en attribuer le mérite aux penseurs hindous qui furent à l'origine de son établissement :

> « Une stupidité ou folie de nos parents, grands-parents ou aïeux se transmettra à nos enfants, et aux enfants de nos enfants. Les penseurs hindous, peut-être par l'effet d'une intuition heureuse ou d'une généralisation empirique, admirent le fait de l'hérédité et encouragèrent les mariages entre gens approximativement de même type et de qualité. Si un membre d'une famille de rang supérieur épouse quelqu'un ayant de médiocres antécédents, la bonne hérédité de l'un s'altère par la mauvaise hérédité de l'autre, et il s'ensuit que l'enfant débute dans la vie avec un grave handicap. Si les parents sont à peu près de même sorte, l'enfant sera pratiquement égal à ses parents. Le sang parle. Nous ne pouvons pas faire un génie avec de la médiocrité, ni susciter de bonnes aptitudes à partir d'une stupidité native, malgré tous les facteurs de l'ambiance. »[73]

Face au conflit qui opposait les Britanniques aux Hindous et aux Indiens islamistes, Radhakrishnan, conscient qu'« aucune autre contrée du monde n'a donné lieu à autant de problèmes de races » (p. 94), énuméra les trois possibilités offertes aux races dominantes vis-à-vis des dominées : l'extermination, la subordination, l'identification ou l'harmonisation (p. 94). Aussi, à la profession de foi proclamée le 25 juillet 1925 dans le *Times* par Lord Milner (1854–1925) au sujet des relations

---

72 La place qu'il accorde aux femmes repose uniquement sur leur fonction biologique génitrice : « Tant qu'on ne pourra pas faire tomber du ciel les enfants, mais qu'ils devront être construits dans la chair de leurs mères, il y aura une fonction propre aux femmes. » Radhakrishnan 1935, p. 88. Pour lui, la femme moderne qui cherche à imiter l'homme se masculinise et, sans plus respecter sa propre individualité, entre en conflit avec sa propre nature (p. 89).

73 Radhakrishnan 1935, p. 103–104.

entre l'Empire britannique et ses États[74], il opposa « la solution du problème des races » développée par l'hindouisme depuis des millénaires et qui toujours reposa, selon lui, sur une « unique saine méthode démocratique, en permettant à chaque groupe racial de développer ce qu'il contient de meilleur sans entraver le progrès des autres » (p. 97). De fait, Radhakrishnan était persuadé que le système des castes mis progressivement en place par la civilisation aryenne avait été la seule solution « démocratique » pour permettre aux différentes ethnies de l'Inde ancienne de se maintenir dans une relative cohésion sociale. Puisque « la caste, sous son aspect de race, est l'affirmation de l'infinie diversité des groupes humains » (p. 97), Radhakrishnan pensait que l'hindouisme pouvait apporter une solution définitive aussi bien aux conflits mondiaux qu'à ceux qui touchaient son propre pays. Car, il était persuadé que le code moral que les penseurs hindous avaient édicté, depuis l'époque védique, pouvait être « applicable à l'ensemble de l'humanité » (p. 97). Ce que dénonça donc activement le philosophe indien, et qui opposait irrémédiablement l'Inde hindoue à l'Occident, était l'intransigeance des monothéistes qui avaient pour fondement idéologique la domination et l'extermination de ceux qui ne croyaient pas à leur dogme :

> « L'intolérance d'un monothéisme étroit est écrite en lettres de sang à travers l'histoire humaine depuis le temps où les tribus d'Israël firent irruption en pays de Canaan. Les adorateurs du Dieu unique si jaloux sont engagés dans des guerres d'agression contre les peuples partisans d'autres cultes. Ils invoquent la sanction divine pour justifier les cruautés infligées aux peuples conquis. L'esprit de l'antique Israël fut hérité par le Christianisme et l'Islam ; à vous d'apprécier, s'il n'eût pas été mieux pour la civilisation occidentale que la Grèce plutôt que la Palestine servît ici de modèle. Les guerres de religion, résultats du fanatisme qui précipite et justifie l'extermination d'étrangers ayant des dogmes différents, furent pratiquement inconnues dans l'Inde hindoue. S'il y eut, de-ci de-là, des explosions de fanatisme, l'Hindouisme d'une façon générale n'a jamais encouragé la persécution pour mécréance. »[75]

---

74 « My patriotism knows no geographical but only racial limits. I am an Imperialist and not a Little Englander, because I am a British Race Patriot. It is not the soil of England, dear as it is to me, which is essential to arouse my patriotism, but the speech, the tradition, the principles, the aspirations of the British race. […] The British State must follow the race, must comprehend it wherever it settles in appreciable numbers as an independent community. If the swarms constantly being thrown off by the parent hive are lost to the State, the State is irreparably weakened. We cannot afford to part with so much of our best blood. We have already parted with much of it, to form the millions of another separate, but fortunately friendly State. We cannot suffer a repetition of the process. ».

75 Radhakrishnan 1935, p. 50–51.

Radhakrishnan en appela donc à l'histoire pour montrer que la chrétienté fit front contre la diversité des autres croyances religieuses et qu'elle considéra ces dernières comme imparfaites (p. 10), alors que le polythéisme hindou fit « preuve de charité compréhensive, au lieu d'une foi fanatique en une croyance inflexible. Il accepta la multiplicité des dieux aborigènes et autres qui pour la plupart venaient d'ailleurs que de la tradition aryenne, et les justifia tous » (p. 30). Les vestiges archéologiques, écrivait-il, notamment les édits du roi Aśoka, témoignaient en faveur de la tolérance que les Indiens préislamistes avaient exercée à l'encontre du pluralisme religieux. L'Inde, dans son histoire, avait aussi été le lieu d'asile de nombreux persécutés (juifs, chrétiens, parsis) que les rois hindous ou bouddhistes laissèrent libres de pratiquer leur croyance (p. 52). De ce fait, Radhakrishnan proposa une nouvelle vision de la société fondée « sur la liberté spirituelle, l'égalité politique et la fraternité économique » (p. 120), en juxtaposant les trois principes fondamentaux de la devise de la République française proclamés en 1790 à la classification sociétale tripartite ancienne de l'Inde et recouvrant les domaines propres aux brāhmaṇa, aux kṣatriya et aux vaiśya. Dans ses cours, prononcés en 1926 au Manchester College à Oxford, Radhakrishnan exposa donc le point de vue hindou sur la diversité des religions et de quelle manière l'hindouisme avait su y répondre tout au long de son histoire. Mais, si Radhakrishnan prit à témoin l'histoire ancienne de l'Inde, qu'il restitua en fonction de la finalité de son propos, il dénonça aussi le conservatisme religieux hindou de son temps qui « méconnaît les fondements de la théorie de la relativité en philosophie et en pratique, dans le goût et en morale, dans la politique et dans la société, – théorie dont les Hindous d'autrefois avaient une lucide compréhension » (p. 132-133). Son approche comparée de l'histoire des religions avait donc un double objectif : montrer l'opposition certaine qui existait entre le monothéisme et le polythéisme, plus particulièrement entre le christianisme, l'islam et l'hindouisme, dans leur gestion du pluralisme religieux et faire mémoire de la brillante civilisation indienne préislamique qui « n'était inférieure à aucune de celles des nations les plus avancées du monde jusqu'au milieu de ce millénaire » (p. 132).

Dans *The Hindu View of Life*, l'histoire ancienne de l'Inde telle qu'elle fut restituée et replacée dans la chronologie globale de l'histoire des civilisations de l'Antiquité par les savants européens, offrit l'opportunité au philosophe indien de démontrer que « l'idée que dans l'Inde le temps est demeuré immuable pendant des siècles sans nombre, et que rien n'a changé depuis que la mer primordiale s'est desséchée, cette idée est fausse d'outre en outre » (p. 133). En effet, Radhakrishnan souhaitait vivement que les Hindous ne se cramponnassent plus à « la carcasse » de leur religion pour y trouver leur sauvegarde face à la colonisation britannique et aux conflits qui les opposaient aux Indiens islamistes (p. 132).

La solution qu'il préconisa alors, était d'accepter un réajustement de la société (p. 134) qui devait nécessairement passer par un « élagage » du bois mort et encombrant de la tradition hindoue. Si l'histoire permettait de comprendre qu'il n'y eut jamais d'hindouisme « uniforme, stationnaire et immuable » et de « révélation fixée » (p. 134), les Hindous devaient alors accepter, selon lui, le mouvement du progrès, celui que l'hindouisme avait toujours fait sien avant le « long hiver de plusieurs siècles » (p. 134) qui le figea dans l'immobilisme et le conservatisme religieux. Fort de sa conviction qu'au-delà des dogmes, l'expérience religieuse est une et, quoi qu'ils fussent « hindous, chrétiens ou musulmans, les mystiques appartiennent à la même fraternité et présentent une ressemblance de famille tout à fait frappante » (p. 27), Radhakrishnan professait que l'acceptation de l'Altérité, dans le but de régler les conflits politiques et religieux en Inde et dans le reste du monde, devait s'appuyer sur l'expérience et l'histoire de l'Inde : « Que la solution hindoue du problème du conflit des religions doive être accepté à l'avenir, cela me paraît certain » (p. 55). Ces réflexions sur l'ouverture à l'Autre, que lui-même opéra par l'acceptation des progrès scientifiques de son temps et la connaissance approfondie de l'histoire des civilisations occidentales et de la sienne propre[76], l'amenèrent dans les années 1930 à établir un pont historique entre l'Inde et l'Occident qu'il publia en 1939 sous le titre *Eastern Religions and Western Thought*.

À la différence de *The Hindu View of Life*, dans lequel l'auteur avait tenté de démontrer que le fondement védāntique de l'hindouisme pouvait garantir à la société indienne et plus largement au monde un nouveau départ dans leurs relations à l'Autre, ce nouvel ouvrage abordait les liens historiques entretenus entre l'Inde et l'Occident durant l'Antiquité qui furent à l'origine du passage de la pensée indienne vers le Bassin méditerranéen. Loin de professer ici ce que l'Inde pourrait apporter à l'Occident moderne, Radhakrishnan revint donc sur ce que l'Inde avait déjà offert aux penseurs, aux philosophes grecs, aux gnostiques et aux théologiens chrétiens durant les périodes hellénistique puis romaine. Mais Radhakrishnan souhaitait également montrer que d'après les dernières découvertes archéologiques, les analyses anthropologiques et les avancées historiographiques récentes, l'Inde avait toujours été une terre de brassages et d'ententes raciales. Comme ses prédécesseurs européens ou indiens, il distinguait quatre grandes périodes dans l'histoire de la civilisation indienne.

---

76 « Here is the truth of things which does not depend on any doubtful scripture or fallible human authority but which all who have the intellectual power to observe and honesty to judge will accept. A life of joy and happiness is possible only on the basis of knowledge and science. », Radhakrishnan 1932, p. 48.

Au cours des années 1920–1930, le travail des archéologues dans la vallée indusienne avait permis de mettre au jour non seulement des sceaux en stéatite sur
lesquels étaient représentés des scènes cultuelles et un personnage assis dans une
posture immédiatement considérée comme yogique et qui en faisait la première
figuration de Śiva, mais aussi des restes humains et des figurines dont les types
australoïde, eurafricain, alpin et mongoloïde attestaient qu'au IVᵉ millénaire av. J.-
C., « the social order was not based on any racial or religious exclusiveness. It permitted the worship of more than one God, exalted yogic perfection, and tolerated
different racial groups » (p. 118). Ainsi, ces découvertes offraient l'avantage certain
de faire remonter l'origine de la civilisation indienne, et plus particulièrement hindoue, par l'intermédiaire de ce proto-Śiva, bien avant l'arrivée des indo-ārya dans
le Panjab au cours du IIᵉ millénaire av. J.-C. : « This figure of Śiva, the great Yogi, has
been there from nearly 3250 B.C. (if not earlier), the date which archaeologists give
to the Indus valley civilization » (p. 36). Si la civilisation indienne pouvait dorénavant rivaliser avec les autres grandes civilisations de l'Égypte et du Proche-Orient
et montrer au reste du monde qu'elle avait développé des contacts commerciaux
avec la Mésopotamie, elle pouvait aussi démontrer qu'elle avait déjà eu affaire au
pluralisme ethnique pour lequel elle avait trouvé des solutions pacifiques.

Pour la seconde période, Radhakrishnan notait qu'au vu des correspondances
évidentes entre les langues et les mythologies indiennes, iraniennes, grecques,
latines, etc., les peuples indiens et iraniens avaient été également en contact avec
les Grecs. Mais ils n'en gardèrent aucun souvenir puisque Grecs et Indiens ne se
rencontrèrent à nouveau que durant la période achéménide (p. 118–119). S'étant
séparés des Iraniens, les Indiens de langue indo-ārya s'installèrent au IIᵉ millénaire av. J.-C. dans la région de l'Indus où ils composèrent les hymnes r̥gvédiques.
Pour leur datation, le savant indien se référa aux travaux des indianistes européens et américains (Müller, Weber, Haug, Whitney, Kaegi) dont les chronologies
variaient entre 2400 et 1200 av. J.-C. (p. 119–120). Là encore, s'il reconnut qu'il
y eut des conflits lors de leur installation et de leur progression dans la plaine
gangétique puis la région du Deccan, il présenta leur assimilation comme le résultat de la capacité des classes védiques à avoir réussi à adapter les croyances des
Dravidiens et des aborigènes à leur propre système pour en faire une civilisation
nouvelle et unitaire. Ce rêve d'unité, que les leaders politiques sécularistes indiens avaient au cours des années 1930, avait donc déjà été celui des chefs et des
brāhmanes des temps védiques qui étaient parvenus à le réaliser :

> « It took so much from the social life of the Dravidians and other native inhabitants of
> India that it is very difficult to disentangle the original Aryan elements from others. The
> interpenetration has been so complex, subtle, and continuous, with the result that there

has grown up a distinct Hindu civilization which is neither Aryan nor Dravidian nor aboriginal. Ever since the dawn of reflection the dream of unity has hovered over the scene and haunted the imagination of the leaders. »[77]

Les recherches de Radhakrishnan vers la fin des années 1930 l'invitèrent donc à voir la civilisation hindoue comme l'harmonisation de trois cultures différentes qui n'en formèrent plus qu'une seule, unitaire et indistincte. Il devenait alors évident que si les Hindous de la période védique avait su trouver le moyen d'unifier la société pluriethnique et plurireligieuse de leur temps, combien plus, à leur exemple, et avec le recul des siècles, les Indiens des années 1930 pouvaient-ils y arriver. Ce fut donc cette civilisation unitaire védique qui entra à nouveau en contact avec l'Occident au temps des rois Hittites, porteurs de noms aryens. Les inscriptions mitanniennes, retrouvées à *Boğazköy*, prouvaient définitivement les relations historiques entre les Indiens et la Cappadoce au XVIᵉ ou au XVᵉ siècle av. J.-C. (p. 121). Radhakrishnan pouvait donc en déduire, tout en extrapolant le rôle civilisateur de l'Inde védique, que « the ethical and religious speculations of the Jews derive largely from the culture which was common to Sumer, Egypt, and the Indus » (p. 121) et que « the Jewish religion can only be properly understood if its vast background is taken into account, if the non-Semitic influences on Palestine and Syria are considered. Indian or Indo-Iranian groups who worshipped the Vedic deities, Mitra, Varuṇa, Indra and others, were found in and to the north of Syria in the middle of the second millennium B.C. » (p. 157–158).

Durant la troisième période, entre 900 et 600 av. J.-C., les auteurs des *Upaniṣad* portèrent définitivement la pensée hindoue à sa pleine maturité (p. 122), et ce fut sous l'Empire perse que les Indiens entrèrent de nouveau en contact avec les Grecs. Dès lors, Radhakrishnan pouvait abondamment citer les occurrences de la littérature grecque relative aux traditions biographiques des philosophes grecs qui assuraient que ces derniers avaient acquis un savoir universel en ayant discouru avec les sages de toutes les nations (prêtres égyptiens et mazdéens, brāhmanes de l'Inde, Druides du Ponant). Pour ce faire, Radhakrishnan s'appuya donc encore une fois sur les travaux des comparatistes européens qui essayaient de saisir au mieux l'histoire de la formation des différentes doctrines philosophiques grecques dont l'originalité les déroutait parfois. Pour certains d'entre eux, l'orphisme, le pythagorisme, voire même le platonisme, avaient trop d'éléments communs avec la spéculation indienne, que l'Europe commençait à mieux connaître, pour ne

---

77   Radhakrishnan 1939, p. 308.

pas y voir de possibles emprunts historiques durant les périodes achéménide et hellénistique.

Enfin, la dernière période recouvrant les siècles qui suivirent l'avènement du bouddhisme et celui de l'Empire Maurya, était pour Radhakrishnan le moment des grands échanges entre les mondes grec et indien. Les rois indo-bactriens et indo-grecs avaient été si indianisés (p. 156) qu'aucun doute ne subsistait sur le passage d'idées hindoues dans le Bassin méditerranéen. Ainsi, le comparatisme encore trop analogique et superficiel dans les années 1920, la difficile recontextualisation historique des textes antiques, la délicate analyse de leur histoire rédactionnelle, la méconnaissance des procédés polémiques et hérésiologiques, les incertitudes des exégètes biblistes européens[78] furent autant de facteurs qui entraînèrent Radhakrishnan dans l'affirmation d'une évidente influence de la pensée indienne sur des groupes méditerranéens, tel celui des Esséniens, et, par leur intermédiaire, sur Jean le baptiste puis Jésus le nazaréen. Les parallèles apparents relevés entre les textes néotestamentaires et les sources bouddhiques, la mention d'ambassades indiennes reçues dans les grandes villes du Bassin méditerranéen sous l'Empire romain, le gnosticisme qui était alors regardé comme « a deliberate attempt to fuse Greek (Platonic) and Hindu elements » (p. 198) ou pour fusionner christianisme et bouddhisme[79], les théologiens chrétiens qui

---

78 En 1937, fut éditée *Religion in Transition* par l'américain Vergilius Ferm (1896–1975) qui contacta, pour former le volume, plusieurs savants dont Radhakrishnan. C'est ainsi que sa contribution (« My Search For Truth ») fut publiée avec celle d'un des plus éminents exégètes européens de son temps, Alfred Loisy (1857–1940) qui fut à l'origine de la crise moderniste en 1902. Excommunié en 1908, il fut nommé professeur d'histoire des religions au Collège de France en 1909.

79 « Though Basilides believed that Christinaity was the main factor of his system, there is no doubt that his interpretation of Christianity is profoundly Buddhist » (p. 204). Radhakrishnan s'était appuyé sur un article dû à James Kennedy, membre de la Royal Asiatic Society of Great Britain and Ireland, dans lequel ce dernier tenta de démontrer que le système de Basilide avait été influencé par celui des bouddhistes tant en ce qui concerne la loi karmique, la transmigration des âmes que le système ternaire sāṃkhya des guṇa. Pour lui, la communauté indienne, essentiellement marchande, qui résidait à Alexandrie, aux dires de Dion Chrysostome, ne pouvait être que de confession bouddhique et originaire de Ceylan ou de Barygaza (Kennedy 1903, p. 387). Si, en 1924 déjà, Hans Leisegang acceptait l'idée que Basilide enseignait la croyance en la métensomatose, il rejetait par contre toute influence indienne : « encore moins est-il permis d'invoquer – comme il s'est vu – son nirvanique 'pas même néant' pour l'affubler d'une étiquette hindoue » (Leisegang 1924, p. 177). Mais il faudra attendre 1974 pour que Pierre Nautin mette fin à ce comparatisme analogique en démontrant définitivement

comme Clément d'Alexandrie ou Jérôme de Sidon faisaient référence au Buddha dans leur traité apologiste, obligeaient inévitablement à reconnaître des contacts historiques entre l'Inde et l'Occident et plus encore une véritable influence de la pensée indienne sur les doctrines gnostiques, néopythagoriciennes, néoplatoniciennes et chrétiennes. Suite aux découvertes, en 1945, de la bibliothèque de Nag hammadi et, en 1947, des manuscrits de la Mer morte, les études sur l'histoire des courants religieux du IIe siècle av. J.-C. au IIIe siècle ap. J.-C. s'enrichirent partiellement, et Radhakrishnan abandonna l'idée première d'une influence indienne sur le christianisme : « Historical research has been revolutionizing our understanding of the Old and New Testaments. From the discovery of the Dead Sea Scrolls in 1947, it is clear that Christian doctrine developed from Jewish sectarianism. »[80]. Néanmoins, il continua de penser que le christianisme avait eu des liens étroits avec le mithraïsme qui s'originait, selon lui, dans les croyances anciennes du culte du dieu indo-iranien Mitra[81] : « Christianity has much in common with Mithraism. The similarities may be due to direct borrowing or common Indian background. »[82].

De fait, l'Inde que Sarvepalli Radhakrishnan voudrait nous montrer est une Inde qui, dans l'histoire globale de l'humanité, participa activement tout autant à son dessein civilisateur qu'à son élévation spirituelle ; une Inde qui avait toujours prôné le respect du pluralisme ethnique et religieux ; une Inde active qui ne resta jamais isolée du reste du monde qui l'entourait de toutes parts ; une Inde qui, à chacune de ses périodes historiques, avait été en contact avec les grandes civilisations d'alors (Mésopotamie, Égypte, Empire perse, Empire hellénistique, Empire romain) et qui avait toujours apporté sa contribution au développement de leurs pensées religieuses et philosophiques tout comme elle continuait alors de le faire à la période moderne par la venue en Occident de Vivekānanda, par la diffusion de sa poésie à travers l'œuvre de Rabindranath Tagore, prix Nobel de littérature en 1913, par l'enseignement de ses pratiques

---

que la croyance basilidienne en la métensomatose n'était qu'une surinterprétation hérésiologique de Clément d'Alexandrie et que Basilide ne l'avait, de ce fait, jamais enseignée (Nautin 1974).

80 Radhakrishnan 1967, p. 38.

81 « Under the dynasty of the Arsacids, the god Mithra found his way into the Roman world. The hymns of the Vedas and the Avesta celebrate his name, and the Vedic Mitra and the Iranian Mithra have so many points of resemblance that there is not any doubt about their identity. [...] The worship of Mithra proved the most dangerous rival to the Christian Church before its alliance with Constantine. », Radhakrishnan 1959, p. 120–121.

82 Radhakrishnan 1967, p. 39.

spirituelles tel le yoga qui commençait déjà à faire quelques adeptes en Europe (p. 36), etc. Mais, dans cet écrit, Radhakrishnan ne fit pas que construire un pont historique entre l'Inde et l'Occident, comme Max Müller en son temps en avait bâti un entre l'Occident et l'Inde[83], il formulait l'espoir que les rencontres actuelles, qu'il considérait possibles, entre les religions occidentales et l'hindouisme pussent aboutir à la construction d'une nouvelle religion mystique (p. ix) et à partir de celle-ci et d'une conscience humaine plus haute, à une nouvelle génération, en somme à une nouvelle civilisation que la mondialisation imposait inévitablement (p. 349). Dans son désir de montrer les capacités intellectuelles, sociales, politiques et religieuses des anciens Indiens, il acheva nécessairement son ouvrage sur la figure du grand roi maurya Aśoka, sur sa conversion à la non-violence (ahiṃsā) et sur son dharma – loi socio-politique – qui avait eu pour finalité de pacifier une société dans laquelle le pluralisme mettait continuellement à l'épreuve la cohésion sociale de son immense empire. Par le déchiffrement des inscriptions aśokéennes, l'Inde avait retrouvé un souverain exemplaire qu'elle érigea immédiatement en modèle. Lorsque l'Inde retrouva son indépendance, le drapeau indien fut alors modifié et ses couleurs furent chargées de nouveaux symboles. Le rouet, apposé par Gandhi, en 1921, sur une bande centrale blanche, séparant les bandes rouge et verte, représentant respectivement les Hindous et les Islamistes fut remplacé par la roue de la Loi (dharmacakra) du roi Aśoka. Ce dernier qui l'avait fait tourner (cakravartin) en son temps en tant que roi universel, l'avait fait représenter symboliquement sur nombre de constructions monumentales. Le 22 juillet 1947, lorsque la Constituent Assembly of India adopta son nouveau drapeau, ce fut Radhakrishnan qui en révéla la nouvelle signification fondée sur des concepts

---

83 Max Müller trouvait dans le vedānta non seulement une philosophie préparant à la meilleure mort mais encore une manière d'accepter l'autre notamment en ces difficiles années de 1870 où la France, en guerre contre l'Allemagne, avait dû lui céder l'Alsace-Lorraine, où l'Empire colonial britannique avait de plus en plus de mal à gérer la stabilité de sa colonie indienne : « Bien que vivant sur le forum, et non plus dans la forêt, nous pouvons, à leur école, nous faire à différer du voisin, à aimer ceux qui nous haïssent pour nos convictions religieuses, ou à tout le moins nous pouvons désapprendre la haine et la persécution contre ceux dont les convictions, les espérances et les craintes, ou même les principes de morales, ne sont pas les nôtres. C'est là encore vivre en vānaprastha, c'est vivre une vie digne d'un vrai sage de la forêt, digne d'un homme qui sait ce que l'homme est, ce que la vie est, et qui a appris à se taire en face de l'Eternel et de l'Infini. », Müller 1878, p. 328. Voir Di Costanzo 2004 ; Ducœur 2009.

et des valeurs hindous et sur le passé historique de l'Inde[84] pour lesquels il avait lui-même lutté intellectuellement. L'Inde était à nouveau en mouvement, celui que Radhakrishnan avait défini dix ans auparavant comme le renouveau de la civilisation hindoue. Porté aux nues par certains, voyant alors en lui le plus grand philosophe des temps modernes[85] ou un rishi du XXᵉ siècle[86], décrié par d'autres quant à son interprétation de l'hindouisme[87], Radhakrishnan parvint finalement, après avoir étudié durant des années l'histoire de sa propre tradition religieuse et celle de la pensée occidentale, afin de contrecarrer les critiques chrétiennes contre l'hindouisme[88], aux plus hautes fonctions. Vice-président de l'Inde, en 1952, il fut élu président de l'Inde, en 1962, et succédant ainsi au premier président Rajendra Prasad (1884-1963). Dans son discours d'adieu qu'il adressa à la nation indienne le 12 mai 1967, Radhakrishnan réaffirma sa foi dans l'esprit de l'Inde en faisant appel encore et toujours à l'histoire et en mettant en corrélation l'héritage de la culture indienne antique et la société contemporaine que les Indiens avaient encore à re-construire :

> « The culture which we have inherited is an ancient one and it has faced many waves of invasion of Yavanas, Sakas, Hunas, Pathans and Mongolas, among others and is still enduring. It is not only the quality of antiquity – prācīnatā – but also of enduring vitality – mrtyunjayata – which has enabled it to last all these centuries. The secret of this staying power is the quality of tolerance and understanding. The saints and sages have been the great integrators of our society. They humanize the universe by humanizing man. We

---

84 « Bhagwa or the saffron colour denotes renunciation or disinterestedness. Our leaders must be indifferent to material gains and dedicate themselves to their work. The white in the centre is light, the path of truth to guide our conduct. The green shows our relation to (the) soil, our relation to the plant life here, on which all other life depends. The *Ashoka Chakra* in the centre of the white is the wheel of the law of dharma. Truth or satya, dharma or virtue ought to be the controlling principle of those who work under this flag. Again, the wheel denotes motion. There is death in stagnation. There is life in movement. India should no more resist change, it must move and go forward. The wheel represents the dynamism of a peaceful change. », *Flag Code of India 2002*.

85 Sarma 1944, p. 585. Voir également Samartha 1964, p. 104.

86 Le journaliste singhalais Diyogu Badathuruge Dhanapala (1905-1971) s'exprimait en ces termes à son sujet : « The tradition of the Rishi is alive in India today. Sarvepalli Radhakrishna is the twentieth century equivalent of the ancient Hindu Rishi. He is a presence felt and known in the councils of the nation. », Brown 1970, p. 152.

87 Samartha 1964, p. 108-114.

88 « The challenge of Christian critics impelled me to make a study of Hinduism and find out what is living and what is dead in it. My pride as a Hindu, roused by the enterprise and eloquence of Swami Vivekananda, was deeply hurt by the treatment accorded to Hinduism in missionary institutions », Brown 1970, p. 152.

are going through a period of doubt and uncertainty but such periods often occurred in our past history. We require a good deal of patience and wisdom to make effective contribution to our age. We have to chart our course by the distant stars and not by the dim street lights. »[89]

Pour de nombreux nationalistes indiens d'avant et d'après 1947, l'Inde eut un passé historique glorieux qui se devait de resurgir afin de redonner confiance à son peuple. Tilak et Radhakrishnan furent des pionniers dans leur domaine respectif de recherche et eurent l'intelligence de s'ouvrir aux résultats des travaux des savants occidentaux afin de restituer l'histoire d'une Inde qui leur appartenait en propre et qui pouvait répondre aux attentes des Indiens. Faire resurgir le passé pour faire bouger de nouveau les esprits, tel fut finalement le but poursuivit par Radhakrishnan qui se languissait de voir le peuple hindou figé dans un immobilisme traditionnaliste et stoppé dans sa propre évolution historique là où « aux grands jours de la civilisation hindoue, il y eut de l'ardeur à vivre, à sillonner les mers, à fonder des colonies, à instruire le monde comme à trouver en lui un enseignement »[90]. Bien que son histoire de l'Inde et de la figure d'Aśoka, telle qu'elle sera constamment reprise et exaltée par les bouddhistes pris dans les conflits militaires et les vives tensions politiques[91], puisse paraître aujourd'hui pleinement orientée et datée, il convient de ne pas oublier que Radhakrishnan fut également victime de ses sources occidentales et des théories idéologiques que les indianistes et les historiens européens développaient, pris qu'ils étaient eux-mêmes dans des faces

---

89 Murty and Vohra 1990, p. 182.
90 Radhakrishnan 1935, p. 132.
91 Le moine bouddhiste thaïlandais Buddhadasa, Tenzin Gyatso – XIVᵉ Dalaï-Lama – ou encore le moine bouddhiste vietnamien Thich Nhat Hanh reprirent dans leur discours socio-politique les mesures édictées par Aśoka. Dans le contexte anti-communiste et pro-américain des années 1960, Buddhadasa (1906–1993) fut le leader politique du socialisme dharmique ou bouddhique fondé en tout point sur le dharma d'Aśoka : « Le meilleur exemple est celui du roi Asoka. Bien des livres ont été publiés sur Asoka, en particulier à propos d'inscriptions trouvées sur des stèles de pierre dans tout le royaume. C'était des édits d'Asoka et ils révèlent un système de gouvernement socialiste du type exclusivement dictatorial. Il purifia le *sangha* en chassant les hérétiques et insista sur la nécessité d'une conduite juste pour toutes les classes de la société. Cependant Asoka ne fut pas un tyran. C'était un homme doux qui agissait pour le bien de la société. Il construisit des puits et des salles d'assemblée, fit planter toute une variété d'arbres fruitiers au profit de tous. Il fut 'autoritaire' en ce sens que si ses sujets ne réalisaient pas les travaux publics comme on le leur ordonnait, ils étaient punis. […] La punition était socialiste dans ce sens qu'elle était utile à la société et non donnée pour des raisons personnelles ou égoïstes. », Buddhadasa 1987, p. 86.

à faces nationalistes et religieux complexes. À la différence des nationalistes extré-mistes qui voulaient imposer la seule culture hindoue, la langue sanskrite, l'écri-ture nagari et qui revendiquaient l'autochtonie en fermant leur pays à tout contact étranger, Radhakrishnan eut assez de discernement pour comprendre qu'il fallait au contraire montrer aux nations dominatrices européennes que l'Inde avait été dans son passé précolonial une grande nation, libre, indépendante, organisée et novatrice dans les domaines de la philosophie, de la littérature et de la techno-logie. Cette Inde « retrouvée » et reconstruite pouvait donc prétendre, selon le philosophe indien, reprendre sa place sur la scène internationale et renouveler le généreux don qu'elle avait déjà accordé aux nations d'alors : l'enseignement de l'acceptation de l'Autre, ce même enseignement que Max Müller avait déjà défini, à la fin du XIXᵉ siècle, comme la contribution la plus fondamentale et la plus utile du vedānta, à la pensée humaine.

Il est certain que dans le long processus d'indépendance de l'Inde, dans la confrontation et le débat d'idées politiques, des plus modérées aux plus ex-trémistes, dans la représentation de ce que pourrait être une nation indienne, Radhakrishnan prit conscience au cours des années 1930 que les sciences histo-riques pouvaient grandement participer à éclairer les Hindous sur l'importance de la restitution du passé de l'Inde, sur l'obligation de réinscrire ce même passé dans une histoire globale de l'humanité et sur l'avantage d'une ouverture et d'une prise de distance que pouvait apporter, en temps de crise identitaire et religieuse, l'histoire comparée des religions.

Salil Misra

Ambedkar University Delhi

Emotions in Politics and Politics of Emotions: the Making of Pakistan and the Decolonization of British India, 1937–46

"We do not choose them [emotions]; rather we are in their grips."

Elster 1989, p. 61

"Men do not only rationalize their feelings; they also emotionalize their reasons."

Gellner, 1992a, p. 67

"The Muslims are determined to have Pakistan. It is a question of life and death to ten crores of Muslims inhabiting this country, and to achieve our goal of Pakistan we will sacrifice everything. If we do not achieve our goal of Pakistan, we will be wiped out of the map of India."

Muhammad Ali Jinnah's appeal to Muslims in Bombay
11 August 1944
Yusufi 1996, p. 1939.

"But the Pakistan concept is not merely six years old. […] The idea that led to the eventual birth of Pakistan is as old as the advent of Islam in India….Let us not think today of traitors within or enemies without, but turn our eyes inward, search our hearts and concentrate only on just how much suffering and sacrifice we ourselves are prepared to endure for the sake of freedom. […] Let Muslim parents steal their hearts in the manner of Ibrahim, the friend of God, and mark out their families' best loved as willing offerings to the nation's service. On them will rest the building up of a free Muslim state."

Editorial in The Dawn on 23 March 1946, the Pakistan Day.

This essay has a two-fold purpose. One, it describes and partially explains a very distinctive type of nation, a Muslim nation, that developed in India in the 20th century. Two, it identifies the role of emotions in the articulations and the dissemination of this Muslim nation. The essay would also argue that the strong use of emotions in the creation of a Muslim nation was not a matter of arbitrary choice but was rooted in the very context. The deployment of emotions was almost inherent in the context in which this nation grew and developed. In addition the paper will also try and evolve a framework in which emotions as a category can be meaningfully employed in historical investigation.

Introduction

It is true that whereas emotions as an analytical category has by now come to be firmly established in the history writing in the West, it is yet to find its due in history writing on South Asia. The major historiographical change that has occurred in South Asia in the last couple of decades is a welcome shift from economic history to social history. In particular caste, gender and environment are three themes that have now received adequate attention from historians working on South Asia. All these studies can benefit by the new emotional turn[1] in two ways. One is by treating emotions as a crucial ingredient in the story, or by looking at the role of emotions as motivator in specific human activities and social phenomena. The other would be by adding emotions as an important theme to the new concerns in history writing. In other words, the new history writing can benefit by the 'emotional turn' by focusing on emotions as a theme and also by looking at the 'emotional angle' behind various human activities in the public spheres. In this approach it would be essential to take emotions out of the 'personal and the private' and extend them to the 'social and the public'. In both the possible ways, 'emotions' should be seen as a welcome and a much needed addition to historical research and knowledge.

While working on emotions in historical investigation, it would be necessary to keep a few points of caution in mind.

It would be essential to make a conceptual distinction between 'emotional history' and a history of emotions. Whereas emotional histories of various events and phenomena have been in circulation for a long time, a history of emotions is of a relatively recent origin[2]. A history of emotions has to consist of emotions as a category constructed from a non-emotional vantage point. The enormous social and political power of emotions in social phenomena and the explanatory

---

1   Plamper 2009, p. 229–237.
2   This may seem an obvious point, but it is not very unusual to make an unconscious switch from one to the other. For example see Ray 2001. In the introduction and the articles, Rajat Ray tends to use the two terms almost interchangeably and as mutually substitutable. He also oscillates between the positions that emotions are timeless and universal, and also historically and culturally specific. See p. vii, xi, xii, 17, 18 among others.

power of emotions as a category of analysis, can be grasped better by adopting a non-emotional approach and by standing 'outside emotions' as it were.

Deployment of emotions in writing social history would be quite useful and understandable. But that would amount to a somewhat restrictive view of emotions. It would be necessary not to let 'emotions' be appropriated by social and cultural history. We should resist the temptation of writing surrogate social history in the name of emotions. Emotions have exercised tremendous power not just in the social sphere but also (and much more so) in the political arena. Therefore emotions need to be brought into the orbit of political history. A history of emotions should not be reduced to social and cultural history and it should be conceptualized as a new ingredient within history writing that would enrich social, cultural, literary and political histories. A history of emotions may not create its own separate domain but would do well to feed into other histories and thus enrich them without creating a separate historiographic constituency.

As a 'historical product' it would be essential to look at emotions ideographically and not nomothetically, i.e., not simply on Emotions but on different types of emotions like fear, anger, hatred, resentment, prejudice, craving for solidarity etc. This would impart a historical distinctiveness to different emotions and their role in history and politics.

Political Scientist Roger Petersen has discussed the role of emotions like fear (perceptions of insecurity), hatred (a carry-over of group prejudices from the past, or sometimes a purely 'modern hatred' masquerading as 'ancient hatred'), resentment (related to status hierarchy and a possibility of a change in this hierarchy as a result of structural change or gradual modernization) and rage (non-instrumental, destructive, violent passion)[3]. He has imparted specific meanings to these terms and thus made it possible for them to be used by historians across time and context. However he tends to use these emotions as a kind of 'switch' or a 'trigger'. This amounts to taking a very restrictive view of emotions. It is somewhat limiting to look upon emotions as an 'instrument' to convert a mere desire into action. The tendency to see emotions as a kind of immediate factor (the last straw as it were), or as a virus that lies dormant within a group or a kind of mechanism that ties social forces to concrete action, is important but somewhat self-limiting on the actual and potential role of emotions in political processes. It should be possible to see the role of emotions not just as immediate motivators but as factors gradually feeding into long-term processes of community and nation formation. This paper finds that emotions such as fear,

---

3   Petersen 2002, p. 24–26. For a similar approach also see, Suny 2004.

hatred and resentment played a major role in the formation of a Muslim nation in colonial India, but certainly not as a 'switch'. On the contrary they worked in a more gradual and sustained way and acted as feeding elements in building a community consciousness and creating political solidarities. The pan-Indian religio-political communities that grew in the initial decades of the 20th century often acted also as emotional communities. In this process the significance of emotions was much more than simply episodic. In the process of community and nation formation in India, emotions worked in a pervasive and a sustained kind of way rather than a dramatic and episodic kind of way.

Nationalism and emotions

The emergence of a 'Muslim nation' in South Asia during the 1930s and 1940s has generally been explained in terms of a) the nature and the role of British policy of promoting and fostering a consolidation of Muslims as a political com-munity[4], and b) weaknesses and shortcomings of Indian nationalism in uniting all Indians under a common platform[5].

As a result, it was argued, a crucial political fault line developed between Hin-dus and Muslims. This divide got deepened in 1920s and 1930s. It resulted in the emergence of an alternative Muslim nationalism that was formally declared in 1940 at the annual session of the All India Muslim League under the leadership of M.A. Jinnah. There are no doubt other explanations but these two constitute a substantive part of the story of Muslim nationalism in India. This paper in-tends to offer yet another set of explanations, which is not meant to be either an alternative to the existing ones, or a substitute to them. It merely seeks to add a new vantage point from where the emergence of a Muslim nation can be looked at. It attempts to add to and enrich the existing pool of explanation for the same phenomenon. The starting point of this vantage point is that in addition to the role and functions of state politics, structures of power, and economic explana-tions, emotions too played a part in the making and consolidation of a Muslim nation in India.

This point can perhaps be generalized to include nationalism in general. Na-tionalism as a political idea may be rooted in a particular doctrine and a set of ideas engendered by 19th century European thought[6], or in an economic

---

4   For authoritative statements on the role of British policy in the making of the Muslim nation, see Smith 1946, p. 187–232; Chandra 1984, p. 237–289; and Page 1982.

5   Hasan 1993.

6   Kedourie 1960.

transformation or the world from agrarian to industrial[7], or other larger social processes creating large imagined communities[8]. But the political idea acquired vibrancy and a transformative potential *only* after it was internalized by the people as a powerful emotion. In other words nationalism became politically explosive and powerful only after a large number of people got mobilized behind the idea and imparted an emotional content to the abstract political idea.

The debate on the place of emotions in the making of nations and nationalisms is old and inconclusive. At one level it resembles and is analogous to the debate between modernists and non-modernists[9]. The modernist position broadly sees nationalism as rooted in certain structures engendered by modernity. The position thus opens itself to the criticism that it negates or underplays the role of emotions as providers of the necessary binding elements in the making of national solidarities. The non-modernist position, on the other hand, either looks at nationalism as a 'state of mind' or focuses on symbols, historical memories and cultural traditions as feeding elements in nationalism. It would thus appear that the non-modernist position allows much greater space for emotions than the modernist one. This certainly was a major criticism made against the theory of Ernest Gellner, the leading exponent of modernist position on nationalism. In an interesting and illumination debate on Gellner's theory of nationalism, his argument was critiqued for displaying a neglect of emotions, among other things.

The crux of some of the criticisms was that his theory of nationalism was dry and arid and did not allow any space for emotions. It was pointed out that his theory was instrumentalist in that it looked upon nationalism merely as an instrument at the service of larger processes and structures. In the same vein it was also highlighted that it was reductionist (reducing it as merely a consequence of certain conditions brought about by modernity), materialist (denying the role of ideas and sentiments) and also functionalist (looking at nationalism as merely serving a function rather than fulfilling some deep emotional craving). All these criticisms were made specifically against Gellner's theory of nationalism but could be generalized to include the modernist position in general. The crux of

---

7   Gellner 2006.
8   Anderson 1991.
9   This is obviously an unsatisfactory classification. It clearly privileges the modernist position and lumps together a whole range of other positions, such as the perennialist, primordialist, evolutionist and the ethnosymbolist, into the umbrella category of non-modernist. The only justification for this arbitrary classification is that it serves as a useful point of dichotomy, as far as the debate on emotions is concerned. For the various positions on nationalism, see Özkirimli 2010.

these criticisms was the inability or refusal to look upon nationalism above all as an emotion. This inability was put down to Gellner's own 'great emotional distance'[10] from nationalism. The argument, to put it simply, was that since nationalist emotions were missing from Gellner's personal life, therefore they were also absent in his theory. Perry Anderson, one of the participants in the debate, accused Gellner's theory of negating nationalism above all as an 'identity': ' ... what it plainly neglects is the overpowering dimension of collective *meaning* that *modern* nationalism has always involved: that is, not its functionality for industry, but *its fulfilment of identity* ... Gellner has theorized nationalism without detecting the spell.' (emphasis added)[11]

Gellner replied to both the connected charges, related to the absence of nationalist emotion from his private life and from his theory. His reply is instructive for our understanding of the role of emotions in nationalism in particular and historical processes in general. He constructed the charge of a lack of emotions from his thesis in following words:

> "It [the criticism] runs roughly as follows: my vision of nationalism grossly underrates the emotional intensity of national identification and perhaps, more generally, the role of identity in human life in general. Their nation means so dreadfully much to men! Love of one's country, love of one's nation, is marked by a depth and intensity of passions, which is shamefully travestied by a theory which would make it a mere consequence of a labour market situation in an occupationally mobile society in which work is semantic rather than physical." *Did men die, suffer, kill, write poetry, merely so as to enhance their career prospects?* (emphasis added)[12].

He then provided clarification on both the charges. On the absence of nationalist emotions form his life, Gellner wrote:

> "I *am* deeply sensitive to the spell of nationalism. I can play about thirty Bohemian folk songs (or songs presented as such in my youth) on my mouth organ. My oldest friend, whom I have known since the age of three or four and who is Czech and a patriot, cannot bear to hear me play them because he says I do it in such a schmaltzy way, 'crying into the mouth organ.' I do not think I could have written the book on nationalism which I did write, were I not capable of crying, with the help of a little alcohol..." (emphasis in the original)[13]

---

10 Stargardt 1996, p. 186.
11 Anderson 1996, p. 425.
12 Gellner 1996, p. 623–624.
13 Gellner 1996, p. 624–625.

Gellner then proceeded to refute the second charge. He did it by frankly recognizing the 'powerful emotional impact of nationalism', but in a manner different from the non-modernists. The emotional power of nationalism derives, not from the working of some atavistic forces residing within humans, but from the major social transformations operative under modern conditions. Gellner looked at nationalism as more historical than 'natural' and certainly did not see it as residing in human heart. It was a product of circumstances marked by the transformation of the world from agrarian to industrial. It is during this transformation, and as result of it, that nationalism acquires its powerful emotional content. In a constantly dissolving and a hectically mobile scenario, congruence of culture becomes a great necessity. 'Non-congruence is not merely an inconvenience or a disadvantage: it means perpetual humiliation.'[14] In other words, industrialization, with its stress on mobility, displacement and atomization, creates an unprecedented crisis for the people.

They find themselves in alien conditions and in the company of cultural aliens. Nationalism provides them with meaning and helps create a new cultural community that the displaced people can now identify with. Industrialization created a great emotional crisis. Nationalism fulfils a great emotional need. The two tasks are indeed interrelated. It is from this scenario that nationalism derives its great emotional appeal. It fills the emotional vacuum created by the process of industrialization. Gellner elaborated in the same debate:

> "Nationalism is not explained by the use it has in legitimizing modernization [...] but by the fact that individuals find themselves in very stressful situations, unless the nationalist requirement of congruence between a man's culture and that of his environment is satisfied. Without such a congruence, life is hell. *Hence* that deep passion which, according to Perry Anderson, is absent both from my theory and my bosom. As it happens, it is very much present in both of them. The passion is not a means to some end, it is a reaction to an intolerable situation, to a constant jarring in the activity which is by far the most important thing in life – contact and communication with fellow human beings."[15]

What relevance does this debate have for our case-study? In the general theories of nationalism, nationalism as a political idea was also a carrier of certain powerful meanings for people and a great source of dignity, solidarity and comfort. This comfort and dignity could be enjoyed only *within* cultural groupings and not outside them. It was in this sense that emotions came to be integrally associated with the practice of nationalism. However, in the case of Muslim

---

14 Gellner 1996, p. 626.
15 Gellner 1996, p. 626.

nationalism, emotions had an additional relevance: they fed into the entire process of the transformation from multiple syncretic communities to a pan-Indian religious community of Indian Muslims, to a political community to eventually a national community. In this mammoth transformation and a great journey, emotions were not simply a *product* of the historical process; they were also the *prime mover* in this process.

This debate is instructive for our understanding of a very specific nation under discussion, viz., Muslim nation in colonial South Asia. Khursheed Kamal Aziz, historian from Pakistan and an ideologue of the Muslim nation, defined nationalism in such a way so as to provide an ideological justification for the Muslim nation that started developing since the late 1930s:

> "[…] nationalism, like so many human experiences, is a state of mind. We know that we are a nation, and therefore we are a nation. It is not logic, it is intuition. It is not dialectics, it is instinct. It is not a thought process approved by the laws of reasoning. It is a conviction, an awareness which comes to us in the flesh of a moment. That is what makes it irresistible."[16]

Aziz then listed 13 preconditions or building-blocs that went into the making of a nation. The list is instructive and throws some light on the nature of the nation he was describing and explaining. A group feeling, love for fellow nationals, common hostility to outsiders, common morals or ideas, common cultural characteristics, religion, common past, common character, common pride and sorrows, devotion to the nation, and hope for the future of the country, were some of the preconditions listed by Aziz[17]. It is quite clear that Aziz's task was not to define nation *as such*, but a very distinctive type of nation, Muslim nation. In his attempted construction of a theory, he was proceeding not from a general theory to a case-study, but precisely the other way round. He had the Muslim nation in mind, and proceeded to construct a theory suitable to his nation.

It should be clear from the general discussion of nationalism, and a very specific discussion by Aziz, that emotions were of crucial significance in the making of the Muslim nation. These emotions should not be seen merely as the offshoots of the macro structures of politics and economy. The relationship between the two was not unidirectional. Multiple emotions (of fear and anxiety) fed into the project of nationalism. And the process of the transmission of nationalist politics was such that it engendered many emotions. Emotions often altered the force and texture of nationalist politics, even as they were influenced by the politics.

---

16 Aziz 1967, p. 12.
17 Aziz 1967, p. 13–15.

It is therefore necessary to look at emotions not as fixed and static but as fluid and volatile. They fed into the political processes and vice-versa. In this mutually dialogical process, both were altered and modified. Emotions were not invested with any fixed innate meaning. New meanings were being imparted to them in the dynamic interaction between the human emotions and the political social processes.

This then is the broad framework in which we see emotions, not as a thing apart, but as part of the complex interplay of various social forces. Emotions played an important role in the shaping of major political events, but *along with other factors*. Needless to say, these various factors did not operate in mutual isolation, but were in a state of constant dialogue with each other. To put it differently these were not separate 'clusters' of factors but formed a consortium. Therefore for the purpose of explanation it is necessary not to ignore emotions or underplay their role by seeing them as passive recipients of political processes. At the same time we should also avoid the pitfalls of 'emotional determinism' by privileging emotions over other factors. It is necessary to recognize that emotions acquire their explanatory power not in isolation but in company with other socio-political factors. Any attempt to locate the role of emotions in popular political processes has to be like a tight rope-walk carrying the risk of tilting a bit much towards one side or the other.

Theories of nationalism in general have said more on what is common to all nations, and much less on what is distinctive about each nation. Twentieth century South Asia underwent different type of nationalist experiences. The emergence of a Muslim nation in India was distinct in many respects. This particular nation was devoid of both, a separate territory and a State for that territory. In other words some of the preconditions conducive to a smooth development of nationalist project were missing. What is more, even a pan-Indian community of Indian Muslims did not exist till the end of 19th century. The story of the making of a Muslim nation in India will therefore have to begin not with the development of nationalism in a community, but the very making of the community. The story will then move towards a transformation of Indian Muslims into an internally standardized and externally differentiated pan-Indian community.

Minority into majority, community into nation

This paper discusses the role of certain emotions in the making of a very unique and distinctive type of nation in modern South Asia. The process of the making of a Muslim nation spanned through three different stages: one, the transformation of Indian Muslims, scattered throughout the country, into a pan-Indian religio-political community; two, the transformation of this religio-political community into a potential national community; and three, the popularization and dissemination of this nation, through a process of a political mobilization, in the 1940s. The three stages should not be seen as mutually exclusive, as they often proceeded almost simultaneously. The contention of the paper is that emotions played an important part in all the three interconnected stages.

Why was this Muslim nation unique and distinctive? It was based on the idea, and a political claim accompanying the idea, that Muslims of India were a nation and were therefore entitled to *their own* nation-state. But on a simple and cursory empirical examination, we find that till the second half of the 19th century, Muslims of India were not even organized as a separate community and could not be characterized as such. India's community profile till the second half of the 19th century was marked by considerable complexity and diversity and it would be difficult to discern a coherently demarcated Muslim community[18]. Moreover, the ideological justification for the claim was made on the ground that Muslims in India were a minority and would be vulnerable to persecution by the Hindu majority in a single unified India. But the geographical area that was claimed for Pakistan consisted of areas where Muslims were a majority and least likely to be persecuted by Hindus or other non-Muslims. This was in some ways inevitable because there was no substantial piece of Indian territory that could be called exclusively Muslim. A substantial proportion of Muslim population was distributed in four provinces (Bengal, Punjab, Sind, North West Frontier Provinces) *as the majority community*. In these provinces Muslims constituted a majority.

The Muslim majority areas were concentrated in the east and north-west, geographically separated from each other by nearly a thousand miles: the Muslim majority provinces of Punjab and Bengal, the two most important provinces, contained significant minorities of Hindus (nearly 44% in Bengal and 31% in Punjab) and Sikhs (around 11% in Punjab). Quite apart from the geographical spread Indian Muslims were also characterized by considerable internal cultural and linguistic diversity. In other words there existed no territorial, cultural or linguistic preconditions necessary for the making of this Muslim nation. The remaining one-third of Muslims were scattered in all the other Indian provinces as minorities ranging from a numerical strength of 5% to 14%. They were deliberately and openly left out of the proposed Muslim nation-state (called Pakistan) by the leaders of the movement.

---

18 The nature of India's community structure is discussed slightly later in this paper.

The irony of such a claim was quite clear: a new nation-state was being claimed for a Muslim majority, on the grounds of Muslims being a minority. The real Muslim minorities were to be consciously left out of the new Muslim nation-state. But the support of the Muslim minorities was very crucial for the success of the movement. Such a movement could only be justified and sustained by strong emotional terms. 'Interests' or other rational principles could simply not be invoked as the substantial body of the supporters of the Pakistan movement consisted of Muslims from the minority areas who were least likely to benefit by the establishment of Pakistan. The movement could only be justified to them in purely emotional terms.

It was partly for some of these reasons that emotions came to acquire a crucial place in the Pakistan movement. It can be argued that emotions constituted the pillars that sustained the edifice of the Pakistan movement.

Transformations: local Muslim into Indian Muslim, community into nation

The emergence of a Muslim nation rested upon certain preconditions. One such precondition was that there should be an internally standardized and externally differentiated community of Indian Muslims. Such a community was also to be vested with a strong solidarity and an emotional make-up. As mentioned earlier, such a community did not exist on the ground. But a 19th century transformation in India's community structure did create conditions for the emergence of such a community. The story of the transformation of India's community structure is quite fascinating. It is part of a larger story of major social changes taking places in India under conditions of colonial modernization. These changes can be related, at a generic level, to the process of urbanization, communication, mobility and migrations. These new changes and migrations created new types of groups and communities and also engendered new solidarities and linkages – both horizontal and vertical, cutting across regions and communities[19]. In this context the new changes initiated by the British rule also played their part. Leading sociologist Mysore Narasimhachar Srinivas writes:

> "During the 19th century the British slowly laid the foundations of a modern state by surveying land, settling the revenue, creating a modern bureaucracy, army and police, instituting new courts, codifying the law, developing communications – railways, post and telegraph, roads and canals – establishing schools and colleges, and so on. The British also brought with them the printing press, and the profound and many-sided changes

---

19 For an elaborate description of this process, see Srinivas 2000, p. 49–95.

this brought about in Indian life and thought deserve a volume in itself. One obvious result was that books and journals, along with schools, made possible the transmission of modern as well as traditional knowledge to large number of Indians – knowledge which could no longer be the privilege of a few, hereditary groups – while the newspapers made people in different parts of the far-flung country realize they had common bonds, and that events happening in the world outside influenced their lives for good or evil."[20]

This may be treated as the general outline of the process that heralded India's transition to modernity. It involved urbanization, migration and mobility, displacement, dismantling of the local community structure, and breakdown of the community isolation. But this transition did not lead to any significant atomization or individualization, as may have happened in the classic Western model of this transition, but to the creation of large religious communities of Hindus and Muslims on the one hand, and a national community of the Indian people on the other. We are in this essay more concerned with the former transition than with the latter. In other words this was a transformation from local communities without fixed boundaries and clear identity tags to pan-Indian religious communities of Hindus and Muslims with neat and explicit lines of demarcation. In this sense, it can be said that Hindus and Muslims, as they are generally seen and understood today and through much of the 20th century, do not go back a very long time in history.

This transformation has many dimensions and has been understood in a whole range of ways. Since it was neither linear nor concentrated around a single event, but more diffused, the various strands in it need to be identified. It can be seen as a transformation from local communities to pan-Indian ones, from syncretic to sharply demarcated ones, from folk and little traditions to great and doctrinal traditions, and from fuzzy communities to enumerated ones[21]. It is however important not to look upon them as *alternative* ways of understanding the transformation, but rather as different strands of the same phenomenon, much like overlapping circles.

The disappearance of syncretic communities

It was asserted in the previous section that a pan-Indian Muslim community did not exist in India. What then was the community profile of Indian Muslims who constituted nearly one-fourth of the population? How were they accommodated in India's traditional community life? India's traditional community life

20 Srinivas 2000, p. 49.
21 On the elaboration of fuzzy and enumerated communities, see Kaviraj 1992, p. 20–33.

was generally marked by twin features of plurality and syncretism. It was simply not possible to talk of 'A Muslim Community' or 'A Hindu Community'. It would be more appropriate to talk of multiple Muslim communities, multiple Hindu communities, multiple communities that were both at the same time, or neither in the strict religious sense. The journey from a complex patchwork of multiple communities to relatively well-demarcated pan-Indian communities of Hindus and Muslims is quite interesting. It was this process that created the conditions for the emergence of a Muslim and a Hindu nation[22]. In order to fully grasp the nature of this transformation, it would be instructive to look at the cultural boundaries of the multiple Muslim groups and communities that inhabited Bengal, a Muslim majority province in eastern India.

In spite of being a Muslim majority area since the medieval times, Bengal never really had an exclusively Islamic flavour. This was largely because the Islam that triumphed and flourished in Bengal was not the high, doctrinal and classical form of Islam, but the low, *Sufi*, ritualistic and the unorthodox variety of Islam[23]. This created openings for the syncretic and composite culture that dominated Bengal's cultural landscape till the 19th century. Many observers noted this aspect of Islam there and commented on it from their own perspective. From the perspective of 'high Islam', these cultural practices, that were neither exclusively Muslim nor exclusively Hindu, appeared as corrupt. For instance as early as in the 16th century, Ihtiman Khan, a Mughal Admiral in Bengal, looked down upon the indigenous cultural practices of Bengali Muslims as he thought they were 'un-Islamic'[24]. The cultural deviations from Islamic practices continued to be commented upon in the 17th and 18th century also. A late 19th century British resident in Bengal, Dr. James Wise, noted the 'corrupt Hinduised rites' of Bengal Muslims. Wise did a survey of Muslims of Bengal and found them to be divided between clean and unclean castes. He found 22 different Muslim communities in Dhaka alone, each under its own *Panchayat*, and some communities including Hindus also[25]. These syncretic elements continued to survive and characterize

---

22 This essay is primarily concerned with the making of a Muslim nation and the role of emotions in this making. The making of a Hindu nation is another interesting story and will be taken up in another essay.

23 On the distinction between the high Islam and low Islam, see Gellner 1992b, p. 9–11.

24 The dominant presence of syncretic cultural influences on the Muslims of Bengal has been the major theme of Asim Roy's work. See Roy 1996, p. 11. For the transition from local cultural rootedness to a trans-local Islamic connectivity in the world of Bengali Muslims, see Ahmed 1996, p. 106–132.

25 Lelyveld 2003, p. 14.

the cultural life of Bengal Muslims till well into the 20th century. For this reason they were variously called imperfect Muslims, 'half-Muslims', or 'census Muslims', i.e., Muslims only for the purpose of census enumeration.

It was quite clear that Bengal Muslims enjoyed considerable autonomy from the tenets of high Islam. The dominant form of Islam that was practised in Bengal through the medieval times and till the 19th century contained strong syncretic elements. This syncretism was also the result of the inability of high Islam, with its stress on Arabic language and scholasticism, to penetrate into the lives of poor Muslims of Bengal. If the Islamic traditions codified in Arabic were not accessible to the lower sections of Bengali Muslims, many non-Islamic indigenous traditions were; it inevitably followed that the poor Muslims would be guided more by the local traditions than by classical Islam. One Syed Sultan wrote: 'There is no dearth of *kitabs* in Arabic and Persian [which were] for the learned alone and not for the ignorant folk [who were] unable to grasp a single precept of their religion [and remained] immersed in stories and fictions of local origin. Hindus and Muslims in every home took themselves with avid interest to the Hindu epic, the *Mahabharata*, rendered into Bengali by Kavindra-Parameswara …and nobody thought about Khoda and Rasul.'[26] The other Hindu epic *Ramayana* was equally popular with the Muslims of Bengal. 'The story of Rama was heard respectfully even by the *yavanas* [Muslims] and they were in tears to hear about the predicament of Rama at the loss of Sita', noted another contemporary commentator.

When the Islamic mediators and propagators tried to make Islam intelligible and meaningful to Bengali Muslims, they could only do it by deviating from the high Islamic norms. Therefore *Nabi* (prophet) and *Rasul* (messenger) were projected not so much as prophets but rather as *avataars* (incarnation). God was depicted as having created Muhammad out of 'his own self'. Krishna, the Hindu god, was depicted as God's messenger. Rama was also portrayed as a prophet. Thus the prophet-based tradition of Islam was combined with the incarnation (*avataar*) – based tradition of Hinduism in order to present a version of Islam that would be intelligible to the poor Muslims of Bengal. All this was done because Rama and Krishna had already reached the Bengali Muslim households through local cultural routes. Such a scenario continued to prevail in Bengal until the 19th century. Even when purification or *Sanskritization*[27] was initiated among the Muslims of Bengal, these syncretic elements did not get totally obliterated from Bengal.

---

26 Roy 1996, p. 20.
27 The adoption of Hindu social customs typical of caste groups considered ritually higher and purer.

Such examples of 'imperfect Muslims' at the level of popular Islam can be easily found in many other regions also. Denzil Ibbetson, the Director of Punjab census in the 1870s found the use of religious categories highly unsatisfactory for the purposes of enumeration. He found different social structures on the east and the west of Lahore city where people followed different cultural practices irrespective of their religion. He found many Muslim landlords retaining and employing Brahmins for ritualistic purposes. Ibbetson actually discovered a category of 'Muslim Brahmin' in west Punjab[28]. Till as late as the census of 1911, a total of 200,000 people from the region of Gujarat described their religious affinity as 'Mohammedan Hindus'[29].

Perhaps the most striking example of this phenomenon can be found from Bombay city where a local community of nearly 10,000 *Kabirpanthis* (Hindu followers of Kabir, the initiator of the *Bhakti* movement in the 15th century) was reported to be in existence. These *Kabirpanthis* were relatively free from the tenets of both high Islam and high Hinduism, hence they could not really be designated as either exclusively Muslim or Hindu. However it was reported at the Census of 1901 that, out of the erstwhile *Kabirpanthis*, nearly eight thousand enlisted themselves as Hindu and 1300 as Muslim[30]. It was a process of internal dissolution of a local community and its subsequent division and reconfiguration as different parts of the large pools of Hindus and Muslims. The result was that the category of '*Kabirpanthi*' disappeared from the census records and the followers of the *Kabirpanthi* faith, upon its dissolution, were subsumed in the newly created and ever enlarging pools of pan-Indian Hindus and Muslims[31]. The category that disappeared from the census records, in time would have also disappeared from the cultural and ritualistic lives of the people. It was through this process of dissolution and assimilation that the pan-Indian communities of Hindus and Muslims were being 'made' out of the raw material of multiple local communities.

The picture constructed above is meant to highlight a contrast between two social settings, temporally situated at the beginning and the end of the 19th century. A world of multiple local communities, devoid of any distinctly religious or other identity markers, gradually gave way to a world that was marked by

---

28 Lelyveld 2003, p. 15.
29 Oberoi 1994, p. 11.
30 Upadhyay 2004, p. 116.
31 The *Kabirpanthi* community should not be seen as exception but part of the larger pattern of Indias community life. The *Meos* of Mewat in Rajasthan were another such community. For syncretic practices among the *Meos*, see Mayaram 1997, p. 36–49.

the presence of internally standardized and externally differentiated pan-Indian religious communities of Hindus and Muslims. The differences pertaining to class, culture, language and region did not entirely disappear but got subordinated to the big religious divide between Hindus and Muslims. It was in this condition that various emotions came into play and helped to create socially and politically separative universes among Hindus and Muslims.

Language identity: the Hindi-Urdu issue

The trajectory mentioned above was not simply a process. It was also a project. It was a process in the sense that it was a product of certain generic trajectories of urbanization, social mobility and other uniformity-engendering elements. But it was also a project. It was a natural outcome of the activities undertaken by a number of individuals, groups and associations. Many of these activities were informed by fears, anxieties and uncertainties of various kinds. The leaders of these activities were not consciously trying to create pan-Indian communities of Hindus and Muslims; they were only trying to consolidate the community as a solution to the perceived problems. In reality they were not just consolidating the community; they were above all *creating* a community.

The two projects, Hindu and Muslim, can be understood like two separate ideological streams that flowed in to create large community-pools of Hindus and Muslims with a degree of self-awareness and an acute community consciousness. The two streams ran parallel to each other with many points of intersection. They also sometimes came close to each other but remained well short of merger at any point. They invariably flowed separately and the presence of one stream created a big incentive for the other stream. The two projects, Hindu and Muslim, were acutely informed by the presence of the other. The fear of the other loomed large on both the projects and cast its shadow. This section discusses the two projects separately in spite of their mutual entanglement.

This project took forms that were both similar and dissimilar among Hindus and Muslims. One area of similarity between the two trajectories was a perception of a 'crisis' that was understood to have gripped their religion. Likewise consolidation of the community was seen as the way out of the 'crisis'. The roots of the 'crisis' were of course different. The Islamic crisis, or rather the crisis of high Islam, was seen to be rooted primarily in the revolt of 1857. Leading Pakistani historian Khursheed Kamal Aziz has prepared a four-volume account of the 'Idea of Pakistan'. The first sentence of the books is quite instructive: 'In 1858

the Muslims of India ceased to be the rulers and became a problem.'[32] The suppression of the revolt of 1857 was a symbolic reminder that the 'Muslim rule'
had come to an end and that India had turned from *Darul Islam* (land of Islam)
into *Darul Harb* (un-Islamic land). This was the crux of the 'crisis'. For the period
1858–1940, Aziz lists a total of 170 schemes, plans and suggestions that were
offered to solve the problem of Muslims created by the events of 1857. The 170
schemes obviously differed in content and focus. But they all concentrated on
one thing: they were concerned with chartering a new and different political,
social and constitutional trajectory for Indian Muslims. All the schemes were
founded on one major line of demarcation, between Muslims and non-Muslims.

According to Aziz, 1857 brought home to the Muslim elite the fear of 'cultural
submergence' into the Hindu religion and traditions. The political crisis was accompanied by a perceived cultural 'crisis' consisting of the fear that a common
humiliation at the hands of the British 'might obliterate differences' between
Hindus and Muslims and 'make the Muslims themselves strangers to their own
identity.... Therefore the differences must be emphasized. The separate feeling
must be made conspicuous. The identity of a people must be shown to be a stark
reality.'[33]

The suppression of the revolt of 1857, end of 'seven centuries of Muslim rule',
and the consequent 'ruin' of Muslims in India became constant themes in the
standard accounts of the Muslim nation and became an integral part of the nation's self-image. In the story of the Muslim nation, as it was told and retold
during the mobilizational campaign for Pakistan during the 1940s, loss of power,
fear of cultural submergence, and anxiety about the future of Muslims became
constant themes. *Aligarh Institute Gazette*, a weekly brought out by the Aligarh
Muslim University, expressed this loss and anxiety very poignantly:

> "At the end of mutiny, Muslims were like a fish out of water. Their land was taken and
> property confiscated. Some were goaded, others were shot down. Consequently thousands
> of Muslims were left to utter ruin and many were rendered homeless and helpless. This in
> turn brought disastrous results. The Muslims became educationally backward, financially
> bankrupt and politically helpless. The Muslim nation in brief was there like ship caught in
> rough of a violent storm and lashed up by the waves of hostile forces on all sides. But out of
> evil cometh good and out of death cometh life. [...] And so it was with the Muslim nation.
> [...] We ought to live on the past, in the present and for the future."[34]

---

32 Aziz 1987, p. 1.
33 Aziz 1987, p. 2
34 *Aligarh Institute Gazette* (paper brought out by the Aligarh Muslim University), 1
    November 1940.

Similar fears, anxieties and resentment were also reflected in the literary crea-
tions written during the second half of the 19th century. They also fed into the
idea of 'Muslim separateness'. Abdul Halim Sharar, one of the early prose writers
in Urdu, wrote nearly 50 books in Urdu on themes revolving around Islam. He
wrote novels on the age of crusades, the Islamic empire in Spain, Arabia in the
pre-Islamic age of 'ignorance' (*jahilia*), Islam in Arabia and early days of Muslim
rule. Sharar created a new genre of historical fiction in Urdu prose in which
the background was provided by history but the characters were created by the
author's imagination[35]. The loss of power for high Islam became an important
theme in Urdu poetry also. Leading 19th century poet Altaf Husain Hali wrote his
famous poem *Ebb and Flow of Islam* (*Madd-i-Jazr-o-Islam*), popularly known as
Musaddas and Muhammad Iqbal followed it with his equally famous *Muslims'
complaint to God* (*Shikwa*) and *God's Reply to Muslims* (*Jawab-i-Shikwa*)[36]. Both
Musaddas and *Shikwa* were concerned with the plight of Muslims, the days of
Islamic glory and the subsequent fall from it. In the introduction to his *Musaddas*, Hali explained: 'This poem … has not been composed in order to be
enjoyed or with the aim of eliciting applause, but in order to make my friends
and fellows feel a sense of outrage and shame'. On the supposed corruptions in
Muslim life, he commented: 'Attached to unbelief, I was permanently disgusted
with faith. I swore allegiance to the Magian elder, became the Brahman's disciple,
worshipped idols, wore the sacred thread, and drew the caste-mark on my fore-
head. I mocked the ascetics and jeered at the preachers. I honoured the temples
and the houses of idols, and scoffed at the Kaaba and the mosques. I was insolent
to God, and disrespectful to the Prophets …'[37].

These anxieties were not simply confined to schemes and poetry. They also
had concrete institutional manifestations. We may refer here to Aligarh Movement founded by Sir Syed Ahmed Khan, and Darul Uloom, popularly known
as *Deoband* School, founded in 1869[38]. The two institutions differed from each
other in their ideological orientations. Aligarh School was a modernist endeavour. It urged Muslims to learn English and modern science in order to equip
themselves for modern conditions engendered by British rule. Sir Syed wanted
to build bridges between British and Muslims and create a new partnership in
order to offset the consequences of the revolt of 1857. Darul Uloom on the other
hand was a revivalist organization and looked upon British rule with suspicion

35 Aziz 1987, p. 42.
36 See Shackle and Majeed 1997; and Singh 1990.
37 Shackle and Majeed 1997, p. 97 and 91.
38 For Aligarh Movement see Malik 1980; and for *Deoband* School see Metcalf 1981.

and some hostility. Both the modernist-cum-loyalist strand of Aligarh Movement and the revivalist-cum-anti-imperialist strand of *Deoband* addressed the same theme – the Islamic 'crisis' that was symbolically understood to have emanated from the events around 1857[39]. The important thing is that in spite of their differences they both resulted in the consolidation of the community on the one hand and its increasing distance from Hindus, on the other[40].

Interestingly, fear, anxiety and resentment characterized not just the Muslim trajectory, but also the Hindu one. The fear of Muslim was as conspicuous in the Hindu project of community consolidation, as the fear of Hindu in the Muslim project. The 'crisis' among the Hindus was engendered by the discovery, provided by the census operations, that their numbers were reducing as a result of conversions to Islam and Christianity. It was hypothesized that the absence of a community, of a sacred book and of doctrinal centralization could be the cause of dissolution among Hindus. In other words, an absence of some of the Semitic religious features was seen as a weakness in the path of the consolidation of the Hindu community. The Hindu 'fear' was engendered by the prospects of decreasing numbers of Hindus and thereby Hindus becoming a minority in India in some distant future. It all began with speculations made by some census officials that the growth rate among the Hindus was slower than among Muslims. This discovery was made on the basis of the first census figures for the period 1872–81. Given the 'declining number' of Hindus, one census official calculated that Hindus would disappear altogether from India in 650 years![41] From here this theme was picked up by some of the Hindu leaders in Bengal and culminated in a book *Hindus – A Dying Race* written by U.N. Mukherji. It was soon translated into Bengali and gradually this idea spread out to become a part of the general common sense of Hindu *communal* politics against Muslims. Dissolution among Hindus, multiple castes and diverse faith systems within Hinduism were

---

39 However, there is *an* argument that dates the perception of the crisis to the earlier century, when Shah Wali Ullah (1703–62), a leading Muslim reformer understood the Muslim 'decline' and 'crisis', as a result of the penetration of un-Islamic, i.e., Sufi and Hindu, values and practices into Islam. He urges his followers to try and revive the pristine glory of Islam by purging it of un-Islamic influences. See Malik 1980, p. 256; and Hardy 1972, p. 28–30.

40 On the role of Muslim revivalism and its implications for politics in the 20th century, see Robinson 2000, p. 216–219.

41 For an interesting story on the scenario that produced this Hindu 'fear', see Datta 1999, p. 21–63. It is important to note that this 'fear' still plays an important role in much of Hindu communal propaganda against Muslims in Indian politics.

understood to be the causes of the problem. Likewise, 'reforms' among Hindus and much more importantly, 'integration of Hindus' were seen to be the solutions to the problem. The fear of being reduced to a minority provided a great stimulus to the project of Hindu consolidation and also to Hindu *communal* politics that developed through the decades of the 20th century.

Three themes would have played an important role in the making of a consolidated Hindu community and imparting it internal coherence: the formation of *Arya Samaj* in 1875, massive cow protection movement undertaken in the second half of the 19th century in various parts of the country, and a Hindi (or Nagari) agitation initiated in the 1860s in parts of north India against Urdu's domination and the British recognition of Urdu as the official language of lower courts. The three themes are interconnected but should be discussed separately, for the sake of clarity.

Aligarh movement was modernist; *Deoband* was revivalist. *Arya Samaj* contained elements of both. It was revivalist in that it advocated an old Vedic form of Hinduism and looked upon subsequent evolution of Hinduism as a form of corruption. 'Back to the Vedas' was its chief slogan. It was also modernist in that a branch of *Arya Samaj* (Dayanand Anglo-Vedic Trust and Management Society, after the name of its founder Dayanand Saraswati) focused on imparting modern education to Hindu students, much like the Aligarh movement. *Arya Samaj* was also opposed to caste divisions within Hinduism. Reconversion of erstwhile Hindus back into the fold of Hinduism was one of its major activities in Punjab.

A notion of pure and pristine Hinduism (Vedic age), its subsequent corruption and the need to purify it again were the central themes of *Arya Samaj*. Given the fundamental changes that had occurred in Hinduism during the period after the Vedas, purifying inevitably implied having to virtually transform Hinduism. Kenneth Jones writes on the founder of *Arya Samaj*: 'Dayanand began to preach a 'purified' Hinduism, one that rejected the popular Puranas, polytheism, idolatry, the role of Brahman priests, pilgrimages, nearly all rituals, and the ban on widow marriage – in short, almost all of contemporary Hinduism.'[42] Activities such as education, re-conversion, starting orphanages for Hindu children and providing famine relief to Hindus fed into a new attitude that began to see Hindus as a distinct community rather than as mere religious sect[43]. At the same time an expansion of *Arya Samaj* network to other parts of country such as the United Provinces (U.P.) in 1889, Rajasthan in 1888, Bengal and Bihar in 1889,

---

42 Jones 1994, p. 96.
43 Jones 1994, p. 100.

the Central Provinces and Berar in 1889, and Maharashtra in 1902 meant that not only was a new Hindu community was being created, it was also acquiring a trans-regional connectivity.

Arya Samaj was undoubtedly a major factor in creating a Hindu 'community' and imparting coherence to it, and creating linkages cutting across regions. The project of creating a Hindu community also benefited greatly by a vibrant cow protection movement that spread in parts of north and western India in the last decade of the 19th century. It was also related to the efforts of *Arya Samaj*. As part of cow protection movement, a number of cow protection societies began to be formed. It was reported that by the last decade of the 19th century, as many as 182 cow protection societies had been formed[44]. These societies generated considerable religions passions and one direct result of these passions was the outbreak of *communal* violence in parts of Eastern U.P. and Bihar in 1891 and 1893. The mushrooming of cow protection societies, display of belligerence over the symbol of cow, and the spread of Hindu-Muslim violence facilitated community formation in three ways. One, it brought together various castes that could be united on the question of cow. It became an opportunity for low caste Hindus to emerge as the champions of the faith and thus aspire for a higher status within the caste hierarchy. Thus internal caste divisions could actually foster the religious ties and solidarities, without any of the segments being dissolved. Two, it also had the potential to bring the Hindus of cities and villages into a common orbit. Three, much more significantly, such symbols could create a grid of solidarity across regions. These solidarities also fed into counter-solidarities among Muslims. Gyanendra Pandey writes: 'The violence of June 1893 in eastern U.P. and Bihar was followed closely by riots in Junagadh and Bombay, where Muslims, some of them Julaha migrants from that very region, came out on the streets at least in part to take revenge for the attacks upon their co-religionists in Azamgarh and elsewhere.'[45]

Yet another contributing factor to this phenomenon was a Hindi (or Nagari) movement launched from 1860s onwards for an official recognition of Hindi language by the British government and against the domination of Urdu language in north India[46]. Why should a language movement contribute to the consolidation of a religious community? How was it that language became an important vehicle in the formation of religio-political identities in the course of the 19th century?

---

44 For a detailed analysis of the cow protection movement and its role in creating a cohesive Hindu community, see Pandey 1990, p. 163–200.

45 Pandey 1990, p. 175.

46 For a detailed account of the Hindi movement, see King 1994.

Hindi and Urdu should be understood as modern literary languages. The two have shared many features in common (roots, speech, grammar and nearly half of vocabulary) but have also differed from each other in certain respects (script, literary trajectories during the 19th and 20th centuries). Whether they should be identified as two different languages or merely as two names for the same language, has been an area of debate among scholars, with advocates on both the sides. However, for the purposes of our argument, we may look upon them as twins, with remarkable similarities and areas of commonness, but also some distinct socio-literary domains of their own.

As Hindi and Urdu grew in the 19th century, they generally came to be normatively identified with Hinduism and Islam, respectively[47]. As the British rulers replaced Persian with English in 1837 as the language of court and administration at the top, they made Urdu the language of administration at the lower level for north India. The Hindi movement developed as a reaction to this measure of the British. The movement generally took three forms. One, the leaders of the movement submitted a number of applications and petitions, signed by many people, to the government to allow Hindi written in the Nagari script in courts. The most important petitions were submitted by the leaders of the movement to U.P. government in 1868, 1873 and 1898. Two, a number of literary and creative works (plays, poems etc.) were written and published in favour of Hindi and to denigrate Urdu. Religious terminology and imagery were invoked both in the defence of Hindi and the denigration of Urdu. Three, associations were formed to propagate the cause of Hindi, *Nagari Pracharini Sabha*, formed in 1893 in Banaras and *Hindi Sahitya Sammelan*, formed in 1910 in Allahabad, being the most prominent.

Soon there began a counter response from the defenders of Urdu. Given the religious association of the two languages, which had by now begun to be established, it was natural for the Hindi-Urdu rivalry to appear like a Hindu-Muslim one. The defenders of the two languages were also drawn from Hindus and Muslims, respectively. The language rivalry was actually *seen* as a religio-political rivalry. Sir Syed Ahmed Khan, dismayed by the Hindi movement, wrote in a letter: 'I understand …Hindus are roused to destroy the Muslim [cultural] symbol embodied in the Urdu language and the Persian script …. This … would destroy

---

47 This too is a contentious theme. The separate religious tags for the two languages should not be accepted as an *a priori* reality, but examined. At the same time it is no use denying the process through which religious connections were imparted to the two languages. For a detailed story of the manner in which these associations came to be formed, see Misra 2005, p. 269–282.

cooperation between the Hindus and the Muslims. Muslims will never accept Hindi and if Hindus persistently demanded the adoption of Hindi in preference to Urdu it would result in the total separation of Muslims from the Hindus.'[48] Similar defences of Hindi were made from the Hindu side. Raja Shiva Prasad, one of the leaders of the Hindi movement, was convinced that the question of language was essentially a question of culture, identity and nationality:

"The Persian of our day is half Arabic; and I cannot see the wisdom of the policy which thrusts a Semitic element into the bosom of Hindus and alienates them from their Aryan speech; not only speech, but all that is Aryan; because through speech ideas are formed, and through ideas manners and customs. To read Persian is to become Persianized, all our ideas become corrupt and our nationality is lost. Cursed be the day which saw the Muhammadans cross the Indus; all the evils which we find amongst us we are indebted for to our 'beloved brethren' the Muhammadans. [...] I again say I do not see the wisdom of the policy which is now trying to turn all Hindus into semi-Muhammadans and destroy our Hindu nationality."[49]

The Hindi movement turned out to be quite successful. In Bihar and the Central Provinces, Hindi replaced Urdu as the language of lower administration and in the U.P., it was granted parity with Urdu. It was thus only in Punjab that Urdu retained its exclusive domination till 1947. But the major impact of the Hindi movement was in creating a language-religion-culture congruence. The language scenario that existed at the beginning of the 19th century was more mixed, plural and syncretic. The multiple speech communities that existed did not really conform to the ideological divide along linguistic lines that prevailed at the beginning of the 20th century. The notion that the speech community, religious community and a cultural community should all be congruent was a product of the major developments of the 19th century, discussed above. In the 20th century such 'communities' were to be treated as 'political communities' as well. It was thus that abstractions like a united Hindu community and united Muslim community were created and legitimized. It was precisely these 'communities' that were placed at the service of *communal* political mobilizations in the 20th century.

The story told so far may be recapitulated as follows: India's encounter with colonial modernity had far reaching effects. One such effect was the transformation in its community structure. One component of this transformation was the emergence of self-consciously pan-Indian religious communities of Hindus and Muslims. The making of these communities was not simply a result of the social

---

48 Malik 1980, p. 240.
49 Quoted in King 1994, p. 131.

processes of urbanization and social mobility. It was also the result of social engineering on the part of various individuals and organizations. These endeavours were inspired by fears and anxieties and perceptions of crisis regarding their future. The Muslim crisis was linked to a loss of power which was believed to have emanated from the suppression of the revolt of 1857 and a symbolic transfer of power from Mughal to British hands. The Hindu crisis, on the other hand, was fostered by the fear that Hindus were destined to remain under the political domination of 'outsiders'. The reasons for this 'perpetual domination' were located in the absence of certain features found in the Semitic religious traditions (a holy book, doctrinal and institutional centralization). These fears were compounded by the 'discovery' about the dwindling numbers of Hindus. A particular reading of the census reports for the years for Bengal helped create the myth the Hindus could be reduced to the status of a minority in some foreseeable future. Both the Muslim fear and the Hindu fear fostered initiatives that resulted in the exclusive consolidation of Hindus and Muslims along separate lines. Such a situation was very conducive for the growth of rival religious nationalisms among Hindus and Muslims. In the articulation and dissemination of these nations, a whole range of emotions were pressed into service. The following section discusses some of these emotions specially in the context of the development of the Muslim nation.

Muslim League and Congress

The period 1937 to 1940 was very crucial in the making of the Muslim nation. It was during this period that all the defining elements, veins and arteries as it were, of this nation were spelt out. Some of the constitutional initiatives taken by the British government provided a major fillip to this nation. The *Government of India Act* of 1935 created an exclusively Muslim domain in the realm of constitutional and electoral politics. This Muslim domain consisted of one-third of seats in the *Central Legislative Assembly*, a majority status in the Muslim majority provinces, weigthage in provinces where Muslims were a minority, and carving out of more Muslim majority provinces. All the Muslim representatives were to be elected exclusively through Muslim votes. Muslim voters were separated from non-Muslim voters. The result of these initiatives was that at the normative level an exclusive Muslim space was created in the electoral politics. Thus it was that Indian Muslims, who had been in the process of being constituted as a pan-Indian religious community, also got constituted as a pan-Indian political community, primarily as a result of the constitutional initiatives undertaken by the British.

The first general elections held in 1937 saw three major claimants for this Muslim constituency – Muslim League, Congress and the regional groups organized in the Muslim majority provinces. The three forces represented three different ideologies. Congress represented Indian nationalism, which consisted of the twin ideas of anti-imperialism and national unity. Muslim League approached the Muslim electorates with Muslim exclusivism and the regional forces focused only on their region. The results of the general election provided a mixed verdict for this Muslim constituency and both – Muslim League and the regionalist forces – gained a foothold into it without being able to claim any monopoly over it. Congress drew a blank in the Muslim constituency. But in the rest of the country it was able to demonstrate its strength and form governments in seven out of the 11 provinces. There was a constitutional obligation to include minorities (read Muslims) in the provincial ministries and Congress fulfilled this obligation by either roping in individual Muslims or giving the ministerial berths to Congress Muslims. For various reasons, Muslim League was not invited or obliged to provide the 'Muslim component' to the provincial ministries under Congress governments. Muslim League responded to this exclusion from structures of power by launching a powerful movement against Congress. The political situation in general was quite favourable for this movement. Hindu-Muslim relations had deteriorated since the 1920s. The elections of 1937 had shown the largest national party – Congress – to be quite unrepresentative of Muslims, the largest national minority constituting nearly 25% of the total population. But this party had captured power in most parts of the country. The largest party of the Muslims had been excluded from power. It was a combination of all these factors which saw Muslim League launching a powerful and emotionally surcharged movement against Congress.

An important aspect of the Muslim League movement was that it projected the Congress-League rivalry as a Hindu-Muslim one. In this way all the religious prejudices and stereotypes could be pressed into the service of the political movement. The movement consciously constructed a long lineage of hatred and dislike between the two communities and turned it into a modern hatred. As mentioned above, the 1920s had witnessed a deterioration in the *communal* situation both at the level of politics and *social* relations between Hindus and Muslims. At the political level, Congress and Muslim League had drifted apart from each other. A series of *communal* riots between Hindus and Muslims had increased the social distances between two religious communities. Quite a few prejudices and stereotypes developed in this period and were established as the general common sense among Hindus and Muslims against each other. They served to reinforce the already existing fear and mistrust between the two communities. Commenting on the nature of these prejudices, historian Bipan Chandra writes:

"The Hindu *communalists* portrayed the Muslim as lacking in culture and as a *goonda*, a bully and a bloodthirsty brute whose natural instinct was to loot, kill, burn and rape. In the communal image, a Muslim was a man of low morals and uncontrolled sexual lust who was ever ready to seduce, abduct and assault Hindu women.... This stereotype of Muslims was then used to create fear and a defensive mentality among the Hindus even though they were a majority in the country. The Hindu communalists also created the stereotype of the 'mild', 'docile' and 'emasculated' Hindu in order to goad Hindus to transform themselves into a 'militant people' by organizing along *communal* and Fascist lines."[50]

A different set of prejudices and stereotypes regarding the Hindus did the rounds among Muslims. The image of a Hindu was that of a 'calculating, crafty, dubious *Bania* (a merchant caste) who could not be trusted and whose every word must be watched for a twist. Moreover, all Hindus were money-mad exploiters in deep contrast to Muslims who cared little for money and had 'no idea of exploitation."[51]

The nature of prejudices and stereotypes between Hindus and Muslims, and their role in contributing to *communalism* has been one of the less researched areas in the political history of modern India. We do not know very much, and for sure, whether these prejudices were a carry-over form pre-modern times or whether they developed during the modern period. We also do not know whether these prejudices were a result of the already existing social distance between Hindus and Muslims or whether they were consciously created and disseminated by motivated political actors and organizations. It is possible that some social raw material may have existed in the form of distant curiosity by one group about another. This social raw material may have transformed into well worked out social knowledge. An increase in *communal* violence and in social gap between the two may have reinforced this 'knowledge'. What appears certain however is that these prejudices and stereotypes were both a product of mutual fear and mistrust and also fed into fear and mistrust between the two communities. These prejudices became politically explosive when they got integrated to the emotional universes of many Hindus and Muslims.

The three interrelated developments of the 1920s – entry of *communalism* in Indian politics, deteriorating Hindu-Muslim relations, and an increase in Congress-Muslim League rivalry – created a fertile ground for the Muslim League campaign after 1937. The campaign was grounded on perceptions of injustice and persecutions practised by the Congress government against Muslims.

---

50 Chandra 1984, p. 202.
51 Chandra 1984, p. 203.

Muslims were sought to be mobilized on the ground that Congress government was a 'Hindu *Raj*'; and Muslims were being persecuted under Congress government. A number of highly emotive issues were picked up. It was emphasized that Congress government would promote Hindi language and suppress Urdu, considered to be a Muslim language. It was also alleged that Congress would Hinduise education and would impose its own cultural symbols on Muslims. Two such cultural symbols that were picked up were the national flag and the national anthem. Both the issues – the flag and the anthem – were considered great symbols of honour. The Muslim League leadership alleged that the Congress government had dishonoured the Muslims by treating its party flag as the national flag and imposing it on Muslims. Likewise it was alleged that Congress had chosen a particular anthem – Bande Mataram – that was considered idolatrous and anti-Islam by the Muslim League leadership. It was issues of this kind, rather than any concrete economic or political grievances, that became the lynchpin of the Muslim League movement against Congress.

There is no conclusive evidence to determine the role these issues played in the popularization of Muslim League and its politics. A few things can however be stated. One, the movement launched by Muslim League against Congress was grounded in strong emotional appeals, rather than economic or political one. Though the movement was primarily political, Muslims were mobilized on emotional basis. Themes like honour and fear of cultural submergence constituted the axis of the movement. Two, Congress did take up some of these issues and replied to the allegations made by the Muslim League. But it is clear that the League's allegations carried greater credibility compared to Congress defence, among Muslims. Three, Muslim League source claimed, as they were expected to, that by 1939–40, Muslim League had truly become a mass force, representative of Indian Muslims. Congress sources denied, as indeed they were expected to, that Muslim League had become truly representative of Indian Muslims. Quite clearly these sources cannot be relied upon to measure the extent of the success of the emotional campaign launched by the Muslim League. But it can be easily concluded on the basis of some independent sources and also British records that the campaign brought the Muslim League from the margins of Indian politics to the mainstream. It also successfully reached out to many Muslims who responded quite enthusiastically to the emotional campaign.

One result of the Muslim League movement was the introduction and inculcation of a political agenda in the religious community of Indian Muslims. This set the stage for the next major development, i.e., the transformation of the political community into a potential national community. At its Lahore session in March 1940, Muslim League passed what came to be known as the historic *Pakistan resolution*. The resolution stated that Indian Muslims were not a minority but a nation and therefore entitled to *their own* nation-state. M.A. Jinnah, the leader of the Pakistan movement, defined Pakistan in following terms:

> "The difference between Hindus and Muslims is deep-rooted and ineradicable, We are a nation with our own distinctive culture and civilization, language and literature, art and architecture, names and nomenclature, sense of value and proportion, legal laws and moral codes, customs and calendar, history and traditions, attitudes and ambitions, in short, we have our own distinctive outlook on life and of life. By all canons of international law we are a nation."[52]

The next stage of the movement was a popularization of this 'nation'. It was simply not enough to create the idea of a nation. This idea had to be taken to ordinary Muslims. As in the earlier phase, emotions played a crucial role in the popularization of the Muslim nation and transform it into an irresistible social and political force.

Towards Pakistan

The year 1939 marked a big shift in the mainstream Indian politics in many respects. World War II had broken out and the British government had unilaterally declared India to be a party in war. In protest Congress governments resigned from all the provinces where they formed a government. This also brought to an end the Muslim League movement against Congress governments. The British government took many strides towards recognizing Muslim League as a force representative of Indian Muslims. Muslim League ended all ambiguities regarding its earlier demands and now demanded a separate nation state exclusively representative of Indian Muslims on the basis of the new assertion that Indian Muslims were not a minority but a nation. This new stand was codified in 1940 in the Lahore resolution by the Muslim League. A new nation was born and Jinnah defined it unambiguously as possible. But when was this Muslim nation born? Why didn't it show up earlier in Indian history? Jinnah's assertion would appear quite incongruent with the social profile of Indian Muslims in the 19th century, as discussed in the previous section. Jinnah had an answer to the question regarding how and when the diverse Muslim communities had metamorphosed into

---

52 Jinnah's Interview to *Associated Press of America*, Bombay, 1 July 1944, no. 534, in Yusufi 1996, vol. 3, p. 1578.

a nation. Jinnah's answer was that Pakistan had already existed for a long time; 'it was not created by Jinnah or anyone else.'[53] He clarified further: 'Pakistan ... was not the product of the conduct or misconduct of Hindus. It had always been there; only they [Muslims] were not conscious of it.'[54]

This was a classic example of nationalism as an 'invented tradition' or rather, a manufactured tradition[55]. Jinnah was portraying his Muslim nation as a continuation in history in a fully accomplished form, almost like the proverbial sleeping beauty who only needed the prince charming to wake her up with his touch. Jinnah himself defined the 'sleeping beauty' as a floating ship:

> "The position of Muslim India during the last 200 years has been that of a ship without a rudder and without a captain, floating on the high seas full of rocks. For 200 years it remained floating damaged, disorganised, demoralised, still floating. In 1936 with the cooperation of many others we salvaged the ship. Today the ship has a wonderful rudder and a captain who is willing to serve and always to serve. Its engines are in perfect order, and it has got its loyal crew and officers. In the course of the last five years it has turned into a battleship. [...] We have to forge our own charter – not the Atlantic charter. But it is Pakistan. Pakistan is here. We have only to take it. [...] I have spoken what was in the hearts of millions of Muslims boldly."[56]

This indeed was a tall claim. There was no discernible indication that this Muslim nation existed in the hearts of millions of Indian Muslims as claimed by Jinnah. Pakistan certainly existed on paper in the form of a resolution passed by the Muslim League. The idea of Pakistan had been born. There was no proof for the claim that the nation in itself was also a nation *for itself*. Were the members of the nation, Indian Muslims, fully aware that they were indeed a separate nation? It would be hard to validate the idea of a Muslim nation as a larger political entity enjoying a consensus among Indian Muslims. The idea had to travel a great distance before it could become an irresistible political and ideological force.

The passing of the Pakistan resolution did not create much of a storm initially. Its opponents condemned it. The British also did not take it very seriously initially and the regional leaders from Punjab and Bengal showed no enthusiasm for it. Indeed there were very few takers for the idea of Pakistan among Indian Muslims in 1940. However, within a period of six years, this idea of a Muslim

---

53 Jinnah's Speech at Karachi, 25 December 1940, no. 411, Yusufi 1996, vol. 2, p. 1295.
54 Jinnah's Speech in Aligarh, 8 March 1944, in Ahmad 1947, p. 2.
55 On how traditions are invented to suit present imperatives, see Hobsbawn 1983, p. 1–14.
56 Jinnah's Speech in Delhi, 25 December 1942, no. 570, in Yusufi 1996, vol. 3, p. 1659–1661.

nation had become such a huge political force that none could ignore it. At the second general elections of 1946, Muslim League won all the seats at the Central Legislative Assembly and captured a large number of Muslim seats in both the Muslim majority and the minority provinces. It was thus in a position to assert itself as a major actor in the political negotiations for a transfer of power. How did this come about?

The general explanations refer to the 'brilliant strategy' of Jinnah, tactical mistakes of both Congress and the British at crucial moments[57], and the support provided to the Muslim League by the British. However some part of the explanation should also focus on the mobilizational campaign carried out by Muslim League among Indian Muslims. It was an emotionally surcharged campaign that made various appeals to Indian Muslims and tried to capture their hearts and minds through these appeals. In this campaign, an extremely emotionalized from of history was used and propagated. Pakistan was projected as the only way in which the 'Muslim honour' that had been injured during the history of the last hundred years could be reclaimed. Religious appeals were made using religious symbols and imageries. It was through all this that an exclusive Muslim patriotism was invoked. Let us look at some of these aspects in some detail.

In the Muslim League campaign, history was both invoked and emotionalized to convey to Muslims that they were a historically formed special national community. Not all religious communities could be considered nations. The national status of Indian Muslims were conferred upon them by history and by the distinctiveness of the Muslim community. Making a special reference to their historical memory of domination, Liaqat Ali Kahn told his audience in Karachi: 'Muslims had governed India for over 800 years. Having been rulers for several centuries, they could never reconcile themselves with the prospects of a permanent minority...'[58]

Whether this was a case of an instrumental manipulation of emotions, or an endeavour conducted under the influence of the same emotions, is an important and a contentious question. The point can be argued both ways. Do political leaders employ certain symbols and imageries to instrumentally construct a particular political universe for the consumption of their followers, or do they operate under the influence of the same politico-emotional universe? Do they manipulate emotions or operate form *within* the conceptual boundaries of those

---

57 Jalal 1985, p. 253.
58 Speech in Karachi, *Star of India* (An English Daily sponsored by Muslim League and brought out from Calcutta), 25 October 1945. For a study of that newspaper concerning the idea of Pakistan, see Di Costanzo 2011.

emotions?[59] Whatever be the answer to the question, it is clear that the two – the appeal made by the leader and its internalization by the same leader – cannot remain wholly distinct from each other for long. The very act of making an emotional political appeal commits the leader to disseminated emotions and brings him within their orbit.

The idea of Pakistan was criticized by its opponents on the ground of being economically unviable. Interestingly, this charge was rebutted by the Muslim League leadership, not by demonstrating the economic feasibility of Pakistan, but by emphasizing the irrelevance of the economic criterion. Mufti Fakhrul Islam, a Muslim League leader from U.P., said in a speech: 'To hold that Pakistan is an economic impossibility is to ignore realities....A nation lives by its ambition to live and not with economic resources. When Islam started about 1300 years ago as an international movement it did not draw inspiration from bread and butter.'[60] On another occasion Jinnah openly admitted to the members of the Muslim League Planning Committee that Pakistan 'may not be as rich as Hindustan.'[61] Evidently, the justification for Pakistan was not to rest on its economic viability but on its emotional sustenance for Indian Muslims.

The Pakistan movement invoked history at two levels, the immediate political history of India and the 1300 years old history of Islam. Referring to the conquest of Sind by Muhammad Bin Qasim in the 8th century, a Shia meeting at Lucknow deplored the 'tragic irony that 1200 men led by Muhammad Bin Qasim could settle their feet in India against heavy odds but a 100 million of Muslims today are not powerful enough to break the chains of slavery.'[62] Quite apart from invoking history, Pakistan was also upheld as the fulfilment of honour that had been wounded during the post-1857 period. In a message to his followers on 'Pakistan Day', Jinnah declared: 'In Pakistan lies our deliverance, defence and

---

59   On this question, there is an interesting debate between two prominent historians of modern India – Francis Robinson and Paul Brass. Whereas Brass imparts an instrumentalist role to the elite leadership, Robinson sees the mobilizing leadership as much more constrained in making its choices and being a part of the same emotional universe involving the masses and the elite. The debate was conducted specifically in the context of the growth of Muslim separatism in north India. See Robinson 1990 and Brass 1990, p. 128–153.

60   Election speech in Allahabad just two days before the elections, *Star of India*, 26 November 1945.

61   Jinnah's address to members of Muslim League Planning Committee, 5 November 1944, in Yusufi 1996, vol. 3, p. 1960.

62   Speech by Shabibul Husain in Lucknow, *Star of India*, 19 October 1945.

honour. If we fail, we perish and there will be no sign or symptom of Muslims or Islam left in this sub-continent.'[63]

As the movement progressed, it developed a major contradiction. Till 1940, major support for Muslim League had come from Muslim minority provinces like UP and Bombay. This support came on the basis that Muslims as a minority were being persecuted, or discriminated against, by the Congress ministries and the fear that they would lose all their advantages in government jobs. But 1940 changed the texture of Muslim League politics in very significant terms. The focus was now on the Muslim majority provinces –Punjab, Bengal, Sind and North-West Frontier Provinces – that were expected to constitute the territory of the proposed Pakistan. It was clear that, upon its fulfilment, Pakistan would sound the death-knell of those Muslim minorities who would remain in India. In demanding Pakistan consisting of Muslim majority provinces, could Muslim League afford to ignore its traditional support base drawn from the minority provinces? Was it not politically suicidal for Muslim League to make a demand, which, upon being fulfilled, excluded its own support base? How was Jinnah to justify the demand for Pakistan to the Muslims of UP and Bihar? It was curious that Pakistan was being claimed for areas that needed it the least. Admittedly the justification for Pakistan came from the minority areas. It was supposedly the 'plight' of Muslims under Congress governments in Muslim minority provinces like UP, Bihar and CP that had engendered the need for a separate Muslim homeland. It was understood in Muslim League circles that the experiences of Muslims of Congress governments in minority provinces would have convinced them of the need for a separate Muslim homeland. It was therefore anticipated that the movement for Pakistan would get major support from the minority provinces. Yet the irony was that the Muslims of minority provinces were destined not to be a part of this Pakistan, upon its realization. It was in this sense that the movement for Pakistan defied logic or any other rational considerations. How could Jinnah justify Pakistan to Muslim minorities of UP? It was partly for these reasons that emotions came to occupy an axial position in the movement for Pakistan.

It is interesting that, contrary to expectations, Jinnah did not try to paper over or underplay this anomaly. He handled it by confronting it directly. He displayed no ambiguity in defining Pakistan in his public utterances. Jinnah made it clear that the demand for Pakistan was *by* the Muslims of minority provinces, not *for* them. He made an appeal to Muslims of minority provinces

---

63 Message on Pakistan Day, 22 March 1945, in Yusufi 1996, vol. 3.

to make a sacrifice for their Muslim brethren from the majority areas[64] because 'it was better to have a homeland for some Muslims than for none.' Jinnah narrated another story of a Muslim peasant in CP, a minority province, who understood Pakistan very well and was willing to make the required sacrifice:

> "Then I asked him because he was in CP where Muslims are only 4 per cent, what will happen to you. [...] He said 'It is my misfortune that I am born here, let my brethren have their own Hukumat [rule] and let them at least be free. God will protect us here."[65]

He assured the Muslims of minority provinces that their condition would be better upon the fulfilment of the Pakistan scheme as there would be reciprocity between the two independent states of India and Pakistan regarding the treatment of their respective minorities and that the presence of substantial minorities in both the states would act as a deterrent on both the states[66]. 'The Muslim minorities in Hindu provinces would put up with their fate, but they would not stand in the way of Muslim majority provinces becoming free'[67]. However if the Muslim minorities of India were subjected to ill treatment, even an exchange of population between the two sovereign states could be considered[68]. In other words, no obstacles of any kind were to be allowed to come in the way of the realization of Pakistan. If however worse came to worst, Jinnah was even prepared to abandon Muslims of minority provinces to their fate: '...in order to liberate 7 crore of Muslims where they were in a majority he [Jinnah] was willing to perform the last ceremony of martyrdom if necessary and let two crore of Muslims be smashed.'[69] From his side a Muslim League leader from UP assured the Muslims of majority provinces that UP Muslims will not betray them and support them in the struggle for Pakistan: 'What guarantee is there in a united India that Muslim rights will not be trampled upon? Are the Muslims of UP whose sympathies are with the Muslims of the whole world, prepared to let down six and a half

---

64 Statement on the Lahore resolution of Muslim League, 1 April 1940, no. 357, in Yusufi 1996, vol. 2, p. 1191.

65 Jinnah's Speech in Quetta, 3 July 1943, No. 598, in Yusufi 1996, vol. 3, p. 1750.

66 Jinnah's Speech in Bombay, 8 December 1940, no. 404, in Yusufi 1996, vol. 2, p. 1284.

67 Jinnah's Speech at a Public Meeting in Ahmedabad, 28 December 1940, No. 413, in Yusufi 1996, vol. 2, p. 1298.

68 Statement by Jinnah on the Lahore Resolution of Muslim League, 1 April 1940, No. 357, in Yusufi 1996, vol. 2, p. 1190.

69 Jinnah's Address to Muslim Students of Kanpur, 30 March 1941, no. 444, in Yusufi 1996, vol. 2, p. 1376.

crores of their Muslim brethren in north-west and north-east of India by voting against the League and Pakistan?'[70]

It was partly for this reason that the Pakistan movement in Muslim minority regions focused on ideas of Pan-Islam and presented Pakistan as a partial fulfilment of Pan-Islamic ideals, particularly during election campaigns. In UP elections, there was a special emphasis on the Palestinian question, the Jewish settlements in Palestine and the struggles being waged by Muslims the world over. A speaker in an election meeting in Sitapur (UP) said: 'Today the whole Muslim world is marching towards freedom. In Java, Sumatra, Egypt and Palestine Muslims are aspiring for a free and sovereign state. Muslims in India are a part and parcel of the great Muslim *millat* [community] and they rightly deserve to be free in their homeland.'[71] At a special meeting in Aligarh Muslim University, a resolution expressed full support to the Arab cause in Palestine and viewed with alarm the illegal migrations of Jews in Palestine and the British inability or refusal to stop it: 'It [the meeting] unequivocally condemns the uncalled for and ill-advised intervention of President Truman and warns the British government that the slightest deviation from the White Paper [on the Palestinian Question] would be intolerable to Muslim India.'[72] The meeting ended with an appeal to UP Muslims to support Pakistan and vote for Muslim League candidates. At another meeting in UP the speaker referred to the Zionist demand in Palestine and asserted that the entire 'Muslim world' would flare up if the British succumbed to the Zionist demand: '... the main fact that Nazi Germany persecuted the Jews does not mean that they should be thrust upon other people whose land cannot absorb them any longer....If America and Britain sincerely desire that a solution of the problem is necessary, it can be found by sending Jews to other parts of the world. The USA is a vast country and if the Americans are really sympathetic to the Jews, they should welcome the Jews in their own country.'[73] 'Palestine day' was held in many cities of UP[74]. A large 'Quit Palestine' procession of Muslims was carried out in Lucknow, attended by over 15,000 Muslims[75]. The procession was followed by an election meeting. There are many other instances to suggest that there was a special focus on the pan-Islamic ideas during the election campaign in Muslim

---

70 Jamal Mian's election speech in Sitapur, *Star of India*, 23 October 1945
71 Jamal Mian's election speech in Sitapur, *Star of India*, 23 October 1945.
72 Jamal Mian's election speech in Sitapur, *Star of India*, 23 October 1945.
73 Speech by Maulana Ahmad Said, *Star of India*, 26 October 1945.
74 Speech by Maulana Ahmad Said, *Star of India*, 31 October 1945.
75 Speech by Maulana Ahmad Said, *Star of India*, 31 October 1945.

minority provinces like UP. It was from such ideas that the main justification for Pakistan was derived[76].

In yet another emotionally surcharged election speech in Kanpur, Raja of Mahmudabad said: 'We may die in the battle of Pakistan without seeing even a glimpse of it, but as long as a single Muslim is alive we cannot accept the Hindu Raj.... Pakistan is not an election slogan but a struggle for existence... If the Muslims did not exert themselves their position would become like that of the Jews who having all the wealth in their possession could not claim a single place on the globe as their homeland.'[77]

The heavy stress on the emotional appeal was am important part of the movement for Pakistan. It could be related to the possibility that in Muslim minority provinces like UP, local and politically pragmatic arguments in favour of Pakistan were simply not available. By all rational criteria the Muslims of UP were to be the losers in the eventuality of Pakistan being established. Yet their wholehearted support was considered essential for the success of the movement. It was hoped by the Muslim League leadership that powerful religious emotions would succeed in transcending local and pragmatic political considerations and create a huge passion for the ideal of a Muslim homeland. Muslim League performed remarkably well at the general elections of 1946, winning all the seats for the central legislatures and 439 out of 494 seats reserved for Muslims in the provincial assemblies. It won a large share of Muslim votes. Muslim League thus lived up to its claimed status of being the exclusive representative organization of Indian Muslims. It also demonstrated that there was a substantial consensus among Indian Muslims for Pakistan. Decks were thus cleared for the establishment of Pakistan. The major question was not whether, but *when*, Pakistan would be born. It was eventually born in August 1947. The making of this Muslim homeland was a remarkable journey. In this long journey from 'cradle to state', emotions of various kinds played a very crucial role.

---

76 The extent to which pan-Islamic held sway over the minds and hearts of Indian Muslims is a contentious theme. That these ideas were influential is however undeniable. But it is always possible to overstate this influence. For an argument that recognizes this power over Indian Muslims, see "Strands of Muslim Identity in South Asia" of Ralph Russel, in Russel 1999, p. 176–188.

77 *Star of India,* 9 November 1945.

Summary and conclusion

This essay is not meant to provide a comprehensive explanation for the emergence of a Muslim nation in South Asia. The main purpose of the essay is confined to exploring the role of certain emotions – such as fear, anxiety, resentment, solidarity craving, and religious passions – in the making of this nation. In this sense the purpose of the essay is to supplement and enrich the existing explanations by adding a new ingredient. It is meant neither to be an alternative nor a substitute to the existing explanations.

It is possible to see the actual life span of the Muslim nation as very brief covering merely seven years from 1940 to 1947. A Muslim nation was formally declared in 1940 and at the general elections of 1946, Muslim League demonstrated that there existed substantial consensus among Indian Muslims behind this idea. In August 1947 the Muslim nation state was formed through a negotiated settlement. But for a full account of the making of this Muslim nation, it is necessary to stretch the story back in time by a few decades.

If we jump a few decades back we find that none of the preconditions in the making of the Muslim nation existed in the 19th century. There did not exist a cohesive and internally homogenous Muslim community. There was no piece of territory exclusively or even substantially occupied by Muslims. Considerable diversity – both cultural and linguistic – prevailed among Indian Muslims. In many cases it was difficult to distinguish a Muslim from a non-Muslim.

The decades of the late 19th and early 20th centuries witnessed major transformations in the Indian society. These transformations were linked to structural changes, political turmoil, social instability and economic dislocations and they affected the lives of Muslims and Hindus in a whole range of ways. Entirely new pan-Indian communities of Hindus and Muslims were created. The structural changes also affected the emotional universes of these Hindus and Muslims by imparting new fears and anxieties to these groups.

It was from this socio-cultural raw material that a Muslim nation grew and developed. It happened through stages. A transformation in India's community profile resulted in the making of relatively neat and coherent pan-Indian communities of Hindus and Muslims. During the initial decades of the 20th century these religious communities were transformed into political communities. New political organizations sprang up claiming to represent these communities and putting forward political demands on their behalf. Major political changes in the 1930s set the stage for a transition of Indian Muslims from a political community to a potentially national one. In the 1940s the idea of this nation was propagated and popularized and eventually became an irresistible political ideological force by 1946–47. This was the long journey. It created a whole range of emotions, and the emotions in turn facilitated the journey. It was argued and demonstrated in the paper that fear, anxiety, resentment, honour and a craving for internal solidarity played an important role in the forging of a pan-Indian Muslim community. An emotional viewing of history, a sense of persecution, and nostalgia for the past (along with other factors, of course) helped in the transformation of this religious community into a national community. Likewise strong prejudices (social stereotypes), a constant invoking of history and passionate appeals along religious and political lines played a role in the dissemination of this 'nation' and mobilizing the people around it.

Any study of the Pakistan movement must take into consideration the rival *communal* campaign undertaken among Hindus to politically mobilize them. The two campaigns fed into, and provided justification for, each other. The role of emotions in the Hindu *communal* mobilization is an interesting and instructive story and would be taken up on another occasion.

Saradindu Mukherji
Delhi University

Unanticipated Catastrophe: Bengal in the 1940's

Introduction

Whether empire was created in a 'fit of absent-mindedness' or happened to be part of some benevolent project on 'civilizing mission', its denouement might well reveal another dimension of colonial rule–that when exit appeared imminent, empire could be left to lurch, perhaps in another fit of absent-mindedness! In the historiography of decolonization[1] there are dimensions which need to be re-visited both from the purely academic and administrative/management angles. Study of the past may not be entirely devoid of an applied dimension!

This paper looks back to the late colonial India, to see why even the best-managed systems go off the rails causing disastrous consequences which perhaps were avoidable or would have perhaps passed off with lesser damages only if they could have been anticipated[2]. The paper seeks to examine the failure of the much vaunted British administration with its 'steel frame" (the Indian Civil Service), the Indian Police, the provincial civil services, and the intelligence network to anticipate the cataclysmic events, and take timely preventive/remedial measures. Alertness might have saved thousands of lives, prevent panicky mass exodus of millions of people, enormous destruction of properties and myriad other socio-religious problems like forced conversion/marriages of hapless women etc. Though the army used to be deployed at times, but it was often requisitioned late, and by then colossal damages had already been caused.

---

1   R. F. Holland suggests that "ramshackle political coalitions in the underdeveloped world were only one element-and not the most vital-in determining the end to twentieth-century empires. Decolonization happened because colonialism as a set of nationally orchestrated systems (by the British, French, Dutch, Belgians and Portuguese) ceased to possess the self-sustaining virtue of internal equilibrium, and the spate of disequilibria can best be observed on a time-scale more extended than that provided by the post-1939 decades', Holland 1985, p. 1–2; Low 1991, p. 58–100.

2   Mukherji 1996a; Mukherji 1996b. Both to anticipate the human tragedy involved in the partition as well as the "undue haste for grabbing and enjoying power" exhibited by India's national leaders and the role of Mountbatten were pointed out.

It is suggested that the colonial authorities were perhaps casual about their principal responsibility to maintain "law and order" at the end of their long innings in India. They usually sided with the separatists, and were reluctant to come to the defence of the beleaguered nationalists, who abjured violent means and also appeared confused.

The article looks at the then Presidency of Bengal, which incorporated the present Indian state of West Bengal, and Bangladesh. The eastern part of British Bengal became East Pakistan in 1947, and thereafter an independent country in 1971 after it broke off from West Pakistan, geographically separated by more than thousand miles at the time of partition in August 1947. Since Bengal was part of the British Indian Empire, there would be references to only those developments in all-India politics which had their bearings on Bengal. The course of events involving the communal confrontation in 1946–1947, and the stance of the British authorities are brought under focus in this article. It is suggested that the official attitude was a decisive factor in shaping the course of events in those critical times that resulted in a disaster. The unfolding scenario, in the western parts of India, was on broadly similar lines but with the worst possible manifestation on a more extensive scale[3].

This culpability of the leaders of the national movement, inclusive of the Bhadralok elite of Bengal, oblivious of the writings on the wall, and chalk out a contingency plan before they were hurtled towards disaster is also examined. The youth in Bengal, many of them with impeccable revolutionary past got involved in organizing the Communist party in the Muslim majority Faridpur district in eastern Bengal[4] and elsewhere without ever realizing that the communal tide would swamp both the nationalist-revolutionaries and the Stalinists, and they would be rendered refugees soon. To that extent, it was a case of collective political myopia on the part of all the parties involved.

Socio-religious and cultural background: the Bengal scenario

To understand the politics of Bengal/India in the 1940s, one has to look back to Bengal's history following its conquest by the Turkish invader Bakhtiyar Khilji (late 12th and early 13th century). The Islamisation/Arabisation of Bengal followed. Why is this our starting point? Because partition of India was brought about basically on the basis of religious demographic composition both in the east and the west and this had roots in the past.

---

3   Mukherji 2000.
4   De 1980; Mukherji 2012a.

Muslim rule came to an end following the British conquest of Bengal (1757). Their administrative system and official support for "Orientalism" in 1780s, associated with Warren Hastings and William Jones, provided a political-cultural space for the Hindus[5]. Modern education and English language became popular with Bengal's Hindu intelligentsia leading to the so called Bengal "Renaissance". Availability of new employment opportunities in government/commercial sectors, education, law, journalism, medicine etc helped the Bengali Bhadralok in a big way. Social/religious reformers like Raja Rammohan Roy, Vidyasagar and Swami Vivekannada and literary figures like Bankim Chandra Chatterjee, Rabindranath Tagore and many more promoted the idea of an enlightened society.

Hindus of Bengal were the pioneers of modern politics along with their compatriots in Bomaby, Pune and Madras. Surendranath Banerjee, "Prophet" of Indian nationalism, Romesh Chandra Dutta, Aurobindo Ghose, Bipin Chandra Pal, Subhas Chandra Bose and a host of revolutionaries were the leading activists in the vigorous anti-colonial movement[6]. Many of them were ardent admirers of the British parliamentary system, ideas of French Revolution, Irish revolutionaries and the Italian ideologue Mazzini.

On the other side, Wahabis/Farazis in the first half of 19th century with their militant campaign for purifying Islam, weeding out the Hindu-Buddhist-animist remnants from their religio-cultural baggage, coupled with a strident Jihadi campaign, linkages with Arabia, deepened the existing divide between Hindus and Muslims[7]. Thus emerged a fault-line over and above the historical divide. The Muslim community, exceptions apart, remained cut off from the Indian resurgence mentioned earlier[8]. Assassination of Acting chief Justice of Calcutta High court Norris and Governor-General Lord Mayo in 1871/72 by the Wahabbis further added to the charged political scenario. The National Mohammedan Association, leaders like Syed Ameer Ali coupled with the visit of Jamal-al Afghani, and spread of Pan Islamic ideas in India in the late 19th century strengthened the separatist/communal trends[9].

---

5   Mukherji 2012b. My on-going work on certain dimension of Rammohan Roy's life
     and achievements; Majumdar 1963–1965. On Rammohan Roy: Kopf 1969; Marshall
     1970, p. 1–8; Gleig 1841.
6   Banerjea 1925; Majumdar 1962–1963; Seal 1968; Bose and Sinha 1969.
7   Chopra 2001; Smith 1946; Kaviraj 1982 argues that it was an agrarian movement,
     without any communal strand; De 1994; Chattopadhaya 2002.
8   Seal 1968, p. 298–340.
9   Pal 2004; Pal 1916; Ahmad 1967.

Surendranath Banerjea, records how he had worked hard and travelled all over India in 1876–77 for the "establishment of friendly and fraternal relations between Hindus and Muhammadans as the first indispensable condition of Indian progress"[10].

Separatist trends

Sir Syed Ahmad talked of a distinct Muslim politics, opposition to the Indian National Congress, loyalty to the British with threats of violence to the Hindus, particularly to the Hindus of Bengal with reference to the Islamic conquest of India. He threatened to "make rivers of blood to flow from the frontier on the north to the extreme end of Bengal" and preferred to remain "subjects of the people of the Book than the Hindus/Congress". His Aligarh Muslim university was one of instruments in his separatist policy[11].

The census operations in 1881, revealed that Muslims composed almost half of Bengal's population, concentrated mostly in eastern Bengal while Hindus were a community in decline. While the majority of the peasantry happened to be Muslims many of the landlords were Hindus provided another source of tension.

With Muslim separatism finding a territorial basis through the partition of Bengal (1905), its reversal in 1911, and the foundation of the Muslim League (1906), the Hindu-Muslim differences continued to grow. Banerjea, held Lord Minto responsible for introducing "communal representation" in the Legislative Councils through the Reform Act of 1909. In the aftermath of Montagu's declaration in 1917, Banerjea continued to cherish the hope, that the Hindus and Muhammadans were bound to form, sooner or later, a united nationality – "[12].

In September 1918, when a mob came out on the streets of Calcutta, following a call given from the Nakhoda mosque leading to widespread mayhem and destruction of property, the army was called in. Broomfield says that "For the first time in modern Bengal-for the first time in modern India-an attempt was made to use mob violence as a political weapon, and this riot provided a model for many of the vicious techniques which were later brought to perfection by Calcutta mobsters"[13]

The communal situation elsewhere worsened further in the wake of Gandhi's Khilafat/Non cooperation Movement leading to the Moplah attacks on Hindus,

---

10 Banerjea 1925, p. 201.
11 Khan 1982; Robinson 1974.
12 Banerjea 1925, p. 304–305.
13 Broomfield 1968.

anti-Hindu Kohat riots, the assassination of Swami Shraddhanand (1926). In the meantime, Lajpat Rai, opposing the Muslim League demand for according statutory majority to Punjab and Bengal, (as this was not being done in the Hindu majority provinces), warned if they insisted on it Punjab should be divided-one for Hindu/Sikhs and the other for the Muslims[14].

Subhas Bose as the Chief Executive Officer of Calcutta Corporation, (with Chittaranjan Das as Mayor, and Suhrawardy as deputy Mayor) in 1924 sought to please the Muslims by giving 23 out of 25 jobs eliciting praise from Gandhi. The 1935 Constitution providing for 119 seats for Muslims in Bengal legislature, based on separate Muslim electorate, 80 to Hindus (39 to Europeans/ Anglo- Indians etc) clearly showed the British were cutting down the influence of the Hindus, while Hindu-Muslim relations continued to deteriorate[15]. Subhas Chandra Bose (Haripura, Feb 1938) assured the Muslims that they had "nothing to fear in the event of India winning her freedom-on the contrary , they have everything to gain"[16].

Communal violence and separatist tendencies

In India, communal violence has been centuries- old, dating from the Sultanate/ Mughal eras. Along with syncretistic tendencies at various levels, there were also differences between the Hindus and Muslims. Communalism was not a creation of the British masters as some historians have argued in recent times[17]. In Bengal itself, there have been a large number of communal fracas and bloodshed including those by the Wahabis /Faraizis, and many cases of rioting over music-before mosque, cow sacrifice during Bakrid festival etc. British were sometimes impartial, sometimes partisan, sometimes took advantage of the existing divisions as and when they required, and in the process widened the gap[18].

---

14 *The Morning Post* (London), on 11 March 1921, scoffed at the artificiality of the Congress approach. *The Nation* and *The Athenaeum* (London), on 16 July 1921, commented that Gandhi seems more interested in destroying the Treaty of Sèvres than in pursuing Indian self-government; Nanda 2002; Minault 1982; Niemeijer 1972; Saradindu Mukherji examines the views of Bose, Gandhi and Nehru on the violence unleashed by the Moplahs in Mukherji 2007; Prasad 2001; Prasad 2009a; Prasad 2009b; for Tagore's assessment of Hindu-Muslim relations, see Tagore 1990.

15 Bose 2011, p. 114.

16 Bose and Bose 1997a, p. 203.

17 Majumdar 1943; Sarkar 1977; Dimock Jr. 1972; Eaton 1993; Ahmad 1981; Roy 1983; Bayly 1998; Prasad 2009a.

18 Mishra 1990, p. 366–370 and 372; McLane 1977; Gilmartin 1988, p. 3–4, 111–114 and 158–163; De 1982; Das 1993.

Nirad Choudhury, (originally from eastern Bengal,) says that ever since the Twenties he had been advising his sisters to leave East Bengal because he did not want them to live "under the social domination of the Muslims – and come away to Calcutta realizing all their assets in time", but they refused to come saying 'there was perfect harmony and friendliness between the Hindus and Muslims"[19]. Chaudhury's assessment of the emerging scenario was realistic and his sisters were wrong ultimately.

The idea of a distinct Muslim territorial entity and political Muslim supremacy first achieved through the partition of Bengal in 1905 continued to create ripples. In 1927, Malcolm Hailey, Governor of Punjab, "recorded that he noticed 'some curious movements going on in the Mohammedan world of Northern India,' and they were 'thinking about the desirability of having a federation of their own embracing the Punjab, parts of U.P., NWFP, Sind and Baluchistan' as a preparatory step towards "a larger federation with Afghanistan and also Persia". Subsequently, as the Governor of U.P. he also found similar sentiments. A few books were written in the late 1920s by some Muslim thinkers talking about similar concepts[20].

Nawab Khan Bahadur Saiyid Nawab Ali Chaudhuri, a leading gentry from Eastern Bengal, and a member of the Imperial Legislative Council stated in 1920, "Hitherto the whole history of India since the advent of the Mussalamans in this country is a history of a continued antagonism of the two communities."[21]

Separatist politics outside Bengal

H.T. Lambrick, an ICS official reported from Karachi in August 1932, "My fears are for the Punjab – The Sikhs are in a ferment—and do you know what they are saying among themselves, if not openly? They do not mind living under British domination, but will never live under Muslim domination. That I fancy, is the feeling of every minority in every corner of India – ,"[22] Jinnah's speech at Lucknow (15 Oct 1937), referred to the possibility of 'a communal war'. Raja of Mahmudabad, his key aide projected the Congress refusal to form a coalition with them as a refusal 'to recognize even the existence of the Muslim community as such'[23]. At the Sind Provincial Muslim League meeting at Karachi presided

19 Chaudhuri 1990, p. 825–826.
20 Prasad 2009a, p. 332–333.
21 Broomfield 1968, p. 217.
22 Lambrick 1970, p. 510–511.
23 Mishra 1990, p. 320.

over by Jinnah (Oct 1938) , Fazlul Haque, the then Premier of Bengal said, "If Mohammad bin Qasim, an eight year old lad with 18 soldiers could conquer Sindh, then surely nine crores of Muslims can conquer whole of India"[24]. Only if his opponents had taken him seriously, they could have saved themselves and there would have been lesser loss of life and related trauma.

It was reported (January, 1940) from the Hindu minority province of Sind: " – Hindus everywhere tell me that they have no sense of security in the smaller villages since Provincial Autonomy was introduced, and Law and Order is non-existent ! – All are asking for European officers now"[25]. The Muslims in the UP were also complaining of atrocities inflicted by the Congress which Jinnah had been projecting as Fascists. But it was always known that no such thing was done as the Pirpur report had sought to highlight[26].

In fact, Subhas Chandra Bose, by no means a Hindu communalist, took Sind as a synonym for Muslim communal intolerance. Writing to the Governor, Chief Minister and his Council of ministers in Bengal, in 1940, he urged them, "To the Government of the day, I say, 'Cry halt to your mad drive along the path of communalism and injustice. There is yet time to retrace your steps. Do not use a boomerang which will soon recoil on you. And do not make another Sindh of Bengal'"[27].

Broomfield points out, " – the Muslims' assertion, at every point, of their community's right to a separate political existence." – and maintain a distinct political identity was "throughout the basic factor in Muslim thinking"[28].

As for Hindu Mahasabha, (founded in 1915), Rashtriya Swayamsevak Sangh (1925), Savarkar and Hindu communalism, they always remained on the fringes of the Hindu society as most of the politically conscious and active Hindus were with the Indian National Congress. The Hindu Mahasabha and the RSS were however, wedded to Indian nationalism and opposed the policy of appeasement of Muslims by both the Congress and the British. The politically active Muslims of India, from the time of Sir Syed Ahmad to Jinnah had dubbed Banerjea, Naoroji, Gokhale Gandhi-Bose- Nehru led Congress as a Hindu party and Fascists. In the vast literature of Muslim separatism / Muslim League and partition,

---

24 Mehrotra 1970, p. 206.
25 Mehrotra 1970, p. 206.
26 Azad 1988, p. 22, denied the accusations of Jinnah and the Muslim League. With Deobandi inclination, Azad may have had other thoughts. See Mukherji 2003; Mishra 1990, p. 316–318.
27 Bose and Bose 1997a, p. 268.
28 Broomfield 1968, p. 218.

it was Congress, and neither the Mahasabha nor the RSS is the culprit. Be that as it may, on the whole, Hindu communalism was more of a reaction to Muslim communalism/separatism[29].

British entente with the Muslim separatists

Given the politics of India/ Bengal when the British were looking upon the Muslims as "loyal supporters", this letter from Chief Secretary, Govt of Bengal in 1931 on the need to pamper the Nawab Bahadur of Murshidabad, whom it saw as the "head of the Mohamedan community in Bengal, being the premier nobleman and lineal descendant of the Nawab Nazims who once ruled over Bengal, Behar and Orissa" is revealing. This Nawab's "heavy indebtedness" had become a major source of embarrassment but the authorities were warned not to send him to jail and, moreover was to be saved from "any other indignity" since that "will be deeply resented by the whole Mohamedan community" as that would be seen as "an ungrateful Government deserting its loyal supporters". As against this extreme caution, the British had no hesitation in throwing out the Hindu Maharaja of Alwar after some Hindu-Muslim clashes[30].

Blatant British partiality for Muslims prompted even Bose to complain (26 Nov 1940) to the highest authorities, " May I request you to compare for one moment your attitude towards people like myself and towards Muslims arrested and imprisoned under the Defence of India Rules ? How many cases have occurred up till now in which Muslims apprehended under the D.I. Rules have been suddenly released without rhyme or reason? The latest example of the Maulvi of Murapara is too fresh in the public mind to need recounting. Are we to understand that under your rule there is one law for the Muslim and another law for the Hindu and that the D.I. Rules have a different meaning when a Muslim is involved? If so, the Government might as well make a pronouncement to that effect."[31]

---

29 Prasad 1947, p. 18–19 and 25–29, 144; Malkani 1980; Mishra 1990, p. 285, 290–291, 307, 319, 333, 360; Philips and Wainwright 1970.

30 Also on Bengal, see R.N. Reid to H. Metcalf, Secretary *Government of India, Foreign and Political Department*, 3 August 1931, Confidential Document n° 2541 P. S (File. L/P& S/13/1038: Bengal-on Alwar, see Telegram, *GOI Foreign and Political Dept.* to *Secretary of State for India* from Simla dated 2 June 1932 in F L/P&J/13/1377 Alwar affairs; *The Times* (London), 6 June 1932; F./ P&S/13/379 Pol. Secret Dept British Library; *The Daily Express* (London) 8 July 1933, reported that "this is the first time that any native prince has been banished from his state", British Newspaper Library, London.

31 Bose and Bose 1997a, p. 263–268.

More developments

Promotion of Muslim interests through an alliance with the British was a reality. Jinnah declared , 'I say the Muslim League is not going to be an ally of anyone, but would be the ally of even the devil, if need be in the interests of Muslims'. – he further said, "It is not because we are in love with imperialism; but in politics one has to play one's game as on the chess-board'. Jinnah wrote to Suhrawardy "I am in agreement with you that Bengal has to be made 100% "League-minded"[32].

With an unsuccessful Civil Disobedience Movement (1940), expulsion of Bose, and his escape from India, brutal suppression of the Quit India movement, the Congress was getting weaker and side-lined. The demand for Pakistan (1940) was followed by the Dacca riots (1941), and the Muslim League began eyeing Calcutta as a part of the proposed eastern part of Pakistan. The Communist Party having supported the Muslim League demand for Pakistan earlier, and the British during the Quit India movement, their role in Indian politics was suspect, and "the Government also exploited to the fullest extent such agents, as the erstwhile Communist leader, M.N. Roy, who were prepared to sell themselves to Britain". With political parleys going on, and the devastating man-made famine (1943), there was chaos. However, in 1946, when the Communists were reportedly engaged in various trade union activities among the railway workers and plantation labourers, "encouraging riot in rural areas" that they distracted the attention of the government. [33]

Royle says, "For the police in Bengal it was often an impossible situation" dealing with riots, massive demonstrations breaking out in unexpected places, and "use of the continuing communal unrest as a stick with which to beat the police force". He cites the case of a Muslim District Magistrate of Chittagong, who "ordered all the officials and the police to fly Muslim League flags during the "Day of Action" ; at the same time, Hindu policemen were forbidden to intervene during the day long Muslim demonstrations". Nanda says, "The growth of private armies, the Muslim League National Guards, the Rashtriya Swayam Sevak Sangh and others, showed that popular faith in the impartiality of the instruments of law and order was at a discount"[34].

But then, discipline in the services had not collapsed altogether. One senior British official in Bengal, Stanley Taylor Indian Police found that even when the

---

32 See Nanda 2002, p. 166, footnote 10: Letter from Jinnah to Suhrawardy (whether it
    was 1940 or 1941 is not clear).
33 Bose and Bose 1997b, p. 387; Royle 1989, p. 137.
34 Royle 1989, p. 137; Nanda 1985, p. 102.

police were "sorely provoked by outside influences" they remained unruffled. –
Not for one minute, did they ever thought of following "the example of their
countrymen who mutined or went on strike." [35]

G.D. Khosla, observed, "In the history of communal relations the years 1946–
47 marks a period of unequalled mistrust, acerbity and frenzied warfare in almost all parts of India. Tensions between the Muslim and non-Muslim communities increased till the cords that bound them together snapped and flung them
apart-it seemed for ever"[36].

As early as April 1946, Gandhi had criticized 'loose talk of civil war'. Tarachand,
the Congress historian later on recalled, "Omens of impending calamity were
already visible. The chain of bloody feud which had started on August 16 at
Calcutta was lengthening. East Bengal in October, Bihar in November and the
state of general disquiet, uncertainty and unrest throughout the country were
alarming enough. The nervous tension was intensified by the conflict within the
government. The government services were affected with partisan spirit"[37]. The
question one could raise is if the Congress was so sanguine about the nature of
the dark clouds what measures did it take to prepare the people and warn the
authorities regarding the developing scenario. They did nothing and there was
no sign of any kind of preparation, as far as we know, for the eventuality either
among the British government or the Indian National Congress, except Rajendra
Prasad[38].

"Great Calcutta Killing/Direct Action": August 16, 1946

The "Direct Action" in (16 August 1946) Calcutta, pogrom at Noakhali-Tippe-
rah, communal killings in Bihar certainly gave an idea of the shape of things to
come. In fact, the Hindu Muslim relations were turning quite strained and the
law-enforcing machinery appeared feeble and partisan at times. Hence, when
the "Direct Action" was launched by Jinnah, all except the organizers were totally
unprepared. The Calcutta Mayor, Osman's leaflet talked of Jihad, victory over
kafirs and establishment of Islamic rule in India.

Another pamphlet with Jinnah's photograph warned the "kafirs" of a "general
massacre". Abul Hashim, the Muslim League leader from Bengal declared on

---

35 Royle 1989, p. 139.
36 Khosla 1989, p. vii.
37 Chand 1990, p. 494.
38 See Saradindu Mukherji's review of Rajendra Prasad's book *India Divided* in *The Sun-
    day Pioneer* dated 17 October 2010.

29th July 1946, "Where justice and equity failed, shining steel would decide the issue". Nazimuddin, ex-Premier of Bengal asserted, that "There are 150 different ways to cause trouble particularly as the Muslim League is not restricted to non-violence". One of the aides of Jinnah had called upon the Muslims to adopt the slogan "Larke Lenge Pakistan" (We will take Pakistan by force). Just ten days before the Direct Action, Suhrawrady had openly said, 'Bloodshed and disorder are not necessary evils in themselves, if resorted to for a noble cause. Among Muslims today, no cause is dearer or nobler than Pakistan". A visiting American journalist correctly guessed that Calcutta would see the Muslim fury[39]. Jinnah said, "This day we bid good- bye to constitutional methods" and "Today we have also forged a pistol"[40]. Since apologists/admirers of Jinnah want him to be known as a constitutionalist, many of his pronouncements or declarations of intent and tactics are ignored or smothered. Venkatachar, an ICS official talking about the "Direct Action" says that Jinnah brought in the Muslim mob, "a weapon which Congress had excluded from Jinnah's armoury' and this was the time the Congress "had become weak;" everyone knew the days of British administration were numbered. They were in no position to deal with the civil disorder decisively. Regardless of consequences, Jinnah set the country on a disastrous course. The British were worried. On whom could they depend- the police, Indian army, even British troops? Congress for a time seemed not worried, still hoping to push Jinnah aside. However, realization soon came as civil war spread over the Indo-Gangetic plain"[41].

Nirad C. Chaudhuri, then based in Calcutta recalled, "In every Muslim quarter the Muslims were seen to sharpen their knives and spears and heard to utter their threats. Well-disposed Muslims sent word to their friends to be careful and avoid trouble spots. But nobody could anticipate that the violence would be on such a scale". He further elaborates the "British Governor of Bengal was so timid about his constitutional position that he would not invite the military authorities to take charge of the situation – ", and when asked for it, and that might have

---

39 Talbot 2007, p. 175, 187–189, 192, 223–224, reviewed by Mukherji, in *The Sunday Pioneer* on 16 September 2007; Das 1993, p. 161–192; Sinha and Dasgupta 2011, p. 62–200; Mukhopadhaya 2007, reviewed by S. Mukherji in *The Sunday Pioneer* on 28 August 2011; Sen 1976; Collins (and Lapierre 2007; Ikramullah 1991, she is the sister of Suhrawardy and she makes an unconvincing case proving the innocence of the main culprit; Prasad 2009b, p. 417–492.

40 Mosley 1962, p. 29.

41 C.S. Venkatachar, 1937–1947 "In Retrospect: A Civil Servant's View", in Philips and Wainwright 1970, p. 487.

been prompted by the changing scenario when they "saw that the game of killing was going against the Muslims"[42].

Dalton points out that "No Indian political leader foresaw that event. Indeed, most of them do not appear to have had the slightest inkling of the scale on which the Calcutta riots would occur". A section of the press "was a shade more foresighted" but they also could not guess the extent of violence[43]. Mosley tells that Nehru visited Jinnah at his Bombay house in the morning hours on 16 August itself[44].

Markovits refers to rumours about Suhrawardy's "close links to the Muslim underworld" based on "smuggling, gambling and prostituition".45[45] The new Governor Sir Frederick Burrows, who had assumed charge February 1946 was said to be "no match for Suhrawardy"[46]. As for the casualty figures, they vary from 4000/ 5000 to about 10,000, and perhaps Hindus suffered more because most of the policemen in Calcutta Police Dept were Muslims. According to Tuker, it was "even for both sides"[47].

By any standard it was a huge number. There were also rape of women and abduction of women (mostly Hindus) as had become a standard practice by now, when we look at the role of the Moplahs in Kerala. After the initial attack by the Muslims, Hindus and Sikhs hit back. The army was used, but it was too late and colossal damage had been done.

The Daily Mail, (London) observed, "If the Direct Action of the Muslim League leaders of Jinnah goes on, there will be no real end to murder in Calcutta and a fear has grown with the Muslim 'dictator's' refusal to join in the formation of the interim government with the Congress chief Nehru". This is a crucial testimony from a conservative English newspaper opposed to the Indian nationalists about those behind the "Direct Action"[48]. Interestingly enough, a group of ambulances touring the affected areas were "manned by medical persons of the rebel Subhas Bose's army which was initially raised to fight the British was working on the side of them."[49]

---

42 Chaudhuri 1990, p. 809–810.
43 D.G. Dalton, "Gandhi during Partition: A Case study in the Nature of Satyagraha", in Philips and Wainwright 1970, p. 227–228.
44 Mosley 1962, p. 29.
45 Markovits 2007; Chand 1990, p. 494.
46 Mosley 1962, p. 29.
47 Tuker 1950, p. 46.
48 The Daily Mail, 20 August 1946. British Newspaper library, Colindale, London.
49 The Daily Mail, 17 August 1946.

Noakhali-Tipperah pogroms October 1946

According to Wainwright, after the Calcutta killings, "it was confidently expected that the next outbreaks would be in East Bengal" and a detachment of troops (1/3 Gurkhas) were sent to Chittagong in the third week of August. "During the next six weeks reports received at the eastern command headquarters indicated tension in the rural areas, especially in Noakhali and Chittagong, but civil intelligence was completely lacking". Subsequently, more troops were sent to Comilla, and Fenny to bolster the local police. Wainwright also mentions "alarmist reports" in the "Hindu press" on the deteriorating scenario in the region. The soldiers were further "handicapped by bad communications"[50].

The mayhem which began on 10 October 1946 was spread over a vast area in the district of Noakhali, where the Hindus were a small minority. It is accepted by all that it was engineered by the Muslims of the area on the pretext that Muslims had alone suffered terribly in Calcutta. They were led by Ghulam Sarwar, formerly with the Muslim League and a member of the Bengal legislative Assembly. Again on 13 October there was an organized attack on the Hindus of Tippera[51].

Hindus were subjected to every conceivable form of violence and cruelty. The number of casualties in both Noakhali and Tippera had been estimated at a few hundred from official sources but non-official Hindu sources had put it at 5,000. The total number of people arrested stood at 1,122 from 350 villages by mid-November. Abduction of women, their conversion to Islam and forced nikah with the Muslims, conversion of Hindu males, destruction of their properties, arson, loot besides of course killing were extensively reported[52] It was a thoroughly planned successful genocide!

As Kriplani put it, "The attack on Hindu population of Noakhali and Tipperah was previously arranged and prepared for and was the result of League propaganda-it was absolutely communal and one-sided, the authorities had warnings of what was coming beforehand; the Muslim officials connived at the preparations going on, and a few encouraged, the police did not function during

---

50 Philips and Wainwright 1970, p. 134–136.

51 Sinha and Dasgupta 2011, p. 62–200, book reviewed by Saradindu Mukherji in *The Sunday Pioneer* on 28 August 2011; see Talbot 2007, p. 175, 187–189, 192, 223–224. On the conversion of Hindus to Islam .see E.F. Maicnery (Deputy Commissioner, Noakhali reports to Sir J. Habakkuk recorded on 14 February 1976) in MSS Eur.148 (B.L); Das 1993, p. 198–203.

52 Sinha and Dasgupta 2011, p. 262–277; Philips and Wainwright 1970, p. 134–138.

the riots, there being no orders to fire except in self-defence; there have been many cases of forcible marriages and religious conversion"[53].

Towards a conclusion

According to Choudhury, "The responsibility for all this killing, bloodshed, plunder, ruin and displacement of millions, with their subsequent miseries must be placed squarely on the shoulders of the British authorities-directly – . In the last two years of their rule the British "failed". – That was wholly unjustifiable. So long as British rule lasted even in form, i.e. till August 1947, they had no right to abandon the task and leave it to the fainéant government they had created in August 1946". Nanda suggests, "The real explanation for the violence of 1946–47 is to be sought in the tensions which the Muslim league's seven-year -long campaign for Pakistan aroused in its protagonists as well as opponents"[54].

The British colonial regime in India had been known for its capacity for efficient administration and recourse to timely remedial measures to rectify the defects in the implementation of its policies, and to nip in the bud any emerging fault-line as and when it cropped up[55]. This has been one of the principal justifications, the British offered to explain their rule. However, their fire-fighting capacity was perhaps put to real test only when it involved "law and order" threatening the majesty of the Raj, as one finds in its suppression of the "Quit India' movement when the British faced serious challenge in South Asia[56]. Perhaps such a consideration did not matter to them when they were on the verge of leaving India, and their bitterest adversaries- the nationalists, were at the receiving end but also set to succeed them.

Despite the negotiations between the parties involved regarding the future of the post-colonial Indian state-system, and all -round uncertainty, the Muslim League leaders had been demanding an exchange of population. One may guess that they were perhaps influenced by the Treaty of Lausanne (1923) which had paved the way for an exchange of population between Turkey and Bulgaria. In a report to Jinnah (November, 1944), one Abdul Rashid Khan, proposed an

---

53 Kripalanis's press statement on 26 October 1946 cited in Sinha and Dasgupta 2011, p. 203; Royle 1989, p. 137; Das 1993, p. 199–203.
54 Chaudhuri 1990, p. 815; Nanda 1985, p. 102.
55 Mukherji 1993, discusses the handling of agrarian problems by the colonial authorities.
56 Nehru 1959, p. 412–422; Low 1991, p. 134, 138, 151–152; Mishra 1990, p. 254, 345, 347–348, 345; Talbot 2007, p. 142, 221, 315.

exchange of population which he thought "not such an impossible thing." One of the suggestions was to shift the Muslim population from Jessore to Calcutta or to Hyderabad to turn them into Muslim strongholds. Khan Iftikhar Hussain Mamdot stated that exchange of population was a practical solution. Pir Illahi Box was another votary of the idea of an exchange of population which would bring an end to all communal disturbances. Raja Ghaznafar Ali had asked for the altercation of the population map of India. Incidentally, there exists a document on "The Exchange of Population between Greece and Turkey in 1922" prepared by Noel Barker, Secretary of State for Commonwealth Relations and sent by L.B. Graffley Smith to Liaqat Ali Khan on 8 Dec 1947, which suggests that the idea of an exchange of population between India and Pakistan was possibly alive even after the partition[57].

Though Bengal remained calm on the day of partition/independence unlike Punjab, Sind, Baluchistan and North Western Province, there was no end to the sufferings of the Hindus/ Buddhists in eastern Bengal subsequently[58]. This being beyond the remit of this paper, there is no discussion of the post -1947 dimension. However, for the unending sufferings of the Hindus, Buddhists and Christians in Eastern Bengal/ East Pakistan/Bangladesh including the Chittagong Hill Tracts, and their flight to India, the colonial rulers of India, and all successor governments in Pakistan/Bangladesh are responsible[59].

The Congress stubbornly refused to heed to the repeated warning of a blood-bath from their main antagonists. The colonial authorities, one must admit in fairness to them, had taken firm measures to control the Moplahs just twenty years back. Following the disastrous consequences of Gandhi's major

---

57 Qaid-e-Azam Papers Reel 2, Files 7, 7A, 12 in IOR NEG 10778 (British Library); *The Dawn*, 3 December 1946; *The Dawn*, 4 December 1946; *The Dawn* 19 December 1946. Mudie Papers Mss. Eur. F 164/46. Despatch. No. 15(54) 47 (B. L).

58 Chakrabarty 1990, has shown that by June 1948 1.1 million Hindu refugees had moved out of East Pakistan to India.

59 Ray 1968; Mukherji 2000; Saradindu Mukherji, 'Indian Experience with Forced Migration: Its Lessons and Limitations', Paper presented at the *Conference of Scholars & other Professionals* working on Refugees and Displaced Persons in South Asia, held in Rajendrapur, Bangladesh, on February 9–11, 1998. The conference was organised by the *Regional Centre for Strategic Studies*, Colombo in collaboration with the *Refugee Studies Programme* of Oxford University, the *Refugee and Migratory Movement Research Unit* of Dhaka University and the *Bangladesh Institute of International and Strategic Studies*; Dastidar 2008,, reviewed by Mukherji in *The Sunday Pioneer* on 5 September 2010; Mukhopadhaya's book (see infra) was reviewed by Mukherji in *The Sunday Pioneer*, 28 August 2011.

experiment-Khilafat aspect of the Non-cooperation, the British perhaps could see through the game-plan of the Indian nationalists-their inclination to make use of the primordial to serve the "larger"' nationalist goal-of creating and sustaining an united anti-colonial Pan Indian front. Perhaps a flawed strategy to begin with, but probably the only one available to the Gandhians. One may however, suggest that, therein lies the increasing British fondness for Muslim demands and abetment, if not approval of a certain behavioural style from them. The Muslim League had never shied away from either declaring its intent or method. That perhaps explains the disaster in the 1940s.

Low suggests that. "There can be no doubt too that Muslim separatism was now encouraged", and that "fuelled the megalomania of the Viceroy Lord Linlithgow that only the British could solve India's problems, and that it would be in the country's best interest if – Congress could be 'crushed'. Subsequently, Wavell also "retained the wartime tenderness of the British for India's Muslims"[60].

As mentioned earlier, besides Rajendra Prasad, Syama Prasad Mookerjee (Hindu Mahasabaha) had sensed the impending calamity, and that prompted the latter and other Congress leaders, including Gandhi to keep western Bengal out of the proposed United Bengal as conceived by Sarat Bose and Suhrawardy. A small number gripped by a sense of euphoria generated by the demand for an United Bengal became impervious to the fast-changing developments[61].

Perhaps some of the trauma and tragedy could be attributed to "the difference between abandoning an empire dishonourably and honourably. De Gaulle abandoned Africa out of free will, just in the nick of time, without involving himself in what was to follow. Above all, he risked his life by what he did. Mountbatten risked nothing, rose higher and higher after the abandonment of India, dwelt with satisfaction on his life and his luck"[62].

---

60 Low 1991, p. 96–97.
61 Madhok 1954.
62 Chaudhuri 1990, p. 832.

Sucheta Mahajan
Jawaharlal Nehru University

Towards Freedom: the Making of a History

The theme of this article is how the *Towards Freedom* series took shape as a counterpoint to the *Transfer of Power* series published by Her Majesty's Stationery Office since 1970[1]. British Prime Minister Wilson had announced the publication of records on transfer of power on the twentieth anniversary of Indian independence and British departure. These were selections from historical records from the official holdings made by an editorial team headed by Nicholas Mansergh, widely recognized as an authority in Commonwealth history. The timing of the publication was such that there was widespread interest, both academic and popular, in the end of empire and the attainment of independence by colonies across several continents, Asia, America and Africa. These volumes, eventually numbering twelve for India for the period 1942 to 1947, were limited in the sources they self-confessedly drew upon, to the official papers of His Majesty's Government pertaining to the constitutional relations between the colony and the metropolitan power.

The *raison d'être* of the *Towards Freedom* series conceived by the Indian government, and entrusted to the Indian Council of Historical Research for its execution, was to go beyond the limited perspective of transfer of power to a broader perspective of seeing independence as the culmination of the multifaceted struggle for independence. Diverse sections of society had participated in the struggle, with working class movements intertwined with peasant rebellions, among others. Whereas the *Transfer of Power* series interpreted the British departure as primarily voluntarist[2], for which the term decolonization would be suitable, the *Towards Freedom* project saw independence as a battle, hard fought and hard won. Similarly, while in the *Transfer of Power* series partition came across as the consequence of the division between the two communities, which the colonial power tried ineffectually

---

1   Mansergh 1970a.

2   A revised draft of a statement of policy dated 2 January 1947 set out His Majesty's Government's (HMG's) proposed statement as 'the final stage in their achievement of self-government', which 'for the past thirty years...has been the policy of successive British governments', Mansergh 1970b, p. 441–443.

to bridge; indeed, in keeping with safeguarding their imperial interests, setting up two dominions, with the Commonwealth as a transitional institutional arrangement, suited the British the best. In the *Towards Freedom* series partition was rooted in the growing communalization of society, to which the colonial state, the communal forces and even the nationalist forces, by their weaknesses, contributed.

The intention of the *Towards Freedom* series was to draw upon a wide range of sources, ranging from the private papers, autobiographies and memoirs of political activists to newspapers, photographs and visual materials. The editor was Professor Sarvepalli Gopal, who had earlier been asked by G. Parthasarathy (the first Vice Chancellor of the Jawaharlal Nehru University) to set up the Centre for Historical Studies at the Jawaharlal Nehru University in New Delhi. The *Towards Freedom* series shared the left liberal perspective which informed Gopal's other projects, namely, the history centre at JNU and a multivolume biography of Jawaharlal Nehru, which till today does double duty as an unsurpassed biography as well as a history of twentieth century India. Under his stewardship, the *Towards Freedom* series escaped being a mundane official history of the freedom movement. The rich haul of sources about the multi-hued movement, the umbrella like party, which was more a platform than party, dexterously handled by able editors, transformed what could have been compendiums to veritable histories. In fact the series could be said to have reached its high point with the volumes edited by Partha Sarathi Gupta[3] and Basudev Chatterjee[4].

My association with the *Towards Freedom Series* was from 2007, when I was invited to be editor of the volume on 1947[5], the last and arguably the most important year covered by the series. Having spent two decades researching on and writing on this period, it was expected by the editorial board, headed since 2006 by Sabyasachi Bhattacharya, an eminent historian of modern India, that the 1947 volume would take the least time. After all, "only" seven and a half months were to be covered, from 1 January till 15 August 1947. I found the latter cut-off date most arbitrary and difficult to adhere to. Most processes, be they partition, migration or transfer of population or accession of the princely states, did not heed such officially decreed dates and moved at their own pace. Some developments, like the runaway spread of Hindu communalism after

3   Gupta 1997.
4   Chatterjee 1999.
5   Mahajan 2013. Parts 2 and 3 are in press.

September, culminating in the assassination of Gandhiji, were integrally linked to the pre August events, but fell outside the circumscribed period; indeed, outside the calendar year[6]. Very soon I found, not unsurprisingly, that my research on the relationship between imperialism, communalism and nationalism[7] covered a miniscule part of the story of 1947. In my research work I had pitched for looking evenly at independence and partition – as two sides of the same coin – rather than glorifying one or privileging the other, as many historians were wont to do. I came to realize that there were many sides to the story, beyond the twin stories of independence and partition. Along with political freedom, there were other freedoms, social and economic, towards which our struggle had been enjoined but had a long way to go.

Over time the volume on 1947 kept growing and dividing, finally assuming three parts, in keeping with the many freedoms, political, social and economic, that our people were moving towards in 1947. The organization of the volume ended up being somewhat unusual because the year that it dealt with was unlike any other year of the freedom struggle. Nineteen forty-seven was the year of independence and partition. The conflict between communalism, nationalism, and imperialism, culminating in independence and partition, was dealt with in the first two parts. Important issues to do with nation-building demanded they be addressed. For example, what would be the nature of the polity? Would India be a secular state or a Hindu *rashtra* (nation), given Pakistan's creation on a communal basis? What would be the place of minorities in the new state? How would the princely states integrate into the very different polity of erstwhile British India? How would the anti-colonial movement, which had operated as a broad front, transform into an ideologically distinct party?

In earlier volumes of *Towards Freedom*, the focus was broadly on the nationalist movement, communal politics and peasant and labour movements. In this multipart volume on 1947, those issues pertaining to society, polity, economy, and culture, which would occur in any routine year, have been dealt with in Part 3. It is this part that I intend to focus on in this article.

Before that, let me spend a minute on the sources, which the volumes draw on. As far as the documents go, they emanated from both official and non-official sources. Official attitudes were reflected by documents selected from sources like the records of the *Government of India's Home Department*, its

---

6   This was the subject of Mukherjee, Mukherjee and Mahajan 2008.
7   Mahajan 2000.

Political section in particular[8], copies of *Cabinet Papers* and papers of Viceroys and senior officials from *India Office Records*[9] on microfilm, or as photocopies in *National Archives of India*, and *Mountbatten Papers*[10]. These official documents, particularly the fortnightly reports from each province to the centre, were a valuable source of information on the nationalist, communal, and popular movements. Further, selected published official documents, such as from the *Transfer of Power* series, have been included where they were integrally linked to the story.

A wide variety of newspapers like *Hindustan Times, Dawn, People's Age, Amrita Bazar Patrika*, among others, represented the non-official point of view. Private papers of institutions and individuals like *All India Congress Committee* (AICC), *All India States Peoples Conference, All India Hindu Mahasabha*, the socialist leader Jayaprakash Narayan, the *Mahasabha* leaders, S.P. Mookerjee and B.S. Moonje,[11] also evinced the intricacy of political processes in this period. Further, the numerous instances of individuals voicing their opinions about issues of socio-political and economic importance in their letters and memoranda to various political representatives, institutions, bodies such as the AICC and the *Constituent Assembly*, illustrate the extent of popular involvement in such matters.

Documents have also been included from published collections of primary sources such as *Selected Works of Jawaharlal Nehru*[12], *Sardar Patel Correspondence* [13], *Mohammad Ali Jinnah Papers*[14], *Collected Works of Mahatma Gandhi*,[15] *Constituent Assembly Debates*[16], *Rajendra Prasad Correspondence*[17], so that the diversity of perspectives was available all at one place to the reader.

---

8   These are original files held by the *National Archives of India*, New Delhi.
9   The originals are the holdings of the *National Archives* (formerly *Public Record Office*), Great Britain, London and the *India Office Library and Records*, London.
10   The originals are the holdings of the *Hartley Library* at Southampton, U.K. and the *India Office Library and Records*, London.
11   These papers are held by the *Manuscript Section* of the *Nehru Memorial Museum and Library* (NMML), New Delhi.
12   Gopal 1984.
13   Das 1971–1974.
14   Zaidi 1993–.
15   *The Collected Works of Mahatma Gandhi*, 1884–1948, vol.1–100, New Delhi, first edition, 1960–1994.
16   http://parliamentofindia.nic.in/ls/debates/debates.htm
17   Prasad 1984–.

For instance, Viceroy Wavell's journal[18] gave a day-by-day account of the political developments in early 1947 peppered with the Viceroy's often barbed comments and incisive reactions. Documents have been included relating to the extremely significant issues discussed in the *Constituent Assembly* and its committees, for instance, fundamental rights and constitutional safeguards, which provided insights into the nature of the polity and society of free India.

Wherever possible, preference was given to newspaper reports over official records, to bring out the amazing diversity of opinion in the public domain. Newspapers often threw up delightful letters to the editor, hand drawn maps of proposed boundary lines, cartoons with acerbic wit, and quaint advertisements, such as the one for a balm, titled 'freedom from pain'[19], evidently inspired by the impending freedom of the country.

With the coming of freedom, communities of various kinds demanded recognition and representation. This was not only about fighting for loaves as often suggested. Issues sometimes on the backburner during the course of the freedom struggle – for instance, class – now came to the fore with the end of colonialism. Hence, issues related to caste, labour, or agrarian relations acquired salience. This did not just involve positioning for better or more territory and resources. These issues had been there earlier too but were coming to the fore now, as was the question of the future of *zamindari*. With British rule ending, the emergence of a new polity involved both fashioning of a new constitution and restructuring old institutions. This was part of the process of political churning which the old and new both had to go through.

In the third part of the volume I included a range of issues related to the society and economy, ranging from division of assets and institutions to debates about the form and direction of society, politics, economy, the role of the state, governance, and so on.

The chapter on peasant movements[20] mostly covered the struggles of peasants and workers, which were not against the departing imperialist power, but against feudal landowners and princely despots.

Some of the main movements were the *Tebhaga*, *Telengana* and *Warli* revolts. The demand of the *Tebhaga* movement was, quite literally, for two-thirds of the produce, plus storing paddy in the *bargadar's* (sharecropper) storeroom. The *Tebhaga* struggle was special because of the participation of

---

18 Wavell 1973.
19 *The Searchlight*, 15 August 1947, in Mahajan 2013, Part 3, chapter 56, Document 42.
20 Mahajan 2013, Part 3, chapter 47.

women and peasants from both Hindu and Muslim communities[21]. Gandhiji lent support to the movement but warned against use of compulsion and violence. [22]

A massive struggle of the *Warlis* erupted in western India under the banner of the *Kisan Sabha* and the Communist Party[23]. *Warli* tribals were caught in the landlord – moneylender – official nexus and suffered forced debt, slavery, and sexual exploitation. In the course of the movement, the *Congress* ministry was charged by the Communists with being soft on the *zamindars,* jungle contractors and other intermediary elements and with being repressive against the peasants. [24]

The *Telengana* movement combined agrarian revolt with opposition to princely autocracy. The repression against the *Telengana* movement was most severe in Nalagonda in the state of Hyderabad. Martial law lasted for two months and peasants suffered untold miseries at the hands of police authorities[25]. The Punjab Kisan Morchas were the result of years of work by the *Kisan Sabha*s among the peasants in resistance to *zamindars* and communalism in western Punjab[26]. A *Kisan Sabha* movement was organized in Karnataka in which activists were targeted and externed as *goondas* by the police and Section 144 was enforced across the state[27]. This is also the period when the *Hind Kisan Sabha* was formed[28]. This chapter carries a cache of documents highlighting lesser-known agrarian conflict

---

21 Article by P.C. Joshi, *People's Age*, 12 January 1947 in Mahajan 2013, Part 3, chapter 47, Document 4.

22 Gandhi's speech at a Prayer Meeting in Nabagram, 31 January 1947, *Collected Writings of Mahatma Gandhi (CMWG)*, vol. LXXXVI, pp. 412–13 in Mahajan 2013, Part 3, chapter 47, Document 8.

23 *People's Age*, 19 February 1947, in Mahajan 2013, Part 3, chapter 47, Document 5.

24 Statement issued by Morarji Desai, *Home Minister of the Government of Bombay* on Warli Adivasi Unrest in Thane, 20 January 1947, AICC Papers, File n°G-46(Pt.I)/1946, NMML in Mahajan 2013, Part 3, chapter 47, Document 6.

25 *People's Age*, 11 May 1947 in Mahajan 2013, Part 3, chapter 47, Document 28.

26 *People's* Age, 5 January 1947 in Mahajan 2013, Part 3, chapter 47, Document 1.

27 Letter from P.C. Joshi enclosing a memorandum titled The 'Goondas of Karnatak', to Congress Working Committee, 21 March 1947, File n°CPI-100, P.C. Joshi Archives on Contemporary History, JNU in Mahajan 2013, Part 3, chapter 47, Document 15.

28 Draft Constitution of the *Hind Kisan Sabha*, Circular of *Hind Kisan Sabha* with Enclosure, 12 April 1947, P.D. Tandon Papers, Roll n°4, Acc. n°367, S. n°699, NAI in Mahajan 2013, Part 3, chapter 47, Document 20.

between *Mirasdars* and *Adi-Dravidas* in Tanjore[29] and *jagirdars'* onslaught on tenants in Patiala[30].

The chapter on working class movements[31] focused largely on wages, working conditions, taxes, and legislation. It carried accounts of workers' strikes across the country as well as the different raids, arrests, and repressive measures against the *Communist Party of India* (CPI) and its allied organizations. The CPI presented the string of arrests of Communists as a sort of witch-hunt against the party by the *Congress*[32]. When the question was raised in the *Constituent Assembly*[33], Vallabhbhai Patel defended government action, stating that the searches and arrests were in connection with a case of stolen defence documents and that appropriate procedure was being followed. Jawaharlal Nehru in turn wrote to the British Communist Harry Pollitt about the matter[34]. In contrast to Communist–*Congress* clashes was a strike in Kanpur where Communist and *Congress*men together led the agitation, which was covered by the documents in this selection[35]. The chapter included documents which highlight trade union politics embedded in party rivalries[36]. Further, it provided accounts of numerous workers' agitations and formation of unions in various industrial units, including in distant areas.

In very different ways, nationalism, colonialism and communalism continued to shape societal developments in the post-independence era. Documents in the category of society in transition (Part 3, chapter 49) have been clubbed under the sections of caste (3, 49 [A]), language and politics (3, 49 [B]); education and politics (3, 49 [C]); linguistic provinces (3, 49 [D]); religious and social practices (3, 49 [E]); position of women (3, 49 [G]); and cultural expressions (3, 49 [H]).

---

29 Letter from H.C.M. McLaughlin, District Magistrate, Tanjore to Under Secretary, Government of Madras, Public Department, 7 May 1947, Public Department (General-A), G.O. n°2160, T.N. State Archives in Mahajan 2013, Part 3, chapter 47, Document 26.

30 *People's Age*, 7 May 1947, in Mahajan 2013, Part 3, chapter 47, Document 27.

31 Mahajan 2013, Part 3, chapter 48.

32 Pamphlet titled 'Operation Asylum And You', March 1947, CPI-95, Archives on Contemporary History, JNU, in Mahajan 2013, Part 3, chapter 48, Document 23.

33 Discussion on raids on CPI offices, 3 February 1947, *Legislative Assembly Debates*, vol. I, 1947, pp. 57–59 in Mahajan 2013, Part 3, chapter 48, Document 9.

34 22 January 1947, *SWJN*, second series, vol. I, pp. 617–18 in Mahajan 2013, Part 3, chapter 48, Document 5.

35 *People's Age*, 19 January 1947, in Mahajan 2013, Part 3, chapter 48, Document 4.

36 Letter from Vallabhbhai Patel to Gulzarilal Nanda, 27 February 1947, *SPC*, vol. IV, pp. 93–94 and Letter to Editor, from Rahman Ali, Secretary, District Muslim League, Jubbulpure titled "Muslim League Trade Union", *Hitavada*, 17 May 1947, in Mahajan 2013, Part 3, chapter 48, Document N°s 21 and 58.

One of the major movements was against ordering of public spaces along caste lines. A number of temples were opened up to *Harijans* in South India as well as across the country[37]. Most of these temple-entry movements were led by progressive associations from within the Scheduled Caste community. Then, there were others where *Congress*men led such movements. The reaction from the upper caste community was mixed. In *United Provinces*, in some places resolutions against the temple entry of *Harijans* were forwarded to the All India *Congress* Committee[38]. On the other hand, a prominent figure in Maharashtra went on a fast unto death in support of temple entry[39].

The *Congress* organization and particularly Gandhiji were in correspondence with many of these organizations and movements. Most petitions, letters, and resolutions were copied to the *Congress* President or the AICC. The *Harijan Sevak Sangh*[40] had already been active in this area, initiating self-educating and self-supporting institutions, such as community weaving centres. This met with applause as well as criticism from the organizations of *Scheduled Castes*. Several caste organizations began to work for material improvement in coordination with the government for scholarships, jobs, housing, and so on. In some, there was emphasis on education informed by the Gandhian perspective, which advocated education related to everyday life and to the local economy.

Further, there was a major controversy over the national language and the position of Hindi, Urdu, and Hindustani in the new post-independent state. The arena was public spaces such as All India Radio, public signboards, schools, and so on[41]. While Hindi and Urdu were now seen as languages 'belonging' to Hindus and Muslims respectively, Hindustani was preferred as the national

---

37 *The Hindu*, 8, 21 and 22 January 1947, Notification of the Madras Temple Entry Authorisation Act, 30 January 1947, Home Poll (I), File n°13/8/1947, NAI, in Mahajan 2013, Part 3, chapter 49 (A), Document n°s 1,2,3 and 6.

38 Letter from Swami Yogeshwaranand Teerth to Acharya Kriplani (Resolution enclosed), 16 March 1947, AICC Papers, File n°G-19(KWI)/1946–48, NMML, in Mahajan 2013, Part 3, chapter 49 (A), Document n°14.

39 Press Statement by Jayaprakash Narayan, 9 May 1947, *Jayaprakash Narayan: Selected Works*, pp. 143–44 in Mahajan 2013, Part 3, chapter 49 (A), Document n°18.

40 Letter from K.S. Shivam, General Secretary, Harijan Sevak Sangh to Sadiq Ali, Secretary, AICC, enclosing monthly letter for February 1947, 15 February 1947, AICC Papers, File n°G-19 (KWI)/ 1946–48, NMML in Mahajan 2013, Part 3, chapter 49 (A), Document n°11.

41 Letters from Liaquat Ali Khan to Vallabhbhai Patel, Ghazanfar Ali Khan to Vallabhbhai Patel, Vallabhbhai Patel to Ghazanfar Ali, 8, 21 & 22 January 1947, *SPC*, vol. IV, pp. 63, 68–71, 71–73 in Mahajan 2013, Part 3, chapter 49 (B), Document N°s 1,2,3.

language, including by Gandhiji[42], given the secular character of India and its mixed population. Provincial *Congress* Committees even adopted Hindustani as their language for correspondence and started preparations for its promotion. However, the conflict between promoters of Hindi and Urdu gradually led to Hindustani taking a backseat. The documents map this crucial debate.

While the debate over the national language assumed some communal overtones, education programmes and establishments too were affected by communalism and partition. The reputed Punjab University, including its famed library, based at Lahore, was partitioned between East and West Punjab[43]. Further, there were battles between colonial, nationalist, and communal positions on this terrain around issues like imparting religious education in schools, use of the Roman script, the position of English language in education, the setting up of a new education system, strikes of primary school teachers in United Provinces and Bengal (specifically in Noakhali), exposure of corruption in education departments, bringing back valuable materials belonging to or emanating from India Office in London[44], and the politics of language in literary forms.

Other social issues included removal of illiteracy[45], eradication of untouchability, abolition of beggary[46], promotion of inter-caste and inter-community marriages[47], and promotion of *ayurvedic* and *unani* medicine[48]. The battle was on two fronts – to shed colonial elements and promote indigenous practices as well as adopt progressive measures to do away with social ills emanating from

---

42 Gandhi at a prayer meeting at Goriakhari, 19 March 1947, Valmiki Chaudhary (Ed.), *Rajendra Prasad Correspondence and Select Documents*, vol. II, pp. 260–61 in Mahajan 2013, Part 3, chapter 49 (B), Document n°6.

43 *The Tribune*, 20 July 1947 in Mahajan 2013, Part 3, chapter 49 (C), Document n°15.

44 Memorandum by Listowel to the Cabinet India & Burma Committee, 9 August 1947, *T.O.P.*, vol. XII, pp. 623–27 in Mahajan 2013, Part 3, chapter 49 (C), Document n°18.

45 Press Note from the Directorate of Information, United Provinces, 29 June 1947, AICC Papers, File n°G-10/1947, NMML in Mahajan 2013, Part 3, chapter 49 (C), Document n°13.

46 Letter from Shri Gupta to President of Indian National Congress, 8 March 1947, AICC Papers, File n°G-8(I)/1947, NMML, in Mahajan 2013, Part 3, chapter 49 (E), Document n°2.

47 Letter from Mr. Krishna Mathur to J.B. Kripalani, 18 April 1947, AICC Papers, File n°CL-10/1946–47, NMML in Mahajan 2013, Part 3, chapter 49 (E), Document n°3.

48 Press Note from the Directorate of Information United Provinces, 2 July 1947, AICC Papers, File n°G-10/1947, NMML in Mahajan 2013, Part 3, chapter 49 (C), Document n°14.

economic and social conditions. Hence, there were petitions from women organizations for prohibiting practices of bigamy, allowing divorce for Hindus,
prohibiting the practice of *devadasis*[49], and enquiring into conditions of working women[50].

With the coming of freedom and the dissolution of the internal administrative boundaries of the colonial state, the demand for reorganization of states
along linguistic lines came up. Linked to this was the demand from linguistic
minorities for necessary safeguards[51].

Issues like cow slaughter[52] and religious conversions were raised in the context of the safeguarding of religious and cultural practices. Some of these were
consequences of the communalization of society at that time.

This selection has a cache of advertisements for theatre and motion pictures
and documents that highlight trends of artistic expression in those days, the
role of progressive cultural organizations like *Indian Peoples' Theatre Association*, debates on arts and politics, and the representation of communities in
cinema[53].

The chapter 'Economic Issues and Policies'[54] centred around debates on economic policies and problems of the times. A few months before freedom, all
eyes were set on the economic future of India and Pakistan. Like everyone else,
industrialists had no choice but to opt for either India or Pakistan. The partition
endangered economic assets in both countries and this bred anxieties for those
industrialists who were unsettled by it. A number of petitions, resolutions, and
letters by these industrialists form a section of this chapter.

Another section was based on the private papers of Indian industrialists which
reflected their concerns about nation-building. While Indian business classes
predicted a prosperous future for India, Pakistan was perceived with pessimism.

---

49 Legislation to Prevent the Practice of Devadasis, 24 April 1947, Home Poll (I), File
    n°13/28/47, NAI in Mahajan 2013, Part 3, chapter 49 (F), Document n°4.
50 Renu Chakravarthy to the General Secretary, *All India Women's Conference* with an
    extract from the report on working women, 22 July 1947, AIWC Papers, File n°93,
    NMML in Mahajan 2013, Part 3, chapter 49 (F), Document n°5.
51 Mahajan 2013, Part 3, chapter 49 (D).
52 Gandhi's speech at a prayer meeting at Patna, 25 April 2012, *CWMG*, vol. LXXXVII,
    pp. 357–59 and Letter from Secretary of Jiva-daya Sabha, Hoshangabad to J.B. Kri-
    palani, 7 August 1947, AICC Papers, File n°G-II (KWI)/1947–48, NMML in Mahajan
    2013, Part 3, chapter 49 (E), Document N°s 5 & 8.
53 Mahajan 2013, Part 3, chapter 49 (G).
54 Mahajan 2013, Part 3, chapter 50.

A question widely debated was whether Pakistan would be a sustainable self-sufficient economy[55].

Unlike industrialists, *zamindars* did not look to the future; they were gripped by their privileged present and its protection. *Congress* had a firm policy of land reforms at hand. Threatened *zamindars* wrote a number of letters, passed resolutions, and organized protests against the *Congress* policy, which are carried in this selection[56].

The documents on *Congress* reorganisation[57] covered themes such as the future role of *Congress*; a new constitution for the *Congress*; factions and indiscipline; Socialists and *Congress*; and activities of the *Congress*, such as observance of Independence Day and membership drives.

The primary concern of the party was with its future role. Reorganization had taken a back seat given the involvement of the party in negotiations, in parliamentary work, in the *Constituent Assembly* and Interim Government, among other things. The *Congress* organization ended up playing second fiddle to the 'government' wing, to the distress of the *Congress* President[58]. With independence, a change in the form of the party was on the cards to meet the new challenges. It was expected that the party, from being a platform for the anti-colonial movement, would come to represent a distinct ideology and interests. While some saw this as implying the winding up of the grand old party, others, like the General Secretary, Sadik Ali, initiated a debate on the continued relevance of the organization[59].

The chapter on the provincial ministries[60] highlighted the complex position of the *Congress* as it held office while being a popular organization working for freedom. This dual role threw up a host of issues, ranging from cooperation and rivalry between different levels of the *Congress* organization to emerging corruption in administration.

---

55 Confidential Foreign Report in *The Economist* titled "Will Pakistan Work?", 15 May 1947, *Jinnah Papers*, vol. I, Part I, pp. 762–66 in Mahajan 2013, Part 3, chapter 50 (H), Document 2.

56 Letter from Manzoor Ahamed, President, Thana Congress Committee, Nawadah, Gaya to President, AICC, 20 July 1947, AICC Papers, File n°G-42/1947–48, NMML and Letter from B.N. Jha to R.N. Banerjee, 23 June 1947, Home Poll (I), File n°34/1/47, NAI in Mahajan 2013, Part 3, chapter 50 (F), Document N°s 15 & 13.

57 Mahajan 2013, Part 3, chapter 45.

58 19 July 1947, File *N°*. G-31/1946–47, AICC Papers, NMML, in Mahajan 2013, Part 3, chapter 45(A), Document 11.

59 23 January 1947, File n°G-18 (Pt.-I)/1947, AICC Papers, NMML in Mahajan 2013, Part 3, chapter 45 (A), Document 2.

60 Mahajan 2013, Part 3, chapter 46.

The impending birth of Pakistan on the basis of the League's two-nation theory raised several questions about the nature of its polity. Was Pakistan to be a modern, secular, democratic state, or was it going to eschew the 'western' form of political organization in favour of a theocratic one, in which Sharia or Islamic laws would become the basis of governance, law, and politics? Similar questions were also raised about the nature of the Indian nation state. While Hindu communal organizations did step up their demand for a Hindu *rashtra* in the wake of partition, the *Congress* dismissed all such notions as antediluvian, communal, and against Indian civilizational ethos. Documents relating to these issues have been included in the chapter on Future Visions[61].

The chapter on the national flag[62] comprises primarily of the proposals sent to the AICC and carried in newspapers regarding the composition of the flag. These ranged from a collage of different religious and civilization symbols of the subcontinent to being markedly distinct from national flags of other countries[63]. The focus was on a symbol that could stand for all the stories – the new nation, the uniqueness of India, freedom, sovereignty, and its civilizational legacy.

At the same time, there were proposals for the suitable remodification of the *Congress* flag and also the assertive demand of the *Hindu Mahasabha* that the only flag suitable for the country was the *bhagwa* (saffron) coloured flag bearing the lotus base and yellow Swastika[64]. There was a debate over the national flag when the symbol of *charkha* (spinning wheel) was replaced by *chakra* (wheel). Savarkar, the *Hindu Mahasabha* leader, explained that this chakra was the Dharma Chakra, reminiscent of the golden epoch of 'Hindu' history, and not the *Ashoka Chakra*[65]. The colour white was seen as the ultimate culmination of VIBGYOR and hence symbolic of purity and most suitable for the backdrop of the flag[66].

---

61 Mahajan 2013, Part 3, chapter 54.
62 Mahajan 2013, Part 3, chapter 55.
63 Letter from Rao Sahib Ikshvaku V.K. Viraraghava Acharya to Kripalani enclosing a design for India's flag, 1 February 1947, AICC Papers, File n°G-20/1946–48, NMML, and Letter from Ramesh Chandra Bhargava to the editors of the *Amrita Bazar Patrika*, *The National Herald* and *The Pioneer* on 25 June 1947 in Mahajan 2013, Part 3, chapter 55, Document N°s 1, 2.
64 Letter from Debes C. Ghose to AICC, 2 July 1947, AICC Papers, File n°G-20/1946–48, NMML. and an article by Prof. P.S. Naidu in the *Bombay Chronicle*, 16 July 1947, in Mahajan 2013, Part 3, chapter 55, Document N°s 3, 6.
65 29 July 1947, S.S.Savarkar & G.M. Joshi (Eds.), *Historic Statements-V.D. Savarkar*, pp. 204–6 in Mahajan 2013, Part 3, chapter 55, Document n°15.
66 Rao Sahib Ikshvaku V.K. Viraraghava Acharya to Kripalani, 1 February 1947, in Mahajan 2013, Part 3, chapter 55, Document n°1.

The chapter on the flag included the documents about the National Flag Committees of India and Pakistan and debates in the *Constituent Assembly* regarding their composition[67]. Jinnah, who had initially agreed to have the Union Jack on the Pakistan flag, later retracted, saying that it would not be acceptable to the people of the country[68]. There was an emphasis on the new flag of Pakistan being appealing to the minorities as well[69]. Eventually, the National Flag of Pakistan was inaugurated in the Pakistan *Constituent Assembly* wherein Liaquat Ali Khan, the future Prime Minister, claimed that the flag stood for liberty and equality of all citizens in Pakistan[70].

There was discussion on whether people and organizations that were on the 'wrong side' of the border could salute the flag of their choice or not. The *Congress* left it to the people to decide but warned that the hoisting of the Pakistan flag by private institutions would be tolerated only in the initial state of transition[71].

Eventually, the National Flag was introduced in the *Constituent Assembly* of the Indian Union by Nehru and applauded on an unprecedented scale. The tricolour and the *chakra* on the white background found resonance with the secular imagination of a country embedded in civilizational values as well as modern attributes of liberty, equality, and fraternity. The *Hindu Mahasabha* resolved to respect all flags but recommended that 'real' Hindus salute only the *bhagwa* flag and take a pledge to fight for the reunification of India[72].

As with most events of the year 1947, celebrating 15th August was also very politicized. This volume devoted a chapter to documents wherein different groups and leaders took a stand on the matter, ranging from *Congress*, Gandhiji, AISPC to Shiromani Akali Dal (SAD) in Punjab. The *Hindu Mahasabha* declared

---

67 Extracts from the summary of proceedings of the Congress Working Committee,19–20 July, 1947, AICC Papers, File n°G-30/1946, NMML, *Constituent Assembly Debates*, 22 and 31 July 1947 in Mahajan 2013, Part 3, chapter 55, Document N°s 10, 11, 16.

68 Extracts from record of an interview between Ismay and Jinnah,24 July, 1947, *T.O.P.*, vol. XII, pp. 322–25 in Mahajan 2013, Part 3, chapter 55, Document n°12.

69 Editorial, *Deccan Times*, 10 August 1947, in Mahajan 2013, Part 3, chapter 55, Document n°19.

70 *Dawn*, 12 August 1947, in Mahajan 2013, Part 3, chapter 55, Document n°21.

71 Extracts from the summary of proceedings of the Congress Working Committee,19–20 July, 1947, *AICC Papers*, File n°G-30/1946, NMML, in Mahajan 2013, Part 3, chapter 55, Document n°10.

72 Extract from proceedings of the meeting of the *Working Committee of the All India Hindu Mahasabha*, 9 August 1947, AIHM Papers, File n°C-155, NMML, in Mahajan 2013, Part 3, chapter 55, Document n°18.

Independence Day as a day of mourning[73]. Newspapers carried special numbers, with messages from leaders. The midnight session of the *Constituent Assembly* was held on the night between 14 and 15 August wherein Nehru made his famous 'tryst with destiny' speech[74]. The session began with the singing of *Vande Mataram* and the President's address. The session met again on the morning of 15 August and received messages of congratulations from countries across the globe[75]. Gandhiji spent the day in Calcutta, fasting and spinning[76]. Political prisoners were released[77] and all major cities held their own public ceremonies to mark the day. Most celebrations on this day acknowledged the reality of partition and passed various resolutions to that effect.

Fifteen August 1947, then, was an occasion for both mourning and celebration. It marked independence and partition, which in turn reflected the success and failure of the anti-colonial movement. Success in wresting independence; failure in not being able to bring the majority of Muslims into the national movement.

The documents indicated that there was much discussion on the programmes for celebrating independence on 15 August 1947. The President of the *Congress* was of the view that the areas affected by partition and the ensuing violence could not be expected to rejoice on the day when their homes and villages would fall away from them[78]. There were, however, others like Lallan Prasad 'Insaan' from Gorakhpur in the *United Provinces*, who believed that not celebrating the day of hard-earned freedom amounted to a sin[79]. An advocate from *North-West Frontier Province* derided the ongoing preparations for

---

73 Extracts from the resolution passed by the *Working Committee of All India Hindu Mahasabha* at New Delhi, 9–10 August 1947, AIHM Papers, File n°C-155, NMML, in Mahajan 2013, Part 3, chapter 56, Document n°24.

74 *Constituent Assembly Debates*, 14 August 1947, vol. V, pp. 1–11, in Mahajan 2013, Part 3, chapter 56, Document n°30.

75 *Constituent Assembly Debates*, 15 August 1947, vol. V, pp. 13–23 in Mahajan 2013, Part 3, chapter 56, Document n°31.

76 Letter from Gandhi to Agatha Harrison, 15 August 1947, *CWMG*, vol. LXXXIX, pp. 43–44 in Mahajan 2013, Part 3, chapter 56, Document n°32.

77 'Instructions for Release of Prisoners', report in *The Statesman*, 15 August 1947, in Mahajan 2013, Part 3, chapter 56, Document n°45.

78 Circular letter from Kripalani to Provincial Congress Committees of Bengal, Sindh, Punjab & NWFP, 23 July 1947, AICC Papers, File n°G-8 (KW-I)/1947–48, NMML in Mahajan 2013, Part 3, chapter 56, Document n°11.

79 Open Letter to Hindus, c. August 1947, AICC Papers, File n°G-18(KW-I) (Pt. II)/1947–48, NMML in Mahajan 2013, Part 3, chapter 56, Document n°56.

celebrating 15 August in the face of widespread devastation and massacres. The various hues in which freedom was visualized become poignantly clear from the documents.

The coexisting experiences of triumph and anguish, the creation of new identities, and the questioning of old ties – the documents evoke the multitude of reactions to the dawn of freedom.

Marc Cluet
Université de Strasbourg

Punjab's New Capital City Chandigarh: Aims and Reality

Following the subcontinent's independence from Britain and its partition into India and Pakistan in 1947, the former Imperial Province of Punjab was divided between the two new sovereign states. East Punjab with its Muslim majority came to separate existence as an individual state of Pakistan; West Punjab, where Hindus and Sikhs made up the majority, emerged as an individual state of India. The decision about the fate of the Punjabi towns of Lahore and Amritsar was uneasy for the Boarder Commission. Finally Lahore was given to Pakistan and Amritsar to India. Amritsar, being the spiritual capital of the Sikhs, could hardly become the administrative capital of Indian West Punjab. At the same time, India's first Prime Minister Jawaharlal Nehru blamed Imperial New Delhi for its "un-Indianness" and dreamt about "a new town symbolic of the freedom of India, unfettered by the traditions of the past"[1]. The loss of Lahore which in any case held its architectural splendours from the Moghul era gave him the opportunity to realize at least that dream. In fact a total of 300 new towns was the target by the end of the 20th century, but only a few were to be built. Introducing democracy in a country where 80 per cent of the people were living in villages meant concentrating on rural issues for a start. Yet the question of building a new capital for East Punjab could not be postponed ad calendas graecas. First plans for Chandigarh – its very name had to be coined – as this new capital were designed in 1949-1950 by the American architects Albert Mayer and Matthew Nowicki with the assistance of P.L. Varma, the state's Chief Engineer. Freshly independent India did not want to put up an all-Indian team for lack of recent building experience on such a large scale. Contracting British architects was out of question in the moment of gaining independence. Unfortunately M. Nowicki died in an aviation accident (1950) when preparatory works were about to begin. Since A. Mayer did not want to carry the project on his own without his co-planner, a new team had to be formed. Nehru favoured Swiss-French architect Le Corbusier who had been a major promoter of the so-called International Style in the 1920s and 1930s, along with the German modernists Walter Gropius

---

1   *Hindustan Times* (New Delhi), July 8, 1950. Quoted from Kalia 1987, p. 21.

and Ludwig Mies van der Rohe. The special appeal of Le Corbusier to Nehru
was his supposed ability to take India to the cutting edge of western progress.
As a matter of fact Nehru had adopted the colonialists' view of a static "old India" largely entitled to blame herself for being colonized[2]. Forced modernism
was the warranty for true independence and world significance. In the autumn
of 1950 a two-man delegation from India, P.L. Varma shouldered by State Ad-
ministrator of Public Works Pran Nath Thapar, visited Le Corbusier in his Paris
studio on Nehru's behalf. Le Corbusier was enthusiastic about their offer to take
over the Chandigarh project. He met their modernist expectations by associ-
ating three architects from the *Congrès Internationaux d'Architecture Moderne*
(CIAM / International Congresses of Modern Architecture) which he had initiated in 1928: the British husband and wife professionals Edwin Maxwell Fry and
Jane Beverly Drew, plus Le Corbusier's fatherly cousin Pierre Jeanneret who was
to stay the longest on the Chandigarh site. The problem was that Le Corbusier
himself unexpectedly moved away from radical modernism in the aftermath of
World War II. The Ronchamp Chapel which he built in French Jura in parallel
to the Chandigarh project is a testimonial of his change of mind and vision.
For sure the destructions of war, especially the allied flattening of old French
towns as Caen, Le Havre, Rouen, Tours fostered a certain nostalgia in France.
Le Corbusier did not exactly share the common attitude, but he evolved into a
more flexible modernism in which functionalism no longer excluded the lessons
of the past. Nevertheless his radical reputation barred him from French reconstruction schemes, but the resulting frustration made him all the more receptive
to the Indian offer for Chandigarh. While his youth idol Auguste Perret would
*re*build Le Havre, he would build Chandigarh on a site where nothing had previously stood.

The questions to be asked are: Did Le Corbusier meet Nehru's expectations?
Was he at the height of his own ambitions? Did Chandigarh work out for its
people?

In recent years Le Corbusier has been said to have shaped his architectural
and urbanistic concepts according to the figure of the Rousseauian "noble savage", especially in the Chandigarh project[3]. In my opinion this interpretation
only meets half the truth. In his later days Le Corbusier certainly did endorse a
highly critical attitude towards capitalist industrial "civilization", but he thought
an optimized society could offer the remedies to the ills. The loathed "first

---

2   Prakash 2002, p. 9–11.
3   See Vogt 1998 and Prakash 2002, p. 16, p. 92, p. 153–154.

industrial age" – which he saw as the "iron age", not only for its iron and steel industry but also in the mythological sense – could make place to a "second industrial age" which would restore harmony within people, among people, with surrounding "nature", even with the "deities", the sacred cosmos. His architectural and urbanistic concepts certainly do follow an idealistic anthropological figure, but it rather is the Rousseauian "generic man" whom the "noble savage" helps to circumscribe, but who should never go back to primitive conditions nor be artificially kept under such.

"Generic man" enjoys "natural rights" and natural physical and mental integrity, that is to say he is undeformed by a life of hardship or (excessive) luxury. When Le Corbusier first came to India in mid-February 1951 to get acquainted with the Chandigarh site, he fell to the illusion that ordinary Punjabi people, down to field and construction labourers, incorporated "generic man" in their manner. In his sketchbooks and letters he gets enthusiastic about "superlatively human" India,[4] "[its] human splendours out in the open, without class, outside of class",[5] "people on their feet [...], men and women *upright*",[6] all men "looking intelligent",[7] women "of strong race"[8]. To him "calm, dignity, despise of greed" seemed to prevail,[9] "relations without violence",[10] "brotherhood"[11]. This "orientalist" view of the Punjabi people comes close to the mistaking of universal slavery for equality which Karl Marx had warned against in his analysis of the "Asiatic mode of production". In any case Le Corbusier did not want to be disillusioned. He was quite angry at the communist physicist Pierre-Frédéric Joliot-Curie for his more realistic view of differences in class and wealth in freshly independent India[12]. When confronted with any Indians who did not exactly fit into the frame of fraternal classless India, such as harsh businessmen or ruthless police,[13] he would be in rage as if they were guilty of sacrilege. Perhaps Le Corbusier's strange scheme of raising the three major state buildings of democratic

---

4   Petit 1970, p. 110.
5   Le Corbusier 1982, vol. 2, E 18 (Feb.-March 1951), folio 365.
6   Le Corbusier 1982, vol. 2, E 18 (Feb.-March 1951), folio 362.
7   Le Corbusier 1982, vol. 2, E 23 (27.10.1951–28.11.1951), folio 646.
8   Cf. n. 7.
9   Cf. n. 6.
10 Cf. n. 5.
11 Le Corbusier 1982, vol. 2, E 20 (May 1951), folio 448.
12 Cf. n. 5.
13 Le Corbusier 1982, *Carnets*, vol. 3, J 39 (11.11.1955-Dec. 1955), folio 440, and Le Corbusier 1982, vol. 2, E 18 (Feb.-March 1951), folio 362.

Indian Punjab (the State Secretariat, the Assembly Hall and he High Court), which all together (all *three* of them) materialize democratic separation of powers, in an "intact" rural setting, with field labourers going around, has to do with his idea that these supposedly "generic" men/women are the right citizens for the ideal society. As if he were conscious that the proper city of Chandigarh with its inevitable social stratification – not to speak of the persistent caste-structure! – could never match his utopian hope and self-deceptive grassroot democratic scenography, he curtailed it off the Chandigarh government district. The so-called Capitol complex cannot be seen from the city and vice versa as a result of big earth works Le Corbusier had done[14].

The "horizontal hills" Le Corbusier put up between the Capitol complex and the proper city of Chandigarh strongly suggest that in his mind the latter was abandoned to the ugly reality of social stratification. Such interpretation would be over-hasty. For one thing – as we know – Le Corbusier really believed in Indian fraternity; for the other thing, being an architect dealing with practical problems, he definitely could find a way out of total self-deceit. The result came out as Le Corbusier's attempt to centre the city onto the social middle. The main function of the city as an administrative centre implied a sociology that made this goal comparatively easy to achieve. Perhaps his later opposition against the city developing any industries but the lightest has to do with the envisioned middle class sociology. In 1957 socio-demographic facts were in accordance: the largest number of wage earners in the city (27.6 percent) held administrative and clerical jobs[15]. Even among Chandigarhian private house owners among whom you would expect a great majority of professionals, businessmen or industrialists, these were nearly outnumbered by the administrative and clerical category or other closely related sections (as academic personnel or retired officials)[16].

Le Corbusier's envisionment of Chandigarh as a city of middle class people includes the Proudhonian idea of all Chandigarhians living in private houses designed for a single family and also the idea of housing styles narrowing around medium standards. Chandigarh should count neither marble palaces nor mud huts. To use the words of one of the initial Indian planners with whom Le Corbusier kept on working after his appointment: "We tried to take down the top a little and raise the bottom a little"[17]. Thirteen different categories of housing were initially planned for government employees, varying from two-floored

---

14 Riboulet 1985, p. 92.
15 Kalia 1987, p. 128.
16 Cf. n. 15.
17 Quoted by Korngay 1980, p. 7.

"VIP houses" with kitchen and drawing room on the ground floor and several bedrooms on the first floor, to single-floored row-houses for the "peons" (office boys, watchmen etc.), each unit consisting of a veranda, two bedrooms, a kitchen, and an open-air water closet ("Indian style")[18]. Although the differences are quite notable, and come along with a "downward" segregation in space starting from the northern "VIP sectors",[19] those differences are largely levelled out by common features: all houses are connected to a water sewerage system (unique in Punjab at the time), are linked by pedestrians-only pathways, offer privacy within a minimum of greenery, and – most visibly – bear what might be called the "Chandigarh style". Le Corbusier's requirement to use ordinary local materials (such as brick, lime plaster, lime wash), his preference for austere repetitive designs, his requirement for standardization (down to manhole covers), his insistence on strict implementation of the "Punjab Capital Buildings Rules" of 1952, in order to escape the *"merde générale"*,[20] – all this led to the characteristic (i.e. characteristically *un*characteristic) urbanscape of residential Chandigarh, known as "City Beautiful", but also associated with "matchbox architecture"[21]. To Le Corbusier, the latter probably would not have appeared as a shame. Significantly, he liked to point out that the previously homeless "peons" were now enjoying houses built with the same love and care as the houses of ministers. In Le Corbusier's mind, narrowing onto the social middle was achieved with such consequence in Chandigarh that he could prompt all radical critics to forget about spatial and domestic segregation: "Don't fuss about classes [being segregated, MC]! All that is being done here is merely and purposefully a classification matter." ("Ne chicanez pas sur les classes ! C'est ici, simplement et utilement, du classement.")[22] He even went so far as to say of a temporary "village" for "peons" (in that case probably peasants from a razed village) that that they lived "majestically" ("fastueusement") under conditions "worthy of masters"[23].

Besides narrowing around medium standards, Le Corbusier planned public places where citizens of all kinds should interact. As he put it, the city centre, located in sector 17, was to be *"le cœur de la cité"*, not "the core of the city"[24]. In other terms, it should let people flow in and out and mingle; it should not

18 Prakash 2002, p. 66.
19 Fry 1977, p. 358.
20 Le Corbusier 1982, vol. 3, J 36 (17.03.1955–27.03.1955), folio 304.
21 Wattas 2003.
22 Quoted from Boesiger et Girsberger 1967, p. 194.
23 Le Corbusier 1982, vol. 2, F 27 (28.11.1952–20.12.1952), folio 878.
24 Le Corbusier 1982, vol. 2, E 21' (07.07.1951–17.07.1951), folio 494.

be an entrenchment for the social or administrative elite as a maharaja's palace district or a colonial town centre. Around the central *"chowk"* or "plaza" are clustered the Town Hall, the Central Library, the GPO, commercial buildings, all housed in standardized four story concrete-frame buildings. In Le Corbusier's mind, standardization was not appalling to people, but on the contrary would contribute to social interaction. The place was to become "an entity of sociability" where people (men, women, children alike) would engage in "friendly and productive relations" ("rapports aimables et fructueux")[25] and combine to a "social bouquet" that would be colourful indeed and show "profusion and harmony"[26]. To tell the truth, it took some time to even start evolving in that direction and certainly never met the Corbusian ideal in its full extent. Other places for people to gather and mix were designed with varying success, such as the "Leisure Valley", a succession of gardens deployed downward from the Capitol complex over six sectors, the man-made Sukhna Lake with an embankment ten times broader than necessary in order to provide a convenient promenade, an excavated forum within the Capitol complex, which Le Corbusier called *"la Fosse de la Considération"* (usually rendered by "the Trench of Consideration")[27]. In his mind this place was to be some sort of Chandigarhian equivalent of Orators' Corner in London, where anyone can speak out freely, get the public consideration he or she may attract, possibly inspiring a movement of opinion. While this "forum" had a difficult start (the Open Hand structure which Le Corbusier wanted to crown the pulpit was completed only decades later) and has rather become a tourist attraction than a platform for discussion, Sukhna Lake promenade rapidly came closest to the Corbusian ideal of an urban public space.

In an early letter to the Indian Embassy in Paris (dated November 25, 1950), just at the point of being commissioned, Le Corbusier praised himself for "the *raison d'être* of his life [...] expressed by one word: HARMONY", which of course he would also pursue in India[28]. As far as we could see, a reduced scope of housing types, a tops-down and bottoms-up policy in matters of living standards were Le Corbusier's main tools to promote the social harmony that originally came by with "generic man". In his innermost thoughts he must have known that this figure was no more than a figment, at the best a (regulative) heuristic idea. The very fact that he designed urban public places for the "social bouquet" to

25 Cf. n. 24.
26 Le Corbusier 1982, vol. 2, E 21' (07.07.1951–17.07.1951), folio 496.
27 Petit 1970, p. 116–117.
28 Quoted from Sarin 1977, p. 398.

dazzle proves that he was aware of social differences. Beyond feasibility the problem is: what happens with the sections that have been forgotten while narrowing onto the social middle? We immediately think of the poorly skilled workforce, especially building and road workers or diggers, but we should not, either, forget the wealthy. The first were quite numerous from the beginning because of all the construction work going on. Manual labour was performed by 19 percent of the local wage earners, mainly in construction activities[29]. Le Corbusier had pledged that no *"banlieue"* (working-class or lower middle-class suburb), which he loathed altogether with the whole "first industrial age", would ever be possible in a planned city like Chandigarh,[30] but he had to face a dilemma: on one hand, offering "substandard" houses (below the lowest of the "official" standards) was contrary to human dignity; on the other hand, offering all the low-paid workers in the area even the lowest of the thirteen housing types, actually even a fourteenth type that was temporarily added at the bottom,[31] was economically unbearable, especially since Le Corbusier himself eventually appreciated the advantage of cheap labour: thus he was able to do and *undo* own blueprints in reality without notable extra costs[32].

Le Corbusier's de facto exclusion of the actual builders task force from the city that was just being built was pointed out fittingly (but in somewhat accentuated form) by the Indian architectural historian Ravi Kalia:

> "The assumptions of the Chandigarh master plan were based on the consumption patterns of the middle classes of the industrialized countries of the West [...]. The physical constructs of the master plan comply with these assumptions [...]."[33]

As a result slums sprung up, mostly on peripheral locations out of sight of the actual residents. In May 1957 there already were 655 improvised houses without water and electricity in Chandigarh[34]. As slums were absolutely "unthinkable" for Le Corbusier in a city like Chandigarh, little was done to improve living conditions for their inhabitants. Bigger cities like Delhi, Calcutta or Madras designed policies towards their slums while Chandigarh simply turned away from the problem. Persistent protest from the slum dwellers finally led to the legalization of some "colonies" and the grant of minimal facilities as water taps, latrines,

---

29 Kalia 1987, p. 128.
30 Sarin 1977, p. 406.
31 Sarin 1977, p. 402.
32 Le Corbusier 1982, vol. 3, H 34 (08.11.1954–11.12.1954), folio 195.
33 Kalia 1987, p. 148.
34 Kalia 1987, p. 129.

lamp-posts[35]. Yet, by 1971, 15 percent of the population lived in unauthorized settlements lacking any facilities[36].

At the top end of Chandigarh society, life certainly was worth living. Still the Corbusian idea of narrowing onto the social middle – alongside with the fact that from its very function the city was an intellectual and administrative centre, rather than an economic one – made it less agreeable a place for the well off (as far as there were any) than the old maharaja towns or the former colonial quarters of Anglo-India. In the early days Chandigarh had a remarkable cinema and literary café culture, but did not allow any "serious shopping". Affluent people in need of expensive items for occasions like weddings had to rely on Delhi[37].

While the poor were banned from the proper city and the rich remained un-catered for in town, the relatively homogenous middle class majority was increasingly ridden by tensions and strains. From the beginning, differences in housing types from sector to sector also meant differences in population density. The standard sector measures 1,800 m x 800 m, but the northern sectors were supposed to accommodate about 5,000 and the southern sectors about 20,000[38]. The intended one-to-four density ratio may, at first sight, seem harsh on the lesser advantaged, but in fact it is extremely people friendly by the standards of any older major city in East and West alike. The problem is that the comparatively low disparity grew with the years. The main reason was rent subsidies to all government employees who could not be offered a home within the public housing scheme[39]. These employees were offered an additional 12.5 percent income as compensation and thus could find rented accommodation in the private house market. An unwanted side effect was that non-government employees who were uneligible for provided accommodation or financial help from government were forced to share dwelling space with their alike. Consequently, homes, initially meant for one family, now sometimes housed up to four or five families a room. The sectors where all this was happening drifted away from the others. The social gap which had been kept narrow broadened again. Yet middle class values continued to prevail. According to a survey carried out in 1963-1964, 41.7 percent of the households sending children to primary schools sent them outside their own sector,[40] that is to say in supposedly better sectors. The rickshaw wallahs

---

35 Sarin 1977, p. 390.
36 Kalia 1987, p. 130.
37 Prashar 2002.
38 Sarin 1977, p. 380–381.
39 Sarin 1977, p. 407.
40 Sarin 1977, p. 383.

who were in charge of conveying the children upward in the city were carrying the hope of the parents who wanted to secure a position close to the escaping social middle.

In the 1990s decade which brought "IT-led development" to Chandigarh as to India altogether (a unit of the National Informatics Centre was established in Chandigarh that very year, 1990), Le Corbusier's ideal of centring onto the social middle became an open lie. A comfortably well off upper middle class emerged in the face of a ballooning lower class. The influx of migrant workers, lured by a city topping Delhi in terms of per capita income, turned the slums from unseen to all-too-visible. The strength of the trend is clear by the over 30 percent of slum dwellers that were to be reached in Chandigarh at the eve of the new century (1999)[41]. Le Corbusier compromised with the concept of "generic man" from the beginning, but the illusion held to some extent for about three decades. Significantly Tarun J. Tejpal's partly autobiographic first novel *The Alchemy of Desire* (2005) hardly registers any other stratification in 1979 Chandigarh (which T.J. Tejpal knows from his student days at Punjab University) than the stepwise down decrease in amenities between north and south sectors and the difference between cinema audiences. While the students from the surrounding small towns "lived by the Hindi film", the "real cool crowd" used to show up on Sunday mornings for the new English-language releases[42]. In the same novel, Tejpal also evokes 1999 Chandigarh which the first-person narrator comes to visit again. Besides heavy traffic and "new money", the one notable change for him is the transformation of homes into strongholds[43]. This change in a city which Le Corbusier had envisioned as open and most convenient for people to socialize and harmonize, at least within its specific sociology, started to happen in the year 1984. The fatal string of violence and counter-violence that marked that year is well known: from Indira Gandhi's order to expel Sikh separatists from Amritsar's Golden Temple to the Indian army's assault on the sacred shrine with artillery, combat helicopters and vehicles (3-8 June), and then from Indira Gandhi's assassination by Sikh body guards (on October 31st) to anti-Sikh riots in New Delhi and various parts of the country like Haryana. In this dramatic context, Chandigarh "VIPs" were offered personal protection and allowed to raise the front-side walls of their homes above the previously mandatory 4 feet[44]. Even barbed wire fences were permitted under the condition they were hidden by shrubbery.

---

41 Singh 1999.
42 Tejpal 2007, p. 491–492.
43 Tejpal 2007, p. 510–511.
44 Singh 2000.

dinary citizens followed the example on the motive of preventing burglary
squatting (if they are to stay away for a longer time). Many installed window
les, some went as far as raising parapets on road berms or even side-walks.
r since 1984, the social and urbanistic continuum which Le Corbusier wished
Chandigarh has been subject to further and further fragmentation.

s late as 1977 the British architect and academic Robert Furneaux Jordan
had praised the great Le Corbusier and the work of his life: Chandigarh, and the
30 years independent India all together in one lyrical *envolée*:

> "Chandigarh is like the man [Le Corbusier, MC]. It is not gentle. It is not pompous.
> It is hard and assertive. It is riddled with mistakes. Le Corbusier found fulfilment in
> the scorching heat of India. Lutyens' New Delhi was the end of an era; Chandigarh the
> beginning."[45]

For sure R. Furneaux Jordan could not foresee that Sikh separatism and unwise
government response to the problem would also compromise ideal Chandigarh.
Yet, celebrating a superhuman accomplishment – which (minor) mistakes don't
tarnish, but on the contrary make appear even greater – seems to miss the fundamental error or even moral fault of Le Corbusier: as we saw, the lower classes, all the building and road workers, all the wallahs of any kind had no place
in "his" Chandigarh. Fragmentation which just happened to occur because of
changed times is one thing; exclusion from the beginning an entirely different
thing. "City Beautiful", as Chandigarh was soon to be called, indeed rests on a
paradox concept of "human dignity" which ends in making "inferior people"
to "out people". On the other hand, it should perhaps also be remembered that
the "(vulgarly) rich" are equally left aside in Le Corbusier's "ideal" Chandigarh.
This emphatic notion of "(true) human dignity" now retains a utopian "appeal"
which paradoxically may be at work in today's supposedly fully materialistic
India. My theory is that Chandigarh's repeatedly self-fixed goal to become the
first "slum-free" city in India[46] results from the tension between both the city's
emphatic "human rightness" and its striking omission of the lowest sections.
In other words, Le Corbusier could have initiated a dialectics of absence which
will result in the integration of the "insistingly missing". Besides the city's pledge
to rehabilitate its slums, a recent story about Chandigarh's Sukhna Lake suggests

---

45 Article on "Le Corbusier (Charles-Edouard Jeanneret)" for Richards 1977.
46 NN 2009; Malik 2012. Significantly, the latter press article is illustrated by an older
    black and white photograph of the Open Hand structure Le Corbusier wanted to
    overlook and most probably "bless" the "Trench of Consideration" that is of free
    speech and democratically granted consideration.

that subverting Le Corbusier's restrictive sociology in a superiorly Corbusian spirit is on its way to the minds. In December 2009 itinerant low-caste (male) road workers from Uttar Pradesh were hired for cleaning the lake of weeds from pedal boats (*"pédalos"*) which were originally designed by Pierre Jeanneret and are normally used for fun rides. The Chandigarh-based, previously Lahore-based, venerable daily newspaper The Tribune never misses an occasion to re-mind Chandigarhians of Le Corbusier's ideal expectations towards the city and consequently its inhabitants. This time, it was "lifestyle" columnist Mrs. Sreed-hara Bhasin who sprang in[47]. Using pleasure boats to do work on lake cleaning impressed her for the "brilliance of the scheme", but as she saw "one man [leave] his crying baby on the shore and [jump] into the boat", she had to think of "Co-lumbus setting off for new continents" and was brought to deeper views:

"If Pierre Jeanneret was here today, he would have approved. The lake is for one and all of us. It is of the people, by the people and for the people."

The word "caste" is not spelled out, but any Indian understands that "caste" is at issue. Family ties could be strained (see the crying baby), but there is hope that a society of individuals is emerging where inhuman segregation, for the threat of "caste pollution" and the sake of "caste purity", will be fully dismissed as silly superstition of the past: the same boat can be used by anyone for pleasure or for labour, so long as the money is right. If a Sunday columnist thought this story worth telling and commentating on, it is because it reaches deeper than one may think at first glance. Of course, any bigger Indian city contributes to dissolve the caste system for its crowding and unstructured intermingling,[48] yet the time of separate election booths for upper and lower caste voters is not that far away and "in-groupism" remains so strong in cities across North India that special residen-tial societies keep emerging for lower caste families because other cooperatives stubbornly refuse to rent or sell to them[49]. Le Corbusier's positive effect on the Chandigarh situation in the long-run seems unquestionable.

Chandigarh results from a series of misunderstandings and mistakes. Le Cor-busier agreed with Nehru in refusing Imperial New Delhi as a cityscape making people understand at each step (in so far as they could walk around) that liberty will not descend to them. Parallels to Albert Speer's later plans for Hitler's Berlin ("world capital Germania") are evident[50]. Nehru and Le Corbusier abhorred all

---

47 Basin 2009.
48 Nilekani 2009, p. 230.
49 Nilekani 2009, p. 158 and p. 153.
50 Larsson 1978, p. 116–117.

that, but while Nehru envisioned Chandigarh as a friendlier version of a Soviet new town, Le Corbusier tried to establish in India a liberal middle class utopia borrowed from the West. Both concepts were well-intentioned, but unsuitable for India at the time. Nevertheless it must be said and repeated that Le Corbusier has been a good tutelary spirit to Chandigarh. His "obviously limited openness" makes true openness a lasting want, even after a lengthy period of forced closing (from the 1980s).

Sonia Cordera
University of Florence

The long-term effects of Decolonization of the British Empire in South Asia:the 1971 secession of Bangladesh and its international consequences

Introduction

In 1971 India and Pakistan fought their third war in less than thirty years. The history of hostile relations between the two countries is not sufficient to understand the genesis of the 1971 conflict, which was not fought, as the first two were, to rule over Kashmir. The key to comprehension lies rather in the domestic situation of Pakistan. This article demonstrates that the third Indo-Pakistani war originated from the actions of the authoritarian Pakistani governments that repeatedly negated and repressed regional identities and claims for decentralisation. The direct consequence of these policies was the eruption in East Pakistan of a civil war in 1971, which ended up involving India and triggering the third Indo-Pakistani war.

In the first section of the article the causes of the East Pakistan civil war are analysed to provide the tools for understanding the 1971 events. Cultural, sociological, political and economic disparities between East and West Pakistan were the bases for the regional political movement that emerged in East Pakistan. Some of these imbalances, like the territorial conformity of Pakistan, the sociological dominance of the Punjabi ethnic group in the military and civilian administration, the vice-regal pattern of government, and the lack of strong and rooted political parties were inherited from the colonial period. However, colonial legacies alone cannot fully explain this discord. The second section of this article indeed shows that by worsening these imbalances and by repressing democratic claims for major regional autonomy, the Pakistani authoritarian governments rather exacerbated them further. In the third section, the developments of the civil war are briefly summarised in order to show how a domestic question rapidly became an international problem, which not only directly triggered India's military intervention, but also threatened a military confrontation between the Soviet Union and the United States.

The roots of the East Pakistan crisis and the colonial legacies

To understand the reasons for the political and social crisis that Pakistan faced, it is crucial to consider first and foremost those historical territorial, sociological and cultural aspects inherited from the colonial period.

The first evidence of weakness was that Pakistan was the first state in the world to have emerged with two different territorial wings, divided by nearly 1,610 km of Indian territory[1]. The difficult communications between the two wings of Pakistan were also complicated by the fact that East and West Pakistan were connected by air or sea communication lines only along routes much longer than the effective line of sight, because of the antagonism with the Indians. The physical distance evidently contributed to obstructing the creation of a sense of national identity fundamental in bridging the regional differences.

One of these differences was that in 1951 East Pakistan was the smaller wing, but with the larger portion of the entire Pakistani population and with 22% of Hindu population[2], a much greater proportion than the 3% in West Pakistan[3]. The polarisation of religious identities in competing groups, such as Hindus and Muslims, had begun during the colonial era, when for example in the name of efficiency the Muslim districts of the Bengal presidency were divided from the Hindu ones, and unified to Assam to form a new province in 1905[4]. Religious identities had later been further reinforced by the communitarian violence experienced during the first partition of the Indian subcontinent in 1947, when India and Pakistan gained independence from the colonial power[5]. Those traumatic events obstructed the construction of a cohesive state where different religious groups could live together in peace. Religious differences in independent Pakistan had thus remained alive and emerged again in 1971 when, during the violent repression of the East Pakistan political demands, the Pakistan Army indulged in communitarian violence[6], which

---

1   Dixit 1999, p. 9.
2   Ahmed 1998, p. 227.
3   Jaffrelot 2009, p. 246.
4   On the conflicting relations between Hindus and Muslims in Bengal during the colonial rule, and on the partition of Bengal realised by the British in 1905 see for example Torri 2007, p. 493–497.
5   Torri 2007, p. 573–616.
6   Even if there is debate on the possibility of using the word 'genocide' (see note 38), what seems plausible is that the Pakistan Army, during their work of violent suppression of the political dissent in East Pakistan, worked to up-root the Hindu population. On this topic see Zaheer 1994, p. 261; and Bose 2005, p. 4465. Moreover, in the

resulted in the majority of the Hindu community searching for shelter in India in order to escape[7].

The rivalry between Hindus and Muslims was not the sole exacerbating factor of the Pakistan civil war. Cultural and sociological differences were the basis for the formation of regional identities competing with the national one among the Pakistani Muslims themselves. For example, the identity of East Pakistani Muslims was deeply rooted in the linguistic and cultural traditions of Bengal, which were significantly different from those of West Pakistan. The colonial rule had indirectly enhanced the differences in some cases. The East Pakistan socio-economic context was different from the Western one, for instance, and not only because of its different climatic characteristics. After the colonial period the Eastern wing indeed turned out to be dominated by a much smaller land-holding than West Pakistan[8], thus preventing the convergence of socio-economic interests between the landowners of the two wings. Another case was that the new Pakistani administrative centre "became increasingly identified with Punjab because of the region's dominance of the two main institutional structures of the state – the Army and the civil bureaucracy"[9]. This aspect came directly from the colonial period when Punjab and the North-West Frontier Province were the areas from which the major part of the colonial Indian army had been recruited. British politics of racial classification into martial groups, and the privileged treatment conceded to these classes in the allocation of land and public jobs shaped the social order of these areas[10]. As a result after Independence Punjabis were 80% of the new Pakistan military forces, while East Pakistanis were only 5% of the officer corps of the Pakistan Army, and 7% of the other ranks, doing slightly better in their air force representation[11].

"Telegram sent by American Embassy in Islamabad to Department of State sent on 2nd August 1971", the American Embassy reported that "persecution of Hindus appears to have ceased" due to the "drastic decrease in number of Hindus available to persecute", and that "the main instance of de-Hinduization was expulsion of Hindus". See Khan 1999, p. 624–631.

7   The percentage of Hindus in the entire number of refugees was considerable, around 80%. Sisson and Rose 1991, p. 296.

8   It had been the process of land reforms promoted by the British that produced a society in East Pakistan where the size of land-holding was much smaller, and the power of landowners more fragmented than in West Pakistan. On this see for example Torri 2007, p. 368–495.

9   Talbot 2005, p. 126.

10   Taylor 2011, p. 420.

11   Sisson and Rose 1991, p. 10.

Moreover, Punjabis covered 55% of the entire civil service, while East Pakistanis working in this field were only 16%[12].

As the final colonial legacies, three political aspects contributed to worsen the imbalances between East and West Pakistan. First, the vice-regal pattern of government inherited from the colonial period directly favoured the centralisation of state power. The Governor-General led the country until 1956, thus encouraging the Pakistan political system to become authoritarian and less inclined to accommodate regional disparities[13]. Second, the lack of well-established political institutions at the time of Independence also did not favour the democratization process of the newly formed state. The Muslim League (ML), the largest Muslim party that during the colonial period represented all Muslims in the dialogue with the Indian National Congress and the colonial power, did not have a mass participation until 1940–7, and not even a strong local and territorial organization in the territories that became Pakistan[14]. Deprived by Partition of "the platform of religion as a political mobiliser", the ML even lost the element of cohesion that was central in its previous political struggle to guarantee Muslims a protected position, and faced the emergence of other parties based on regional and provincial identities, like for example the Awami League (AL) in East Pakistan[15]. Naturally, the latter demanded a more fair representation in civil and military jobs, a more equitable distribution of economic resources, and a proportional political representation of the provinces in the National Assembly. Third, the premature deaths soon after Independence of the only nationally recognised leaders of the whole of Pakistan, Mohammed Ali Jinnah and Liaquat Ali Khan, created a political vacuum in the ML that was not so easily filled by the other emerging political leaders who had only regional support[16].

Political responsibilities of the Pakistani governments

The responsibilities for the failure of the Pakistani national state have not, however, to be linked only to the legacies of the colonial period: political developments in Pakistan after 1947 were directly responsible for the explosion of conflicting identities. In fact, "successive bouts of authoritarian rule have reinforced centrifugal ethnic, linguistic and regional forces", and enhanced economic and political

---

12 Jaffrelot 2004, p. 18.
13 Sayeed 1998, p. 300.
14 Rizvi 2000.
15 Aziz 2008, p. 15.
16 Taylor 2011, p. 420.

imbalances between West and East Pakistan, paving the way for the violent division of the state[17]. For example, the attempt made by the Governor General in 1948 to impose Urdu as the only national language in order to suppress the different regional identities of Pakistan had the opposite effect. The strong resistance to replacing Bengali with Urdu became indeed the ground on which the East Pakistani regional political movement of the AL was built.

Moreover, the bureaucratic and military institutions of the state controlled just by the Punjabis exploited the fact that no agreement in the Constituent Assembly on the rules for the formation of the National Assembly could be reached among the political parties of Pakistan until 1954[18]. Being threatened by the request from regional parties for a more equitable distribution of military and civil jobs[19], they gradually assumed the control of the state politics. A triumvirate based on the Western Pakistan military-bureaucratic nexus, and composed of Ghulam Muhammad (Governor-General from 1951 to 1955), General Ayub Khan (Commander in Chief of the Army), and Iskander Mirza (an Army officer who was Defence Secretary, and later President) assumed power in 1954, after the Governor dissolved the Constituent Assembly and the provincial governments elected previously, and named a new government[20]. Therefore the promised elections for the National Assembly did not take place, and were definitively cancelled by President Mirza's imposition of martial law in 1958. Justified by the necessity to save the nation from political disintegration[21], the subsequent coup of Ayub Khan imposed a new Constitution that further exacerbated East-West tensions. This indeed recognised the concept of equity between the two wings, which damaged the representation of the Eastern wing. Moreover, it gave only limited powers to the provinces, thus subjugating them to the presidential executive located in West Pakistan. By favouring the introduction of military officers into the bureaucracy, the Ayub government reinforced the Western Pakistanis' dominance in the administration[22], thus worsening regional imbalances.

---

17 Talbot 2005, p. 1.
18 The issue was whether to adopt the proportional method for the formation of the National Assembly, which would have favoured the larger populated East Pakistan, or instead the concept of parity between the two wings of Pakistan to avoid the East becoming dominant. Sisson and Rose 1991, p. 10.
19 Jalal 1990, p. 298.
20 Jalal 1990, p. 196.
21 See for example Ayub Khan's speech given on 8th October 1958, quoted in Jones 2009, p. 77.
22 Rizvi 2004, p. 194.

Regional dissatisfaction and resentment were also strengthened by economic factors. If in 1947 East and West Pakistan were not characterised by critical differences in terms of development, after Independence resources were mainly directed towards the industrial development of West Pakistan. This took place even though East Pakistan had the larger reserves of foreign exchange and was the larger exporter of jute and tea. The East received only 20% of the entire developmental expenditure during the 1950–1951/1954–1955 period, and 36% during the 1965–1966/1969–1970 period, though it had 60% of the total population[23]. Therefore, while East Pakistan's industrial production grew only marginally until 1970, West Pakistan's tripled, producing growing income disparities[24]. As a result, not surprisingly, in the 1960s the East Pakistani population started to feel they were being treated as a colony by the West. These feelings of dissent in turn revolved around the East Pakistani identity, reinforcing the linguistic and cultural traditions.

Divergences were further sharpened during the 1965 war when the central government decided to interrupt the supervision of defence and economic matters of East Pakistan; thus enhancing its geographical isolation and vulnerability[25]. In this context, the demand for a more political and economic autonomy for the East was clearly formulated in the Six-Points Programme by the leader of the AL, Sheikh Mujibur Rahman, in February 1966[26]. This programme not only asked once again for the recognition of more autonomy to the province of East Pakistan, but also for its full fiscal independence, and for the creation of a separate militia or paramilitary force for the security of East Pakistan. The Pakistani government reacted by arresting the AL leader, and beginning a trial in 1968 against him and 35 other political figures, civil servants and army officers accused of having taken part in the "Agartala conspiracy", a plot to bring about the secession of East Pakistan with Indian help. Although there were some grounds for these accusations[27], no solid evidence was presented. When in 1969

---

23 Dixit 1999, p. 12; and Rahman 1968, p. 32–36.

24 As a consequence disparities in per capita income significantly grew (the disparity ratio passed from 21% in 1949–50 to 61% in 1969–1970), as well as the disparities in infrastructures such as power generation, transport facilities, health and educational services. Dixit 1999, p. 12.

25 Talbot 2005, p. 189.

26 For the text see Government Of India 1972, p. 23–33.

27 The name of the conspiracy came from the Indian city in the Tripura state where the accused were supposed to have met Indian army officers. The fact that Mujibur Rahman had had meetings with representatives of the Indian government since 1962

the government of Ayub Khan became highly contested both in East Pakistan and in West Pakistan, it was forced to free the Sheikh.

On that occasion Ayub Khan was also constrained to pass on his powers to another general of the same faction, Yahya Khan, who imposed martial rule again in order to maintain political control. Nevertheless, the new President Yahya Khan apparently seemed ready to recognize more autonomy to the East Pakistan province. He declared his intention to give proportional political representation to the two wings of Pakistan[28] and the first free elections of Pakistan were then fixed and held on December 1970. The AL won in East Pakistan, running a political campaign on the basis of the Six-Points Programme, while the Pakistan Peoples Party (PPP), a political party led by the previous member of the Ayub government, Zulfikar Ali Bhutto, emerged as the major party in the West. The AL won 160 of 162 seats available for the East Pakistani candidates, ensuring the control of the majority of seats in the National Assembly, while the PPP secured 81 seats, becoming the second party[29].

However, these results left Pakistan politically divided: on one hand, the day after the elections Bhutto declared that the PPP and the AL had to share the authority of the national government and that the AL could not lead alone; on the other hand, Mujibur Rahman claimed his right to lead a government in autonomy[30]. Therefore, the first free elections of Pakistan dramatically ended in a new political stalemate which left room for the military to intervene again on the political scene[31].

---

in different secret locations in India is widely recognised. See: *The Bangladesh News,* 23rd February 2011 (http://www.bdnews24.com/details.php?id=188118&cid=2), or *The Daily Star,* 12th June 2010 (http://www.thedailystar.net/newDesign/news-details. php?nid=142345), both retrieved on 6th August 2012). What remains unclear is whether the two parts were really acting with the same goal of the division of Pakistan in the Sixties, or if the Indians were just keeping alive their relations with the East Pakistani political exponents.

28 On 30th March 1970 Yahya promulgated the Legal Framework Order (LFO), giving 120 days to the Constituent Assembly to frame a new Constitution where 162 seats out of 300 (the majority) had to be given to the elected representative of East Pakistan. Choudhury 1975, p. 92–93.

29 Baxter 1971, p. 206.

30 Government Of India 1972, p. 132–133 and p. 137–142.

31 Although Sisson and Rose claimed that the electoral results surprised all the actors, leading President Yahya Kahn to be driven just by events, it is possible to argue that the army, as the principal actor controlling the political scene in Pakistan at that time, was aware of the probability of such a result and interested to then intervene to assume direct political control. Jalal 1990, p. 310–313.

President Yahya Khan seized the opportunity: he first postponed the National Assembly to 3rd March 1971[32], and, on 21st February, he decided to dismiss the civilian government he had named in 1969, to rule just with his personal military advisers, and to consider the option of making a display of power in East Pakistan[33]. Even though the Governor of East Pakistan had informed him of the risks of a further postponement of the National Assembly, the President then dismissed the Governor, and on 1st March 1971 announced the postponement *sine die* of the National Assembly, and a sharper imposition of martial law.

The reaction in the East was harsh: people started marching on the streets, protesting strongly. On 3rd March, the AL launched a non-violent non-cooperative movement, blocking all governmental and commercial activities, and resorting to violence on some occasions[34]. As a consequence, the central authority in East Pakistan collapsed, the Pakistan Army found it difficult to control the situation, and a civil war erupted. Yahya reacted by shifting the responsibilities again to the political parties, and fixing the date for the inaugural session of the National Assembly on 25th March. He then flew to Dhaka on 15th March officially to try to find a last agreement with Mujibur Rahman. Even if the negotiations apparently seemed to come close to defining an interim government, they not surprisingly failed when Bhutto, who had not been consulted right at the beginning[35], joined the discussions. Therefore, officially justified by the failure of the political negotiations, on 25th March 1971, after having left Dhaka with the West Pakistani politicians, President Yahya ordered the Army to launch a violent and repressive operation, *Operation Searchlight*. The aim was to bring East Pakistan back under control as had been successfully done in 1969 when Yahya Khan had replaced Ayub Khan and imposed martial rule on the country[36].

---

32 Privately meeting Bhutto several times, and repeatedly modifying his position over the Six-Points programme, Yahya gave the impression of preferring Bhutto, and thus increased the AL political distrust that led to the stalemate.

33 Talbot 2005, p. 206.

34 Bose 2005, p. 4464. Highlighting the complexity of the situation, Bose's recent work reinforces in part the official Pakistan position, sustained in the Government Of Pakistan 2007 (http://www.pppusa.org/Acrobat/Hamoodur%20Rahman%20Commission%20Report.pdf, retrieved on 5th May 2012).

35 President Yahya indeed invited Bhutto only on 16th March, when negotiations had already begun. Sisson and Rose 1991, p. 119.

36 Blair 1971, p. 2559.

A 24-hour curfew was therefore called, and the Army forces were got out of their barracks with the order to suppress by force the political demonstrations, to arrest Awami League members, students, and all those suspected of supporting the AL claims for more autonomy for East Pakistan. Violence was then indiscriminately used, and women and Hindus became the primary target of the Army repression[37], which has been often defined "genocidal"[38]. However, unlike in 1969, the military crackdown this time triggered the mutiny of the East Bengal regiment led by Major Ziaur-Rahman and a popular revolt that claimed the secession of East Pakistan[39]. Due to the opposition of the East Pakistani (Muslim and Hindu) population, it thus took the Pakistan Army almost six weeks to bring back all East Pakistani cities under control. The resort to a brutal suppression reportedly caused thousands of deaths among the East Pakistani people by December 1971, although the exact numbers are contested[40], and almost ten million refugees who largely found shelter in India[41]. Despite Mujibur Rahman being captured, the majority of AL members were in fact able to escape to India, together with the surviving nucleus of the East Pakistan Army that had opposed the military crackdown, and millions of Hindus who felt physically threatened by the violence. These events directly involved New Delhi, which offered hospitality to the secessionist forces and to the refugees, and affected the already tense Indo-Pakistani relations, thus leading to the third Indo-Pakistani war.

The international development of the East Pakistan crisis

The relations between India and Pakistan had been characterised by profound distrust and rivalry since the foundation of the two states. However, they were

---

37 For a selection of eye-witness accounts and newspaper reports see Government Of India 1972, p. 280–445. For a complete account from an East Pakistan point of view, see Zaheer 1994; Loshak 1971. For an account much closer to the official Pakistan view, see Bose 2005 and Bose 2011a.

38 See for example Moses 2011, p. 258–280. The term "genocide" however has been contested. See, for example, Bose 2011a, and Bose 2011b, p. 393–419.

39 In some cases killings of Urdu-speaking minorities also occurred, like those of the West-Pakistani and Bihari people (the non-Bengali Muslims who had moved from India to East Pakistan after partition). Bose 2005, p. 4464–4465.

40 For example, the Bangladeshi conventional view gives 3 million deaths, while more objective studies, such as Sisson and Rose's, estimates 500,000 deaths. Sisson and Rose 1991, p. 306.

41 Blechman and Kaplan 1978, p. 189. As noted before, the large majority of the refugees was Hindu.

spoiled completely by the developments that followed the launch of *Operation Searchlight* on 25th March.

India officially reacted to the launch of *Operation Searchlight* by assuming a neutral position and declaring the intention to "follow proper international norms"[42]. The Indian government thus defined the crisis as a "domestic affair" of Pakistan, though it also highlighted the violations of human rights[43]. However, New Delhi proved its empathy towards the East Pakistani people through the use of the term "East Bengal", rather than "East Pakistan", when referring to them in public, and officially offering them humanitarian help[44]. Hospitality was thus granted to the East Pakistani refugees, including the AL members escaping from Bangladesh. The latter were also enabled to establish their headquarters in Calcutta and to proclaim on 17th April the formation of the Government in exile of Bangladesh. Moreover, reflecting India's intentions to exploit the opportunity created by the military crackdown, from April New Delhi also organized and trained the *Mukti Bahini* on its own territory with the clear aim to sustain the East Pakistan secessionist forces, and thus to weaken Pakistan's power[45].

Following the consistent growth of the refugee influx, in May the situation began to challenge India's own security. According to the Indian Minister of Labour and Rehabilitation the refugees who fled to India numbered 3.43 million by 21st May, and 6.33 million by mid-June[46]. By the end of May, the Indian government decided not to rehabilitate the refugees on a permanent basis, but to establish 330 temporary camps close to the borders, where refugees were theoretically ready to go back to their homes as soon as possible[47]. Nevertheless, the influx of refugees soon became a serious concern for New Delhi at different levels: economically because of maintenance costs[48]; at the humanitarian level since several diseases

---

42 Gandhi 1975, p. 11.

43 *Times of India*, 31st March 1971.

44 See the speech by the Prime Minister on 27th March, the resolution of the Working Committee of the All India Congress of 29th March, and the resolution of the Lok Sabha on 31st March. Government Of India 1972, p. 669–672.

45 Literally meaning "Freedom Fighters", this name was generally used to describe the forces that were trained in unconventional ways by either Indian or Bangladesh Army officers, and that later directly contributed to the liberation of Bangladesh. Sisson and Rose 1991, p. 145.

46 Government Of India 1972, p. 446.

47 Government Of India 1972, p. 673.

48 Official statistics of the Indian Government showed 18.5 million Rupees as the daily maintenance cost: a sum of money significant for a country like India that had just reached a precarious situation of food self-reliance. Mukherji 1974, p. 341. The first

began to spread in the camps[49]; and at the social and political level since the concentration of so many refugees into specific areas created problems with the local population[50]. Moreover, in May the Pakistan Army regained firm control over East Pakistan, complicating the return of the refugees and hampering a rapid solution to the crisis. This complex situation led India to seriously consider the option to resort to a war to resolve matters.

As a consequence, the Indian government first tried to further increase the organization of the guerrilla forces, which were divided into several political rival factions, and to reinforce their military capabilities[51]. As a result, by the end of June 30,000 *Mukti Bahini* recruits were trained, and by September 59 training camps were organised by the Indian Army along the borders[52]. The activities of the guerrillas during June-August caused the communication system to collapse and East Pakistan's economy to come practically to a halt[53]. Second, India also increased its efforts to sensitize world opinion and the great powers

---

allocation of resources made in April-May in the national budget was for 600 million Rupees, but this was later increased by 2,000 million in August, when the refugees were about 8.2 million, and by 1,430 in December 1971 with supplementary budgets, reaching 5.5% of the total outlay (including planned and not planned expenditures) of the Union budget. Government Of India 1971/1972, p. 9 and p. 100 (http://indiabudget.nic.in/es1971-72/esmain.htm, retrieved on 16th October 2012).

49 The Indian government indicated that by 4th June there had been approximately 9,500 cases of cholera, with 1,250 deaths (Sisson and Rose 1991, p. 153), and by the end of September 46,000 reported cases, with 6,000 deaths (*The New York Times*, 30th September 1971).

50 By the end of May in the state of Tripura 900,000 people had indeed found refuge in the camps, compared with an indigenous population of only 1.5 million (*The New York Times*, 30th September 1971); in Assam communal tensions emerged (*Economic and Political Weekly*, 12th June 1971), and in West Bengal, the radical Indian communists and Naxalite insurgents began to establish direct links with the extremist communist groups of the East Pakistan forces, creating an explosive situation that led the state government to intervene with draconian measures (Frankel 2005, p. 458).

51 Lifschultz and Bird 1979, p. 21–30. India indeed tried, although unsuccessfully, to set up an institutional forum, called the War Council, where all the East Pakistan secessionist forces could be represented. On this see: "RAW note on the situation of the Bangladesh Army dated 5th July 1971", and "Letter from Principal Secretary of Prime Minister, P. N. Haksar, to Prime Minister on 5th May 1971", in Haksar papers, III inst., f. n. 227. On the military strategy see: "Note for the Chief in Command about the Bangladesh forces undated", in Haksar papers, III inst., f. n. 227.

52 Sisson and Rose 1991, p. 84–85.

53 Banerjee 1971, pp. 818–819.

over the growing challenge the refugees were posing to India's security. This gave positive results, bringing the total international aid to India to $160 million by 30th June[54], while resulting in the Pakistan Aid Consortium and all the Western countries suspending their assistance programmes to Pakistan. Finally, India approached the Soviet Union on 7th and 8th June 1971 proposing the signing of a bilateral treaty with Moscow, which strengthened political and economic ties between the two countries, and (more importantly for New Delhi) protected India with Soviet military help in case of a Chinese intervention in an Indo-Pakistani conflict[55]. The Soviets, who since 1969 had been interested in a bilateral treaty with New Delhi, did not hesitate and when consulted immediately communicated their availability to sign such a treaty[56].

During the summer the situation did not improve, further convincing India of the necessity to resort to a war on Pakistan. Despite Islamabad's formulation of a conciliatory political strategy to repatriate the East Pakistani refugees, the refugees in India grew, becoming 7 million by the end of July[57]. This, added to the Soviet declared availability to sign a treaty, led both the Indian Defence Minister, Jagjivan Ram, and the Foreign Minister, Swaran Singh, to release aggressive statements from late June, as they had never done before, which openly considered resorting to an open war as the only solution to the East Pakistan crisis[58].

When in July Pakistan invoked UN intervention in East Pakistan[59], it received the support of the UN General Secretary who in late July also showed his intention to bring the issue to the Security Council[60]. This fact directly threatened India's plans. UN intervention would have been indeed an obstacle for the military actions of the Indian Army and of the *Mukthi Bahini* in the case of a military conflict against Pakistan. Therefore, the support of the Soviets also became crucial for New Delhi, in order to prevent the Security Council from approving UN inter-

---

54 Zaheer 1994, p. 263.
55 "Record of conversation between Foreign Minister and Mr. A. A. Gromyko, Minister of Foreign Affairs, U.S.S.R. on 7th June, 1971", p. 5–6, in Haksar papers, III inst., f. n. 203.
56 "Record of conversation between Foreign Minister and Mr. A. A. Gromyko, Minister of Foreign Affairs, U.S.S.R. on 7th June, 1971", p. 6, in Haksar papers, III inst., f. n. 203.
57 Government Of India 1972, p. 446.
58 Government Of India 1972, p. 688. This came along with the reportedly regular movement of Indian Army units along the border (*National Herald*, 21st June 1971; and *The Hindu*, 26th June 1971).
59 Jackson 1975, p. 50.
60 "Secretary-General's Memorandum to the President of the Security Council, dated 20th July 1971" in Government Of India 1972, p. 658–669.

vention in East Pakistan. Finally, the development of the Sino-American normali-
sation process[61] also pushed India to accelerate the finalisation of the Indo-Soviet
treaty. On 15th July 1971 China and the United States announced that the secret
visit made a few days before to Beijing by Nixon's advisor, Henry Kissinger, had,
thanks to the mediation of Pakistan, successfully paved the way for the establishment of direct relations between the two states, and for Nixon's visit to China by
the spring of 1972[62]. This news led India to suddenly comprehend the rationale
of the Nixon administration's support for Pakistan that had been evident since
March even in relation to the East Pakistan crisis[63]. New Delhi began to fear that
the new alignment between Washington, Islamabad, and Beijing could prevent a
military solution of the East Pakistan crisis[64].

Therefore, on 9th August India, exploiting Cold War dynamics in its favour,
signed the *Treaty of Friendship and Cooperation* with the Soviet Union: the
agreement strengthened economic, technological, and cultural cooperation, and
assured India of Soviet support in case of an attack (or a threat of attack) from a
third country[65]. This diplomatic step gave India a free hand to deal with the East
Pakistan crisis: it allowed India to rely on the support of the Soviets both at the
UN Security Council to avoid UN intervention, and at the military level in case
of an escalation of the Indo-Pakistani war. Thus, when the last hope of finding a
political solution acceptable to the East Pakistan forces with the Pakistani President went by the board in August[66], New Delhi decided to prepare its military
forces for the conflict. At the end of November New Delhi authorised its troops
to cross the borders of East Pakistan[67], purposely provoking Pakistan to launch
an air strike on 3rd December, after which open war was declared.

Although during the conflict India clearly demonstrated its complete military
superiority on the Eastern front and resisted the Pakistani attacks in the Western
sector, international tensions grew when the United States took the decision to

---

61 Since 1969 Washington and Beijing had communicated through the Pakistan dip-
    lomatic channel in order to find a way to normalise their relations. Chen 2001,
    p. 238–276.
62 Dallek 2007, p. 299.
63 Warner 2005, p. 1097–1118.
64 On this see the following unpublished documents: "Letter of T. N. Kaul to Prime
    Minister on 3rd August 1971" in Haksar papers, I&II inst., f. n. 49; and "Letter of P. N.
    Haksar to Prime Minister dated 8th August 1971", in Haksar papers, III inst. f. n. 170.
65 The entire text of the Treaty can be found in Jackson 1975, p. 188–191
66 Sisson and Rose 1991, p. 194.
67 Jackson 1975, p. 102.

send a task force equipped with a nuclear aircraft carrier to the Bay of Bengal[68]. The aim was to demonstrate American power and to symbolically reassure their Pakistan ally of the fact that the United States would not allow India to continue the war in West Pakistan. The American act fortunately triggered only some Soviet aggressive statements and gestures[69]. On 17th December, the day after the surrender of the Eastern Pakistan Commander, New Delhi declared a unilateral ceasefire also for the Western front, thus definitively ending the war and all risks of an international escalation.

Pakistan was amputated, and a new state, Bangladesh, led by those secession-ist forces that India supported in their fight, emerged out of the ashes of East Pakistan. As the war was officially ended, in a few months most of the refugees who had escaped to India spontaneously returned to their homes in the new state of Bangladesh[70].

Conclusion

Considering the origins that brought about the third Indo-Pakistani war, this paper shows how the 1971 war was caused by Pakistani domestic political prob-lems. Territorial factors, and socio-political imbalances inherited from the colo-nial period had favoured the emergence of several competing regional identities in Pakistan. Failing to accommodate these imbalances and to democratically recognise the East Pakistan claims for decentralisation, the Pakistani govern-ments pointedly paved the way for the explosion of the political situation. By resorting to a brutal repression of the democratically-based demands, in 1971 they thus directly triggered the eruption of a civil war in East Pakistan, which led millions of East Pakistani refugees (largely Hindu) to escape to India. New Delhi not only hosted the refugees, but it also militarily supported the East Pakistan secessionist forces, and in the autumn, in order to favour the secession of East Pakistan and to solve the refugees' issue, resorted to war against Pakistan. As a result, these events reveal how regional identities, when repeatedly repressed and negated by authoritarian central state authorities, can lead to atrocious and

---

68 Warner 2005, p. 1114. The UK instead maintained a neutral position during the con-flict. On this see Smith 2010, p. 451–470.

69 The Soviet Ambassador in India, N. M. Pegov, on 13th December reassured India that they "will not allow the seventh fleet to intervene", in *Daily Telegraph*, 10th January 1972. Moreover, the Soviet Union reinforced its naval presence in the Indian Ocean sending a special task force there. Walter 1979, p. 293–306.

70 Datta 2011, p. 70.

intolerable bloodshed; and how they can also significantly influence regional and international relations, at the risk of provoking conflicts and even confrontation among great powers.

Bibliographie

Adarkar (Bhalchandra Pundlik) 1939, *The Indian Fiscal Policy*, Allahabad, Kitabistan Publishers.

Ahmad (Aziz) 1967, *Islamic Modernism in India and Pakistan: 1857–1964*, Karachi, Oxford University Press.

Ahmad (Jamiluddin) [ed.] 1947, *Speeches and Writings of Mr Jinnah*, Lahore, Sh. Muhammad Ashraf.

Ahmad (Rafiuddin) 1981, *The Bengal Muslims 1871 to 1906: A Quest for Identity*, Delhi, Oxford University Press.

Ahmed (Ishtiaq) 1998, *State, Nation and Ethnicity in Contemporary South Asia*, London, Pinter.

Ahmed (Rafiuddin) 1996, *The Bengal Muslims: A Quest for Identity*, New Delhi, Oxford University Press.

Ahsan (Syed Badrul) 2014, *Sheikh Mujibur Rehman. From Rebel to Founding Father*, New Delhi, Niyogi Books.

Akita (Shigeru) [ed.] 2000, *South Asia in the 20th Century International Relations*, Tokyo, Institute of Oriental Culture of the University of Tokyo.

Anderson (Benedict) 1991, *Imagined Communities: Reflections on the Origins and Spread of Nationalism*, London, Verso (First Edition 1983).

Anderson (Perry) 1996, "Science, Politics, Enchantment", in Hall (John A.) and Jarvie (Ian) [eds.] 1996, *The Social Philosophy of Ernest Gellner* (Poznan Studies in the Philosophy of the Sciences and the Humanities 48), Amsterdam-Atlanta, Rodopi.

Anderson (Perry) 2012, *The Indian Ideology. Three Essays Collective*, Gurgaon.

Anstey (Vera) 1957, *The Economic Development of India*, London, Longmans, Green and Co. (4th edition 1951 reprint).

Ashton (Stephen Richard) 1982, *British Policy towards the Indian States (1905–1939)*, Londres, Curzon Press.

Assayag (Jackie) 2001, *L'Inde. Désir de nation*, Paris, Odile Jacob.

Azad (Abul Kalam) 1988, *India Wins Freedom*, Hyderabad, Orient Longman Press.

Aziz (Khursheed Kamal) 1967, *The Making of Pakistan: A Study in Nationalism*, London, Chatto & Windus.

Aziz (Khursheed Kamal) 1987, *A History of the Idea of Pakistan*, Lahore, Vanguard.

Aziz (Mazhar) 2008, *Military Control in Pakistan: The Parallel State*, New York, Routledge.

Bagchi (Amiya Kumar) 1972, *Private Investment in India, 1900–1939*, Cambridge.

Bagchi (Amiya Kumar) [ed.] 2002, *Money and Credit in Indian History: From Early Medieval Times*, New Delhi, Tulika.

Baker (Herbert) 1912, "The New Delhi – Eastern and Western Architecture – A Problem of Style", *The Times*, Oct. 3, p. 7–8.

Balachandran (Gopalan) 1996, *John Bullion's Empire: Britain's Gold Problem and India Between the Wars*, London, Curzon.

Bandyopadhyay (Sekhar) 2004, *From Plassey to Partition: A History of Modern India*, New Delhi, Orient Blackswan.

Bandyopadhyay (Sekhar) 2009, *Decolonization in South Asia: Meanings of Freedom in Post-Independence Bengal, 1947–52*, New Delhi, Orient Blackswan.

Banerjea (Surendranath) 1925, *A Nation in the Making: Being the Reminiscences of Fifty Years of Public Life*, London, Oxford University Press.

Banerjee (Sumanta) 1971, "Next Phase of the War", *Economic and Political Weekly* 6/16, p. 818–819.

Bannerji (A. K.) 1962, *India's Balance of Payments*, Bombay, Asia Publishing House.

Barthélémy-Saint-Hilaire (Jules) 1887, *L'Inde anglaise, son état actuel, son avenir : précédé d'une introduction sur l'Angleterre et la Russie*, Paris, Librairie Académique Didier, Perrin et Cie.

Basin (Sreedhara) 2009, "Matka Chowk. Sukhna Joyride", *The Tribune*, Dec. 6, Chandigarh.

Bass (Gary) 2013, *The Blood Telegram: Nixon, Kissinger and a Forgotten Genocide*, New York, Alfred Knopf.

Batabyal (Rakesh) 2005, *Communalism in Bengal: From Famine to Noakhali, 1943–1947*, New Delhi, Sage.

Bates (Crispin) 2002, *Subalterns and Raj: South Asia since 1600*, Abingdon.

Baxter (Craig) 1971, "Pakistan Votes – 1970", *Asian Survey* 11/3, p. 197–218.

Baxter (Craig) and Rahman (Syedur) 1996, *Historical Dictionary of Bangladesh*, Lanham, Md. & Londres, Scarecrow Press.

Bayart (Jean-François) 2010, *Les études postcoloniales : un carnaval académique*, Paris, Karthala.

Bayly (Christopher) 1998, "The Pre-history of 'Communalism/Religious Conflict in India 1750–1820", in Bayly (Christopher) 1998, *Origins of Nationality in South Asia. Patriotism and Ethical Government in the Making of Modern India*, Delhi, Oxford University Press, p. 210–237.

Bechert (H.) 1991, *The Dating of the Historical Buddha*, Part 1 (Symposien zur Buddhismusforschung, IV,1), Göttingen, Vandenhoeck und Ruprecht.

Bhagavan (Manu) 2003, *Sovereign Spheres: Princes, Education and Empire in Colonial India*, New Delhi, Oxford University Press.

Bhagwati (Jagdish) and Desai (Padma) 1970, *India Planning for Industrialisation*, Oxford, Oxford University Press.

Birla (Ghanshyam Das) 1944, *Indian Currency in Retrospect*, Allahabad, Kitabistan.

Blair (Harry W.) 1971, "Sheikh Mujib and Deja Vu in East Bengal: The Tragedies of March 25", *Economic and Political Weekly*, 6/52, p. 2555–2562.

Blechman (Barry M.) and Kaplan (Stephen S.) 1978, *Force Without War: U. S. Armed Forces As a Political Instrument*, Washington D. C., Brookings Inst Press.

Blyn (George) 1966, *Agricultural Trends in India, 1891–1947: Output, Availability, and Productivity*, Philadelphia, University of Pennsylvania Press.

Boesiger (Willy) et Girsberger (Hans) 1967, *Le Corbusier 1910–1965*, Zürich, Architecture / Verlag für Architektur Artemis.

Bongard-Levin (G. M.) et Grantovskij (E. A.) 1981, *De la Scythie à l'Inde. Énigmes de l'histoire des anciens Aryens*, trad. Ph. Gignoux, Paris, Institut d'études iraniennes de l'université de la Sorbonne Nouvelle.

Bose (Nirmal Kumar) and Sinha (Surajit) 1969, *Problems of Indian Nationalism*, Delhi, Allied Publishers.

Bose (Sarmila) 2005, "Anatomy of Violence: Analysis of Civil War in East Pakistan in 1971", *Economic and Political Weekly* 40/41, p. 4463–4471.

Bose (Sarmila) 2011a, *Dead Reckoning: Memories of the 1971 Bangladesh War*, Hachette India, New Delhi.

Bose (Sarmila) 2011b, "The Question of Genocide and the Quest for Justice in the 1971 War", *Journal of Genocide Research* 13/4, p. 393–419.

Bose (Sisir Kumar) and Bose (Sugata) [eds] 1997a, *The Essential Writings of Netaji Subhas Chandra Bose*, Delhi, Oxford University Press.

Bose (Sisir Kumar) and Bose (Sugata) [eds] 1997b, *The Indian Struggle 1920–1942. Subhas Chandra Bose*, Delhi, Oxford University Press.

Bose (Sugata) 2003, "Post-Colonial Histories of South Asia: Some Reflections", *Journal of Contemporary History* 38/1, p. 133–146.

Bose (Sugata) 2011, *His Majesty's Opponent: Subhas Chandra Bose and India's Struggle against Empire*, Cambridge (Mass.), Belknap Press of Harvard University Press.

Brass (Paul R.) 1990, "A Reply to Francis Robinson", in Jeffrey (Robin) et al [ed.] 1990, *India: Rebellion to Republic: Selected Writings, 1857–1990*, New Delhi, Sterling Publishers.

Brasted (Howard) and Bridge (Carl) 1994, "Reappraisals. The Transfer of Power in South Asia: An Historiographical Review", *South Asia* 17/1, p. 93–114.

British Parliamentary Debates 1912–1913, *The Parliamentary Debates*. 5th series, vol. 41.

Broomfield (J.H.) 1968, "The Forgotten Majority: The Bengal Muslims and September 1918", in Low (Donald A.) 1968, *Soundings in Modern South Asian History*, Berkeley, University of California Press, p. 196–220.

Broomfield (J.H.) 1968b, *Elite Conflict in a Plural Society: Twentieth-Century Bengal*, University of California Press, Berkeley & Los Angeles.

Brown (Mackenzie) 1970, *The Nationalist Movement. Indian Political Thought from Ranade to Bhave*, Berkeley and Los Angeles, University of California Press (First Edition 1961).

Buddhadasa 1987, *Bouddhisme et socialismes*, Paris, Les Deux Océans.

Çelik (Zeynep) 1999, "Schnittstelle der Kultur: Eine Neue Sicht auf Architektur und Stadt im 20. Jahrhunder", in Ferguson (Russell) [ed.] 1999, *Am Ende des Jahrhunderts: 100 Jahre Gebaute Visionen*, Osfildern-Ruit, Hatje Cantz Verlag, p. 190–227.

Chakrabarty (Dipesh) 2000, *Provincializing Europe: Postcolonial Thought and Historical Difference*, Princeton, Princeton University Press.

Chakrabarty (Prafulla K.) 1990, *The Marginal Men: the refugee and the Left political syndrome in West Bengal*, Kalyani (WB), Lumière Books.

Chand (Tara) 1961–1970, *History of the Freedom Movement in India*, vol. I–IV, New Delhi, Ministry of Information and Broadcasting.

Chand (Tara) 1990, *History of the Freedom Movement*, vol. 4, New Delhi, Ministry of Information and Broadcasting.

Chandra (Bipan) 1966, *Rise and Growth of Economic Nationalism in India: Economic Policies of indian National Leadership 1880–1905*, New Delhi.

Chandra (Bipan) 1979 (1981), *Nationalism and Colonialism in Modern India*, Delhi (New Delhi, Orient Blackswan).

Chandra (Bipan) [ed.] 1983, *The Indian Left: Critical Appraisals*, New Delhi, Vikas.

Chandra (Bipan) 1984, *Communalism in Modern India*, New Delhi, Vikas Publishing House.

Chandra (Bipan) 2009, *History of Modern India*, New Delhi, Orient Blackswan.

Chandra (Bipan) 2012, *Writings of Bipan Chandra, The Making of Modern India: From Marx to Gandhi*, New Delhi, Orient Blackswan.

Chandra (Bipan), Mukherjee (Mridula), Mahajan (Sucheta), Mukherjee (Aditya), Panikkar (K.N.) 1988, *India's Struggle for Independence*, New Delhi, Penguin.

Chandra (Bipan), Mukherjee (Mridula) and Mukherjee (Aditya) 2000 (2008), *India After Independence-1947-2000*, New Delhi, Penguin India (revised and enlarged edition called *India Since Independence*, New Delhi, Penguin India, 2008).

Chatterjee (Basudev) 1992, *Trade, Tariffs and Empire: Lancashire and British Policy in India 1919–1939*, New Delhi, Oxford University Press.

Chatterjee (Basudev) 1999, *Towards Freedom: Documents on the Movement for Independence in India*, 1938, 3 Parts, New Delhi, ICHR and Oxford University Press.

Chatterji (Joya) 2007, *The Spoils of Partition: Bengal and India 1947–1967*, Cambridge, Cambridge University Press.

Chattopadhaya (Rudrapratap) 2002, *Insurgency of Titu Meer. A brief history of Wahabi Movement down to the death of Sayyid Ahmad Barelvi and Titu Meer*, Kolkata, Readers Service.

Chaudhuri (Nirad C.) 1990, *Thy Hand Great Anarch: India 1921–1952*, London, The Hogarth Press.

Chen (Jian) 2001, *Mao's China and the Cold War*, Chapell Hill and London, University of North Carolina Press.

Chopra (P.N.) 2001, "Wahabi Movement", in Majumdar (Ramesh Chandra) 2001, *The History and Culture of Indian People*, Mumbai, Bharatiya Vidya Bhavan.

Choudhury (Golam Wahed) 1975, *India, Pakistan, Bangladesh, and the Major Powers: Politics of a Divided Subcontinent*, New Delhi, Free Press.

Cohen (Jean-Louis) et Burton (Tim) 2008, *Le Corbusier le Grand*, London, Phaidon.

Cohen (Stephen) 2004, *The Idea of Pakistan*, Washington, Brookings Institution Press.

Collins (Larry) and Lapierre (Dominique) 2007, *Freedom at Midnight*, New Delhi, Vikas.

Colum (Padraic) 1959, *Arthur Griffith*, Dublin: Browne & Nolan Ltd.

Copland (Ian) 1997, *The Princes of India in the Endgame of Empire, 1917–1947*, Cambridge, Cambridge University Press.

Copland (Ian) 2005, *State, Community and Neighbourhood in Princely North India c. 1900–1950*, Basingstoke, Palgrave Macmillan.

Curl (James Stevens) 1991, *The Art and Architecture of Freemasonry: An Introductory Study*, London, B.T. Batsford Ltd.

Dallek (Robert) 2007, *Nixon and Kissinger: Partners in Power*, New York, Harper Collins.

Das (Durga) [ed.] 1971–1974, *Sardar Patel's Correspondence*, Navjivan Publishing House, vol. 1–10.

Das (Suranjan) 1993, *Communal Riots in Bengal: 1905–1947*, Delhi, Oxford University Press.

Dastidar (Sachi G.) 2008, *Empire's Last Casualty*, Kolkata, Firma KLM, 2008.

Datta (Antara) 2011, "The Repatriation of 1973 and the Re-making of Modern South Asia", *Contemporary South Asia* 19/1, p. 61–74.

Datta (Pradeep Kumar) 1999, *Carving Blocs: Communal Ideology in Early Twentieth Century Bengal*, New Delhi, Oxford University Press.

Davis (Richard P.) 1959, "Griffith and Gandhi: A Study in Non-Violent Resistance", *Threshold* 3/2, p. 29–44.

Davis (Richard P.) 1974, *Arthur Griffith and Non-Violent Sinn Féin*, Dublin, Anvil Books.

Davis (Richard P.) 1976, *Arthur Griffith*, Dundalk, Dundalgan Press for the Irish Historical Association.

De (Amalendu) 1980, "Formation of Communist Party in Faridpur: A Case study of Communist Movement in a Bengal district", in Panikkar (K. N.) [ed.] 1980, *National and Left Movements in India*, Delhi, Vikas, p. 266–295.

De (Amalendu) 1982, *Islam in Modern India*, Calcutta, Maya Prakashan.

De (Amalendu) 1994, *The Social Thoughts and Consciousness of the Bengali Muslims in the Colonial Period*, Presidential Address at the *Indian History Congress*.

Delisle (Laure) 1891, *Choix de lettres d'Eugène Burnouf, 1825–1852, suivi d'une bibliographie*, Paris, H. Champion.

Dewey (Clive) 1978, "The End of Imperialism of Free Trade: The Eclipse of the Lancashire Lobby and the Commission of Fiscal Autonomy to India", in Dewey and Hopkins 1978.

Dewey (Clive) 1979, "The Government of India's New Industrial Policy 1900–1925", in Dewey and Chaudhuri 1979.

Dewey (Clive) and Hopkins (A. G.) [ed.] 1978, *Imperial Impact: Studies in the Economic History of Africa and India*, London, Athlone Press.

Dewey (Clive) and Chaudhuri (K. N.) [ed.] 1979, *Economy and Society, Essays in Indian Economic and Social History*, New Delhi, Oxford University Press.

Di Costanzo (Thierry) 2004, « L'Inde que Friedrich Maximilian Müller (1823–1900) voudrait nous montrer », Marc Cluet (sous la dir.), *La Fascination de l'Inde en Allemagne 1800–1933*, Rennes, PUR, p. 91–102.

Di Costanzo (Thierry) 2011a, « Essai de Définition du concept de Pakistan dans la presse anglo-musulmane selon le modèle de dominion et selon le modèle irlandais, 1932–1947 », in *Cultures of the Commonwealth: Essays and Studies*, Horizons n° 17, janvier.

Di Costanzo (Thierry) 2011b, « Vers une autre lecture de l'espace sud-asiatique : décolonisation et revendication d'un espace national, le cas de l'Inde colonisée », in *Les Cahiers du GEPE*, n° 3, Hors champ 2011, (http://www.cahiersdu gepe.fr/index.php?id=2011).

Di Costanzo (Thierry) 2011c, *L'idée séparatiste dans la presse anglo-musulmane du Bengale*, Francfort, Peter Lang.

Di Costanzo (Thierry) 2012, "Use and Re-Use of 'Pakistan' in the Indian Muslim Press (1932–1947)", in Hegewald (Julia A.B.) and Mitra (Subrata Kumar) [ed.] 2012, *Re-Use: the Art and Politics of Integration and Anxiety*, Delhi, Sage.

Dimock Jr. (E.C.) 1972, "Hinduism and Islam in Medieval Bengal", in Baumer (Rachel Van M.) 1972, *Aspects of Bengali History and Society*, Honolulu, University Press of Hawaii, p. 1–12.

Directorate of the Chamber's Special Organization 1929, *The British Crown and the Indian States, an outline sketch drawn up on behalf of the Standing Committee of the Chamber of Princes*, Londres, P.S. King and Son.

Dixit (J. N.) 1999, *Liberation and Beyond: Indo-Bangladesh Relations*, New Delhi, Konark Publishers.

Drew (Jane B.) 1977, "Le Corbusier, as I knew him", in Walden (Russell) 1977, *The Open Hand. Essays on Le Corbusier*, Cambridge (Mass.) / London, MIT Press, p. 364–373.

Droit (Roger-Pol) 2004, *L'oubli de l'Inde. Une amnésie philosophique*, Paris, Seuil (1ère éd. PUF 1989).

Drummond (I. M.) 1972, *British Economic Policy and the Empire, 1919–1939*, London, Allen and Unwin.

Duara (Prasenjit) 2004, *Decolonization: perspectives from Now and Then*, Londres, Routledge.

Ducœur (Guillaume) 2009, « Comparatisme orienté et étymologie comparée chez Max Müller : l'équation Bráhman = Verbum », *Revue de l'histoire des religions*, Tome 226, fasc. 2, p. 3–20.

Ducœur (Guillaume) 2013, « Max Müller (1823–1900), de l'édition textuelle du ☐g veda à l'histoire comparée des religions », *Source(s), Cahiers de l'équipe de recherche Arts, Civilisation et Histoire de l'Europe*, Université de Strasbourg, n°2, 2013, p. 81–104.

Dusche (Michael) 2010, *Identity Politics in India and Europe*, Delhi, Sage.

Eaton (Richard) 1993, *The Rise of Islam and the Bengal Frontier*, Berkeley, University of California Press.

Elliot (Henry Miers) 1871, *The History of India, as Told by Its Own Historians. The Muhammadan Period*, ed. by John Dowson, vol. III, London, Trübner and Co.

Elster (Jon) 1989, *Nuts and Bolts for the Social Sciences*, Cambridge, Cambridge University Press.

Ernst (Waltraud) and Pati (Biswamoy) [eds.] 2007, *India's Princely States: People, Princes and Colonialism*, Londres, Routledge.

Evenson (Norma) 1966, *Chandigarh*, Berkeley, University of California Press.

Ferguson (Niall) 2003, *Empire: How Britain Made the Modern World*, London, Allen Lane.

Ferm (Virgilius) 1937, *Religion in Transition*, New York, Macmillan and London, Allen and Unwin.

Feuerstein (Georges), Kak (Subhash) et Frawley (David) 1995, *In Search of the Cradle of Civilization: New Light of Ancien India*, USA (First Indian Edition: Delhi, Motilal Banarsidass Publishers, 1999)

Fischer (Klaus), Jansen (Michael) und Pieper (Jan) 1987, *Architektur des indischen Subkontinents*, Darmstadt, Wissenschaftliche Buchgesellschaft.

Foucher (Alfred) 1922, *L'art gréco-bouddhique du Gandhâra, étude sur les origines de l'influence classique dans l'art bouddhique de l'Inde et de l'Extrême-Orient*, Tome II, second fascicule : L'histoire – conclusions, Paris, E. Leroux.

François (Stéphane) 2011, « La Nouvelle Droite et les Indo-Européens, une anthropologie d'extrême droite », *Terrain, Revue d'ethnologie de l'Europe* 56, p. 136–151.

Frankel (Francine R.) 2005, *India's Political Economy, 1947–2004: The Gradual Revolution*, Oxford, Oxford University Press.

Fry (Edwin Maxwell) 1977, "Le Corbusier in Chandigarh", in Walden (Russell) 1977, *The Open Hand. Essays on Le Corbusier*, Cambridge (Mass.) / London, MIT Press, p. 350–363.

Fussman (Gérard) 2003, « Entre fantasmes, science et politique. L'entrée des Āryas en Inde », *Annales. Histoire, sciences sociales*, 4, 58ᵉ année, éd. EHESS, p. 781–813 (= Fussman (Gérard), Kellens (Jean), Francfort (Henri-Paul), Tremblay (Xavier) 2005, *Āryas, Aryens et Iraniens en Asie Centrale*, Paris, Collège de France).

Gallacher (John), Johnson (Gordon) and Seal (Anil) 1973, "Locality, Province and Nation: Essays on Indian Politics 1870 to 1940", *Modern Asian Studies*, Cambridge.

Gandhi (Indira) 1975, *India: The Speeches and Reminiscences of Indira Gandhi*, New Delhi, Rupa & Co.

Gandhi (Mohandas K.) 1958, *The Collected Works of Mahatma Gandhi*, Delhi, Ministry of Information and Broadcasting, Government of India.

Gast (Klaus-Peter) 2000. *Le Corbusier: Paris-Chandigarh*, Basel / Boston, Birkhäuser Verlag AG.

Geetha (V.) [ed.] 2004, *Soul Force : Gandhi's Writings on Peace*, Chennai, Tara Publishing Ltd.

Gellner (Ernest) 1992a, *Reason and Culture: The Historic Role of Rationality and Rationalism*, Oxford, Basil Blackwell, (First Edition 1983).

Gellner (Ernest) 1992b, *Postmodernism, Reason and Religion*, London, Routledge.

Gellner (Ernest) 1996, "Reply to Critics", in Hall (John A.) and Jarvie (Ian) [eds.] 1996, *The Social Philosophy of Ernest Gellner* (Poznan Studies in the Philosophy of the Sciences and the Humanities 48), Amsterdam-Atlanta, Rodopi.

Gellner (Ernest) 2006, *Nations and Nationalism*, Oxford, Basil Blackwell (First Edition 1983).

Gilmartin (David) 1988, *Empire and Islam: Punjab and the Making of Pakistan*, Berkeley: University of California Press.

Gleig (George Robert) 1841, *Memoirs of the life of the Right Honourable Warren Hastings*, London, Robert Bentley.

Goldsmith (Raymond W.) 1983, *The Financial Development of India: 1860-1977*, New Haven, Yale University Press.

Goody (Jack) 1979, *La raison graphique, la domestication de la pensée sauvage*, Paris, Les éditions de Minuit.

Goody (Jack) 2007, *Pouvoirs et savoirs de l'écrit*, Paris, La Dispute.

Gopal (Sarvepalli) [ed.] 1984, *Selected Works of Jawaharlal Nehru*, second series, vol. 1, New Delhi.

Gordon (A. D. D.) 1978, *Businessmen and Politics: Rising Nationalism and a Modernising Economy in Bombay, 1918-1933*, New Delhi, Manohar.

Gottlob (Michael) [ed.] 2003, *Historical thinking in South Asia: A handbook of sources from colonial times to the present*, Oxford & New Delhi, Oxford University Press.

Government of India 1971-1972, "Economic Survey 1971/1972", Ministry of Finance. (http://indiabudget.nic.in/es1971-72/esmain.htm).

Government of India 1972, *Bangladesh Documents*, New Delhi, Ministry of Information and Broadcasting.

Government of Pakistan 2007, *Hamoodur Rahman Commission of Inquiry Into the 1971 India-Pakistan War, Supplementary Report*, Arc Manor LLC (http://www.pppusa.org/Acrobat/Hamoodur%20Rahman%20Commission%20Report.pdf).

Greenough (Paul) 1982, *Prosperity and Misery in Modern Bengal: The Famine of 1943-1944*, New York, Oxford University Press.

Griffith (Arthur) 1904, *The Resurrection of Hungary : A Parallel for Ireland*, Dublin, James Duffy and Co.

Griffith (Arthur) 1905, *The Sinn Féin Policy*, Dublin, Fowler Printer.

Guha (Ramachandra) 2003, *History and the Limit of World History*, Columbia-Princeton, University Press of California.

Guha (Ramachandra) 2007, *India after Gandhi: the History of the World's Largest Democracy*, Londres, Macmillan.

Guha (Ramachandra) 2011, *Makers of Modern India*, Harvard, Belknap.

Gupta (Partha Sarathi) 1997, *Towards Freedom: Documents on the Movement for Independence in India*, 1943-1944, 3 Parts, New Delhi, ICHR and Oxford University Press.

Habib (Irfan) 1995, *Essays in Indian History: Towards a Marxist Perception*, New Delhi.

Haksar (P. N.), private papers, III inst., f. n. 203, 227 and 170; and I&II inst., f. n. 49, unpublished documents collected at the Archives of the Nehru Museum and Memorial Library (NMML), New Delhi, India.

Hardy (Peter) 1972, *The Muslims of British India*, Cambridge, Cambridge University Press.

Hasan (Mushirul) [ed.] 1993, *India's Partition: Process, Strategy and Mobilisation*, New Delhi, Oxford University Press.

Hegewald (Julia A. B.) 2012a, "Towards a Theory of Re-use: Ruin, Retro and Fake Versus Improvement, Innovation and Integration", in Hegewald (Julia A. B.) and Mitra (Subrata Kumar) [eds] 2012, *Re-use: The Art and Politics of Integration and Anxiety*, New Delhi, Sage, p. 30-54.

Hegewald (Julia A. B.) 2012b, "Building Citizenship: The Agency of Public Buildings and Urban Planning in the Making of the Indian Citizen", in Mitra (Subrata Kumar) [ed.] 2012, *Citizenship and the Flow of Ideas in the Era of Globalization: Structure, Agency, and Power*, Heidelberg Series in South Asian and Comparative Studies, vol. 4, New Delhi, Samskriti, p. 291-337.

Hegewald (Julia A. B.) and Mitra (Subrata Kumar) [eds] 2012, *Re-use: The Art and Politics of Integration and Anxiety*, New Delhi, Sage.

Henry (Robert Mitchell) 1920, *The Evolution of Sinn Féin*, Dublin, The Talbot Press.

Hobsbawm (E. J.) 1969, *Industry and Empire*, Harmondsworth, Penguin.

Hobsbawn (Eric) 1983, "Introduction: Inventing Traditions", in Hobsbawn (Eric) and Ranger (Terence) [eds.] 1983, *The Invention of Tradition*, Cambridge, Cambridge University Press.

Hobson (Bulmer) 1905, *The Manifesto of the Dungannon Clubs*, Belfast, Dungannon Clubs Publication.

Holland (R. F.) 1985, *European Decolonization, 1918–1981: An Introductory Survey*, New York, St. Martin's Press.

Holmes (Michael) and Holmes (Denis) [eds] 1997, *Ireland and India: Connections, Comparisons, Contrasts*, Dublin, Folens.

Iggers (Georg) and Wang (Edward) 2008, *A Global History of Modern Historiography*, Harlow, Pearson Education.

Ikegame (Aya) 2012, *Princely India Re-Imagined: a Historical Anthropology of Mysore from 1799 to the Present*, Oxford, Routledge.

Ikramullah (Shaista) 1991, *Huseyn Shaheed Suhrawardy*, Karachi, Oxford University Press.

Irving (Robert Grant) 1981, *Indian Summer: Lutyens, Baker and Imperial Delhi*, New Haven, Yale University Press.

Jackson (Robert Victor) 1975, *South Asian Crisis: India, Pakistan, Bangla Desh*, Berkeley, University of California Press.

Jacob (Samuel Swinton) 1890–1913, *Jeypore Portfolio of Architectural Details*, 12 vols, London, B. Quaritch.

Jaffrelot (Christophe) 2004, *A History of Pakistan and Its Origins*, London, Anthem Press.

Jaffrelot (Christophe) 2009, *Hindu Nationalism: A Reader*, Princeton, Princeton University Press.

Jalal (Ayesha) 1985, *The Sole Spokesman: Jinnah, the Muslim League and the Demand for Pakistan*, Cambridge, Cambridge University Press.

Jalal (Ayesha) 1990, *The State of Martial Rule: The Origins of Pakistan's Political Economy of Defence*, New York, Cambridge University Press.

Jalal (Ayesha) 1995, *Democracy and Authoritarianism in South Asia: A Comparative and Historical Perspective*, Cambridge, University Press.

Jalan (Bimal) [ed.] 1993, *The Indian Economy: Problems and Prospects*, New Delhi, Penguin.

Jhala (Angma Dey) 2011, *Royal Patronage, Power and Aesthetics in Princely India*, Londres, Pickering and Chatto.

Jones (Kenneth W.) 1994, *Socio-Religious Reform Movements in British India*, Cambridge, Cambridge University Press (The New Cambridge History of India 3.1).

Jones (Owen Bennett) 2009, *Pakistan: Eye of the Storm*, Bodmin, Yale University Press.

Jordens (J. T. F.) 1997, *Dayānanda Sarasvatī: his life and ideas*, Delhi, Oxford University Press.

Kaegi (Adolf) 1886, *The Rigveda: the Oldest Literature of the Indians*, Boston, Ginn and Company.

Kalia (Ravi) 1987, *Chandigarh. The Making of an Indian City*, Oxford *et al.*, Oxford University Press.

Kaviraj (Narahari) 1982, *Wahabi and Farazi Rebels of Bengal*, New Delhi, People's Publishing House.

Kaviraj (Sudipta) 1992, "The Imaginary Institution of India", in Chatterjee (Partha) and Pandey (Gyanendra) [eds.] 1992, *Subaltern Studies (VII)*, New Delhi, Oxford University Press.

Kedourie (Elie) 1960, *Nationalism*, London, Hutchinson.

Keen (Caroline) 2012, *Princely India and the British: Political Development and the Operation of Empire*, Londres, I.B. Tauris.

Kelkar (Vijay) 1980, "India and the World Economy: A Search for Self Reliance", *Economic and Political Weekly* 15/5–7, February, p. 245; 247;249; 251; 253; 255; 257–258.

Kendle (John) 1997, *Federal Britain: A History*, Londres, Routledge.

Kennedy (Dane) and Ghosh (Durba) 2006, *Decentring Empire: Britain, India and the Transcolonial World*, Hyderabad, Orient Longman.

Kennedy (James) 1903, "Buddhist Gnosticism, the System of Basilides", *The Journal of the Royal Asiatic Society of Great Britain and Ireland* for 1902, p. 337–415.

Khan (Roedad) 1999, *The American Papers: Secret And Confidential India-Pakistan-Bangladash Documents, 1965–1973*, Oxford, Oxford University Press.

Khan (Roedad) 2002, *The British Papers: Secret and Confidential India-Pakistan-Bangladesh Documents: 1958–1969*, Oxford, Oxford University Press.

Khan (Sayed Ahmed) 1982, *Present state of Indian Politics and Speeches*, Lahore, Sang-e-Meet Publications (Original in 1888).

Khanna (Madhu) 1994, *Yantra: The Tantric Symbol of Cosmic Unity*, London, Thames and Hudson (First Edition 1979).

Khosla (G.D.) 1989, *Stern Reckoning: A survey of the events leading up to and following the partition of India*, Delhi, Oxford University Press.

King (Christopher R.) 1994, *One Language Two Scripts: The Hindi Movement in Nineteenth Century North India*, New Delhi, Oxford University Press.

Kopf (David) 1969, *British Orientalism and the Bengal Renaissance: The Dynamics of Indian Modernization, 1773-1835*, Berkeley, University of California Press.

Korngay (Sandra) 1980, "Le Corbusier in India", *The Arts at North-Eastern*, Jan. 10, Boston, p. 6-7.

Kumar (Dharma) [ed.] 1983, *The Cambridge Economic History of India*, vol. 2, Cambridge, Cambridge University Press.

Lajpat Rai (Lala) 1915, *The Arya Samaj, an Account of its Origin, Doctrines, and Activities, with a biographical Sketch of the Founder*, London, Longmans, Green and Co.

Lambrick (H.T.) 1970, "Prospects for a United India after the Cessation of British rule, as these appeared in Sind 1930-46", in Philips (Cyril Henry) and Wainwright (Mary Doreen) 1970, *The Partition of India. Policies and Perspectives 1935-1947*, Cambridge, MA, M.I.T. Press.

Larsson (Lars Olof) 1978, *Die Neugestaltung der Reichshauptstadt. Albert Speers Generalbebauungsplan für Berlin*, Stuttgart, Verlag Gerd Hatje.

Le Corbusier 1982, *Carnets*, vol. 2 (1950-1954), Paris, Herscher / Dessain et Tolra.

Le Corbusier 1982, *Carnets*, vol. 3 (1954-1957), Paris, Herscher / Dessain et Tolra.

Le Corbusier 1959, *L'urbanisme des trois établissements humains*, Paris, Minuit (collection « Les Cahiers Forces vives »).

Leisegang (Hans), *La gnose*, Paris, Payot, 1951 (First Edition 1924).

Lelyveld (David) 2003, *Aligarh's First Generation: Muslim Solidarity in British India*, Princeton, Princeton University Press (First Edition 1978).

Levkovsky (A. I.) 1966, *Capitalism in India*, New Delhi, People's Publishing House.

Lewis (David) 2011, *Bangladesh: politics, economy and civil society*, New Delhi, Cambridge University Press.

Lifschultz (Lawrence) and Bird (Kai) 1979, *Bangladesh, the Unfinished Revolution*, New York, Zed Press.

Loshak (David) 1971, *Pakistan Crisis*, New York, McGraw-Hill.

Low (Donald A.) 1991, *Eclipse of Empire*, Cambridge, Cambridge University Press.

Ludden (David) [ed.] 2002, *Reading Subaltern Studies: Critical History, Contested Meaning, and the Globalization of South Asia*, Londres, Anthem Press.

Lutyens (Mary) 1991, *Edwin Lutyens*, London, Black Swan Books, (First Edition 1980).

Lynd (Robert) 1907, *The Ethics of Sinn Féin*, Dublin, Sinn Féin.

Lyons (Francis Stewart Leland) 1983, *Ireland Since the Famine*, London, Fontana.

McCaffrey (Lawrence John) 1995, *The Irish Question : Two Centuries of Conflict*, Kentucky, the University Press of Kentucky.

McCartney (Donal) 1973, "The Political Use of History in the Work of Arthur Griffith", *Journal of Contemporary History* 8/1, p. 3–19.

McLane (J.R.) 1977, *Indian Nationalism and the Early Congress*, Princeton, Princeton University Press.

Maddison (Angus) 2007, *The World Economy*. Vol. 1: *A Millennial Perspective*. Vol. 2: *Historical Statistics*, New Delhi, OECD Indian Edition.

Madhok (Balraj) 1954, *Dr Syama Prasad Mookerjee: a biography*, Delhi, Deepak Prakashan.

Mahajan (Sucheta) 2000, *Independence and Partition: Erosion of Colonial Power in India*, New Delhi, Sage (Series in Modern Indian History).

Mahajan (Sucheta) 2013, *Towards Freedom: Documents on the Movement for Independence for India,* 1947, Part 1, New Delhi, ICHR and Oxford University Press.

Mahajan (Sucheta) and Bhattacharya (Sabyasachi) [ed.] 2013, *Towards Freedom: Documents on the Movement for Independence in India (1947)*, Delhi, Oxford University Press.

Majumdar (Ramesh Chandra) 1943, *History of Bengal*, vol. 1, Dacca, University of Dacca Press.

Majumdar (Ramesh Chandra) 1962–1963, *History of the Freedom Movement in India*, vol. I-III, Calcutta, Firma K.L. Mukhopadhyay.

Majumdar (Ramesh Chandra) 1963–1965, *British Paramountcy and Indian Renaissance*, Bombay, Bharatiya Vidya Bhavan 10/1-2.

Malik (Hafeez) 1980, *Sir Sayyad Ahmad Khan and Muslim Modernization in India and Pakistan*, New York, Columbia University Press.

Malik (Saurabh) 2012, "Master Plan Panel Mulls Sports City, Admn tells. H[igh] C[ourt] Says Plans on Slum-free Walkers' Paradise Underway", *The Tribune*, Feb. 1, Chandigarh.

Malkani (K.R.) 1980, *The RSS Story*, New Delhi, Impex India.

Manela (Erez) 2007, *The Wilsonian Moment: Self-determination and the International Origins of Anticolonial Nationalism*, Oxford, Oxford University Press.

Mansergh (Nicholas) 1970a, *Constitutional Relations between Great Britain and India, Transfer of Power, 1942-1947*. Vol. 1, Her Majesty's Stationery Office, London.

Mansergh (Nicholas) 1970b, *Constitutional Relations between Great Britain and India, Transfer of Power, 1942-1947*. Vol. 9, Her Majesty's Stationery Office, London.

Mansergh (Nicholas), Rawson (Esmond) and Moon (Penderel) 1970-1983, *Constitutional Relations between Britain and India: The Transfer of Power 1942-1947*, Vol. I-XII, Londres, Her Majesty's Stationery Office.

Markovits (Claude) 2007, *Online Encyclopedia of Mass Violence: The Calcutta Riots of 1946*, Paris, Sciences Po-CNRS/CERI (accessed 2 November 2013: http://www.massviolence.org/The-Calcutta-Riots-of-1946).

Marshall (Peter J.) 1970, *The British Discovery of Hinduism in the Eighteenth Century*, Cambridge, Cambridge University Press.

Mayaram (Shail) 1997, *Resisting Regimes: Myth, Memory and the Shaping of a Muslim Identity*, New Delhi, Oxford University Press.

Mayaram (Shail), Pandian (M.S.S.) and Skaria (Ajay) 2005, *Muslims, Dalits, and the Fabrication of History*, New Delhi, Permanent Black (Subaltern Studies XII).

Mehrotra (S. R.) 1965, *India and the Commonwealth 1885-1929*, New York, F.A. Praeger.

Mehrotra (S. R.) 1970, "The Congress and the Partition of India", in Philips (Cyril Henry) and Wainwright (Mary Doreen) 1970, *The Partition of India. Policies and Perspectives 1935-1947*, Cambridge, MA, M.I.T. Press.

Merle (Isabelle) 2004, « Les Subaltern Studies », *Genèses* 3 (n° 56), p. 131–147.

Metcalf (Barbara Daly) 1981, *Islamic Revival in British India: Deoband, 1860–1900*, Princeton (N.J.), Princeton University Press.

Metcalf (Thomas R.) 1989, *An Imperial Vision: Indian Architecture and Britain's Raj*, London and Boston, Faber and Faber.

Minault (Gail) 1982, *The Khilafat Movement. Religious Symbolism and Political Mobilization in India*, New York, Columbia University Press.

Mishra (B.B.) 1990, *The Unification and Division of India*, Delhi, Oxford University Press.

Misra (Salil) 2001, *A Narrative of Communal Politics: Uttar Pradesh, 1937–1939*, New Delhi, Sage.

Misra (Salil) 2005, "Transition from the Syncretic to the Plural: The World of Hindi and Urdu", in Malik (Jamal) and Reifeld (Helmut) [eds.] 2005, *Religious Pluralism in South Asia and Europe*, New Delhi, Oxford University Press.

Mitra (Subrata Kumar) 2011, *Politics in India: Structure, Process and Policy*, Abingdon, Routledge.

Mookerji (Radha Kumud) 1921, *Nationalism in Hindu Culture*, London, Theosophical Publishing House.

Mookerji (Radha Kumud) 1924, *Men and Thought in Ancient India*, Delhi, Motilal Banarsidass.

Moses (A. Dirk.) 2011, "The United Nations, Humanitarianism and Human Rights: War Crimes/Genocide Trials for Pakistani Soldiers in Bangladesh, 1971–1974", in Hoffmann (Stefan-Ludwig) [ed.] 2011, *Human Rights in the Twentieth Century*, New York, Cambridge University Press, p. 258–279

Mosley (Leonard) 1962, *The Last Days of the Raj*, New York, Harcourt, Brace and World.

Mukherjee (Aditya) 1981, "Business and Politics in Bombay", *Indian Historical Review* 9/1–2.

Mukherjee (Aditya) 1990, "Indo-British Finance: The Controversy over India's Sterling Balances, 1939–1947", *Studies in History* 6/2, p. 229–251.

Mukherjee (Aditya) 1992, "Controversy over Formation of Reserve Bank of India, 1927–1935", *Economic and Political Weekly* 27/5, 1 February.

Mukherjee (Aditya) 2002, *Imperialism Nationalism and the Making of the Indian Capitalist Class: 1920–1947*, Sage, New Delhi.

Mukherjee (Aditya) 2007, "The Currency Question in Colonial India", *Yojana* 51, Special Issue, August.

Mukherjee (Aditya) and Mukherjee (Mridula) 1988, "Imperialism and the Growth of Indian Capitalism in the Twentieth Century", *Economic and Political Weekly* 23/11, 12 March.

Mukherjee (Aditya), Mukherjee (Mridula) and Mahajan (Sucheta) 2008, *RSS, School Texts and the Murder of Mahatma Gandhi: The Hindu Communal Project*, New Delhi, Sage.

Mukherjee (Mridula) 2006, *Colonialising Agriculture: The Myth of Punjab Exceptionalism*, New Delhi, Sage.

Mukherji (Partha N.) 1974, "The Great Migration of 1971: II: Reception", *Economic and Political Weekly* 9/10, p. 399–408.

Mukherji (Saradindu) 1993, *Peasants Politics and the British Government: A Study on Eastern Bihar 1930–40*, Delhi, Anamika Prakashan.

Mukherji (Saradindu) 1996a, "The Unwritten Story", *Hindustan Times*, 7 July

Mukherji (Saradindu) 1996b, "Partition: Generous or Hapless Hosts", *Hindustan Times*, 13 October.

Mukherji (Saradindu) 2000, *Subjects, Citizens and Refugees. Tragedy in the Chittagong Hill Tracts: 1947–1998*, Delhi, Indian Centre for the Study of Forced Migration.

Mukherji (Saradindu) 2003, "M.A.K. Azad His Mission and Political Legacy", in Singh (Mahavir) [ed.] 2003, *M. A. K. AZAD. Profile of Nationalist*, Kolkata, Maulana Abul Kalam Azad Institute of Asian Studies, p. 55–82.

Mukherji (Saradindu) 2007, "Netaji's Legacy", First Netaji Subhash Commemorative Lecture, New Delhi.

Mukherji (Saradindu) 2012a, "Bengal Revolutionaries and the Muslims of Bengal. What went wrong and how?", *Journal of Bengal Studies* 1/1, 4 February, Kolkata,. p, 112–126.

Mukherji (Saradindu) 2012b, "New Politics, New Culture: An Exploration into the Origins of the Socio-Religious Ideas of Raja Rammohan Roy", Paper presented at the international conference on 'Indian Pluralism and Warren Hastings's Regime', University of Wales Conference Centre, Gregynog, Powys, 18–20 July.

Mukhopadhaya (Kaliprasada) 2007, *Partition, Bengal and After the Great Tragedy of India*, Delhi, Reference Press.

Müller (Georgina Adelaide) 1902, *The Life and Letters of the Right Honourable Friedrich Max Müller*, 2 vol., London, Longmans, Green and Co.

Müller (Max) 1859, *A History of Ancient Sanskrit Literature So Far As It Illustrates the Primitive Religion of the Brahmans*, London, Williams and Norgate.

Müller (Max) 1878, *Origine et développement de la religion étudiés à la lumière des religions de l'Inde*, Paris, C. Reinwald.

Müller (Max) 1884, *Biographical Essays: Râmmohun Roy, Keshub Chunder Sen, Dayânanda Sarasvatî, Bunyiu Nanjio and Kenjiu Kasawara, Mohl and Kingsley*, New York, Charles Scribner's Sons.

Müller (Max) 1888, *Biographies of Words and the Home of the Aryas*, London, Longmans, Green and Co.

Murty (K. Satchidananda) and Vohra (Ashok) 1990, *Radhakrishnan, his Life and Ideas*, Albany, State University of New York Press.

Nair (Janaki) 2011, *Mysore Modern: Rethinking the Region under Princely Rule*, Minneapolis, University of Minnesota Press.

Nanda (Bal Ram) 1985, *Gandhi and his Critics*, Delhi, Oxford University Press.

Nanda (Bal Ram) 2002, *Pan-Islamism, Imperialism and Nationalism*, New Delhi, Oxford University Press.

Nandy (Ashis) 1983, *The Intimate Enemy: Loss and Recovery of Self Under Colonialism*, Delhi, Oxford University Press.

Nautin (Pierre) 1974, « Les fragments de Basilide sur la souffrance et leur interprétation par Clément d'Alexandrie et Origène », *Mélanges d'histoire des religions offerts à Henri-Charles Puech*, Paris, PUF, p. 393–403.

Nehru (Jawaharlal) 1959, *Discovery of India*, New York, Anchor Books.

Nehru (Jawaharlal) 1965, *Nehru: The First Sixty Years*, ed. by Dorothy Norman, London, Bodley Head.

Niemeijer (A.C.) 1972, *The Khilafat Movement in India*. Dordrecht: Koninklijk Instituut voor Taal-, Land-en Volkenkunde.

Nilekani (Nandan) 2009b, *Imagining India. Ideas for the New Century*, revised and updated, New Delhi, Penguin Books India.

NN 2009, "Housing Scheme for Poor. City Bags National Award", *The Tribune* (Chandigarh), Dec. 4.

Oberoi (Harjot S.) 1994, *The Construction of Religious Boundaries: Culture, Identity and Diversity in the Sikh Tradition*, Chicago, The University of Chicago Press.

O'Hegarty (Patrick) 1952, *A History of Ireland Under the Union*, London, Methuem and Co.

Oldenburg (Philip) 1985, "A Place Insufficiently Imagined: Language Belief and the Pakistan Crisis of 1971", *Journal of Asian Studies* 44/4, p. 711-733.

O'Malley (Kate) 2004, *India and Empire: Indo-Irish Radical Connections, 1919-1964*, Manchester, Manchester University Press.

Özkirimli (Umut) 2010, *Theories of Nationalism: A Critical Introduction*, London, Palgrave Macmillan (First Edition 2000).

Page (David) 1982, *Prelude to Partition: The Indian Muslims and the Imperial System of Control*, New Delhi, Oxford University Press.

Pal (Bipin Chandra) 1916, *Nationality and Empire: A Running Study of Some Current Indian problems*, Calcutta and Simla, Thacker and Spinks.

Pal (Bipin Chandra) 2004, *Memories of My life and Times*, Delhi, UBS Publishers' Distributors Pvt. Limited.

Pandey (Bishwa Nath) 1969, *The Break-up of British India*, Delhi, Macmillan.

Pandey (Gyanendra) 1990, *The Construction of Communalism in Colonial North India*, New Delhi Oxford University Press.

Peers (Douglas M.) and Gooptu (Nandini) 2012, *India and the British Empire*, Oxford, Oxford University Press.

Petersen (Roger D.) 2002, *Understanding Ethnic violence: Fear, Hatred and Resentment in Twentieth Century Eastern Europe*, New York, Cambridge University Press.

Petit (Jean) 1970, *Le Corbusier lui-même*, Genève, Rousseau.

Philips (Cyril Henry) and Wainwright (Mary Doreen) 1970, *The Partition of India. Policies and Perspectives 1935-1947*, Cambridge, MA, M.I.T. Press.

Plamper (Jan) 2009, « Emotional Turn? : Feelings in Russian History and Culture », in *Slavic Review* 68/2, p. 229-37.

Pouchepadass (Jacques) 2010, « Subaltern et Postcolonial Studies », in Delacroix (Christian), Dosse (François), Garcia (Patrick) et Offenstadt (Nicolas) [éd.] 2010, *Historiographies: Concepts et débats (1)*, Paris, Gallimard (Folio Histoire), p. 636-646.

Prakash (Vikramaditya) 2002, *Chandigarh's Le Corbusier. The Struggle for Modernity in Postcolonial India*, Seattle / London, University of Washington Press.

Prasad (Bimal) 2001, *Pathways to India's Partition. Vol. 1: The Foundations of Muslim Nationalism*, Delhi, Manohar.

Prasad (Bimal) 2009a, *Pathways to India's Partition. Vol. 2: A Nation within a Nation: 1858–1937*, Delhi, Manohar.

Prasad (Bimal) 2009b, *Pathways to India's Partition. Vol. 3: The March to Pakistan*, Delhi, Manohar.

Prasad (Rajendra) 1947, *India Divided*, Bombay, Hind Kitabs.

Prasad (Rajendra) 1984-, *Correspondence and Select Documents*, ed. Valmiki Choudhary, vol. 1-, Bombay.

Prashar (A.S.) 2002, "Changing Profile of Chandigarh-1. A Sector Undergoing Quiet Metamorphosis", *The Tribune*, Jan. 14, Chandigarh.

Prinsep (James) 1837a, "Note on the Facsimiles of Inscriptions from Sanchí near Bhilsa, taken for the Society by Captain Ed. Smith, Engineers; and on the drawings of the Buddhist monument presented by Captain W. Murray, at the meeting of the 7th June", *The Journal of the Asiatic Society of Bengal*, vol. VI, part I, January to June, Calcutta, p. 451–477.

Prinsep (James) 1837b, "Interpretation of the most ancient of the inscriptions on the pillar called the lát of Feroz Sháh, near Delhi, and of the Allahabad, Radhia and Mattiah pillar, or lát, inscriptions which agree therewith", *The Journal of the Asiatic Society of Bengal*, vol. VI, part I, January to June, Calcutta, p. 566–609.

Racine (Jean-Luc) 2002, *La question identitaire en Asie du Sud*, Paris, éd. de l'EHESS, « Purusartha 22 ».

Radhakrishnan (Sarvepalli) 1920, *The Reign of Religion in Contemporary Philosophy*, London, MacMillan and Co.

Radhakrishnan (Sarvepalli) 1932, *An Idealist View of Life*, Being the Hibbert Lectures for 1929, London, George Allen and Unwin Ltd.

Radhakrishnan (Sarvepalli) 1935, *L'Hindouisme et la vie*, trad. P. Masson-Oursel, Paris, Félix Alcan (*The Hindu View of Life*, Oxford, 1927).

Radhakrishnan (Sarvepalli) 1959, *Eastern Religions and Western Thought*, New York, Oxford University Press (First Published 1939).

Radhakrishnan (Sarvepalli) 1967, *Religion in a Changing World*, London, George Allen and Unwin Ltd.

Raghavan (Srinath) 2014, *1971: A Global History of the Creation of Bangladesh*, Cambridge (Mass.), Harvard University Press.

Rahman (Muhammad Anisur) 1968, *East and West Pakistan: a Problem in the Political Economy of Regional Planning*, Harvard, Harvard University, Center for International Affairs.

Raj (K. N.) 1965, *Indian Economic Growth: Performance and Prospects*, New Delhi.

Ramusack (Barbara Nelle) 1978, *The Princes of India in the twilight of Empire: dissolution of a Patron-Client system 1914–1939*, Columbus, Ohio State University Press.

Ramusack (Barbara Nelle) 2004, *The Indian Princes and their States. The New Cambridge History of India*, vol. 3.6, Cambridge, Cambridge University Press.

Ray (Jayanta Kumar) 1968, *Democracy and Nationalism on Trial: A study on East Pakistan*, Simla, Indian Institute of Advanced Studies.

Ray (Rajat) 1979, *Industrialization in India*, New Delhi, Oxford University Press.

Ray (Rajat Kanta) 2001, *Exploring Emotional History: Gender, Mentality and Literature in the Indian Awakening*, New Delhi, Oxford University Press.

Renou (Louis) 1928, *Les maîtres de la philologie védique*, Paris, P. Geuthner.

Riboulet (Pierre) 1985, « Sur la composition du Capitole à Chandigarh », in Association française d'action artistique [éd.] 1985, *Architectures en Inde*, Catalogue de l'exposition de l'école nationale supérieure des Beaux-arts de Paris (27.11.1985–19.01.1986), Milan / Paris, Electa Moniteur, p. 91–98.

Richards (James M.) [ed.] 1977, *Who's Who in Architecture*, London, Weidenfeld and Nicholson.

Riddick (John F.) 2006, *The History of British India*, Westport, Praeger.

Rizvi (Hasan Askari) 2000, *Military, State and Society in Pakistan*, New York, Macmillan Basingstoke.

Rizvi (Hasan Askari) 2004, "Pakistan: Civil-military Relations in a Praetorian State", in Selochan (Viberto) and May (Ronald James) [eds.] 2004, *The Military and Democracy in Asia and the Pacific*, Canberra, Australian National University.

Robinson (Francis) 1974, *Separatism Among Indian Muslims: The Politics of the United Provinces, 1860–1923*, Cambridge, Cambridge University Press.

Robinson (Francis) 1990, "The Brass thesis and Muslim Separatism", in Jeffrey (Robin) et al [ed.] 1990, *India: Rebellion to Republic: Selected Writings, 1857–1990*, New Delhi, Sterling Publishers.

Robinson (Francis) 2000, "The Congress and the Muslims", in Robinson (Francis) 2000, *Islam and Muslim History in South Asia*, New Delhi, Oxford University Press.

Rothermund (Dietmar) 1992, *India in the Great Depression, 1929–1939*, New Delhi, Manohar.

Rothermund (Dietmar) 2006, *The Routledge Companion to Decolonization*, Abingdon, Routledge.

Roy (Asim) 1983, *The Islamic Syncretistic Tradition in Bengal*, Princeton, Princeton University Press.

Roy (Asim) 1996, "The Interface of Islamisation, Regionalisation and Syncretisation: The Bengal Paradigm", in Roy (Asim) 1996, *Islam in South Asia: A Regional Perspective*, New Delhi, Oxford University Press.

Roy (Tirthankar) 2000, *The Economic History of India:1857–1947*, New Delhi, Oxford University Press.

Royle (Trevor) 1989, *The Last Days of the Raj*, London, Michael Joseph (Penguin).

Russel (Ralph) 1999, *How Not to Write the History of Urdu Literature and Other Essays on Urdu and Islam*, New Delhi, Oxford University Press.

Samaddar (Ranabir) 2001, *A Biography of the Indian Nation, 1947–1997*, New Delhi, Sage.

Samartha (Stanley Jedidiah) 1964, *Introduction to Radhakrishnan. The Man and his Thought*, New York, Association Press.

Sarasvatī (Swāmi Dayānanda) 1940, *Satyārtha Prakāsh : le livre de l'Arya Samāj*, traduction de Louise Morin, Frameries, Union des imprimeries.

Sarin (Madhu) 1977, "Chandigarh as a Place to Live in", in Walden (Russell) 1977, *The Open Hand. Essays on Le Corbusier*, Cambridge (Mass.) / London, MIT Press, p. 374–411.

Sarkar (Jadunath) 1977, *The History of Bengal: Muslim Period (1200–1757)*, Patna, J. Prakashan.

Sarkar (Sumit) 1983a, *Modern India, 1885–1947*, New Delhi, Macmillan.

Sarkar (Sumit) 1983b, *Popular Movements and Middle-Class Leadership in Late Colonial India. Perspectives and Problems of a History from Below*, Calcutta, K.P. Bagchi.

Sarkar (Sumit) 1985, *A Critique of Colonial India*, Calcutta, Papyrus.

Sarma (D. S.) 1944, *The Renaissance of Hinduism*, Banaras, Hindu University Press.

Savarkar (Vināyak Dāmodar) 1969, *Hindutva*, Bombay, Savarkar Sadan (First Edition 1923).

Sayeed (Khalid B.) 1998, *Pakistan: The Formative Phase, 1857–1948*, London, Oxford University Press.

Schopenhauer (Arthur) 1908, *Parerga et Paralipomena. Sur la Religion*, trad. A. Dietrich, Paris, F. Alcan.

Schrader (Otto) 1890, *Prehistoric antiquities of the Aryan peoples*, London, C. Griffin.

Schumann (H. W.) 1989, *Der historische Buddha*, Munich.

Seal (Anil) 1968, *The Emergence of Indian Nationalism*, Cambridge, Cambridge University Press.

Seal (Anil) 1973, "Imperialism and Nationalism in India", *Modern Asian Studies*, vol. 7/3, p. 321.

Sehrawat (Samiksha) 2007, "'Hostages in our camp': Military collaboration between princely India and the British Raj, c.1880–1920", in Ernst and Pati 2007, p. 118–138.

Sen (Amartya) 1982, *Poverty and Famines: An Essay on Entitlements and Deprivation*, Oxford University Press, Delhi.

Sen (Shila) 1976, *Muslim Politics in Bengal*, Delhi, Impex.

Shackle (Christopher) and Majeed (Javed) [transl.] 1997, *Hali's Musaddas (The Flow and Ebb of Islam)*, New Delhi, Oxford University Press.

Shah (Ghanshyam) [ed.] 1990, *Capitalist Development: Critical Essays*, Bombay.

Shaikh (Farzana) 2009, *Making Sense of Pakistan*, New York, Columbia University Press.

Shams-i Siráj 1891, *Táríkh-i Fíroz Shahí*, Calcutta.

Silvestri (Michael) 2000, "The *Sinn Féin* of India: Irish Nationalism and the Policing of Revolutionary Terrorism in Bengal", *Journal of British Studies* 39/4, p. 460–461.

Silvestri (Michael) 2009, *Ireland and India: Nationalism, Empire and Memory*, New York, Palgrave Macmillan.

Singh (Anita Inder) 1993, *The Limits of British Influence: South Asia and the Anglo-American Relationship, 1947–1956*, Londres, Pinter.

Singh (Anita Inder) 2006, *The Partition of India*, New Delhi, National Book Trust.

Singh (Khushwant) [transl.] 1990, *Shikwa and Jawab-i-Shikwa: Iqbal's Dialogue with Allah*, New Delhi, Oxford University Press.

Singh (Prabhjot) 1999, "City Beautiful is Fast Decaying", *The Tribune*, Feb. 28, Chandigarh.

Singh (Prabhjot) 2000, "No More Fencing of Madhya Marg", *The Tribune*, Feb. 16, Chandigarh.

Sinha (Dinesh C.) and Dasgupta (Ashok) 2011, *1946: The Great Calcutta Killings and Noakhali Genocide: A Historical Study*, Kolkata, Tuhina Prakashani (accessed 2 November 2013: http://www.eastbengal.org/bengal1946_calcut ta_noakhali_killing.pdf).

Sinn Féin [ed.] 1907, *The National Council*, Dublin, Sinn Féin.

Sisson (Richard) and Rose (Leo E.) 1991, *War and Secession: Pakistan, India, and the Creation of Bangladesh*, Berkeley, University of California Press.

Sivasubramonian (S.) 2000, *The National Income of India in the Twentieth Century*, New Delhi, Oxford University Press.

Smith (Simon C.) 2010, "Coming Down on the Winning Side: Britain and the South Asia Crisis, 1971", *Contemporary British History* 24/4, p. 451–470.

Smith (Vincent Arthur) 1920, *Asoka, the Buddhist Emperor of India*, Oxford, The Clarendon Press (Third Edition, revised and enlarged).

Smith (Vincent Arthur) 1970, *Oxford History of India*, Oxford, Oxford University Press.

Smith (Wilfred Cantwell) 1946, *Modern Islam in India: A Social Analysis*, London, Victor Gollancz.

Srinivas (Mysore Narasimhachar) 2000, *Social Change in Modern India*, New Delhi, Orient Longman (First Edition 1972).

Stargardt (Nicholas) 1996, "Gellner's Nationalism: The Spirit of Modernisation?", in Hall (John A.) and Jarvie (Ian) [eds.] 1996, *The Social Philosophy of Ernest Gellner* (Poznan Studies in the Philosophy of the Sciences and the Humanities 48), Amsterdam-Atlanta, Rodopi.

Stierlin (Henri) 2002, *Hindu India: From Khajuraho to the Temple City of Madurai*, Köln, London, Madrid, New York, Paris and Tokyo, Taschen.

Subramanian (S.) and Homfray (P. W. R.) 1946, *Recent Social and Economic Trends in India*, New Delhi, Government of India Publications.

Suny (Ronald Grigor) 2004, "Why We Hate You: The Passions of National Identity and Ethnic Violence", in Berkeley Programme in Soviet and Post-Soviet Studies 2004, *Working Paper Series*, Berkeley, University of California.

Tagore (Rabindranath) 1990, *Kalantar*, Delhi, Vishwa Bharti Prakashan.

Talbot (Ian) 2005, *Pakistan: A Modern History*, London, Palgrave Macmillan (Second Ed.).

Talbot (Phillips) 2007, *An American Witness to India's Partition*, Delhi, Sage Publications.

Taylor (David) 2011, "Pakistan: The Military as a Political Fixture", in Burnell (Peter) and Randall (Vicky) [eds.], *Politics in the Developing World*, New York, Oxford University Press.

Tejpal (Tarun J.) 2007, *The Alchemy of Desire*, New York *et al.*, Harper Perennial.

Thomas (P. J.) 1939, *The Growth of Federal Finance in India: Being a Survey of India's Public Finances from 1833 to 1939*, Madras, Oxford University Press.

Tilak (Bal Gangadhar) 1893, *The Orion or Researches into the Antiquity of the Vedas*, Mrs Radhabai Atmaram Sagoon.

Tilak (Bal Gangadhar) 1903, *The Arctic Home in the Vedas, Being Also a New Key to the Interpretation of Many Vedic Texts and Legends*, Poona, Tilak Bros Gaikwar Wada.

Tilak (Bal Gangadhar) 1936, *Śrī Bhagavadgītā-rahasya or Karma-yoga-śāstra*, (English Translation), volume 1, Poona, R. B. Tilak, Lokamanya Tilak Mandir (First Edition in Marathi 1915).

Tillotson (G. H. R.) 1989, *The Tradition of Indian Architecture: Continuity, Controversy and Change since 1850*, Delhi, Bombay, Calcutta and Madras, Oxford University Press.

Tomlinson (B. R.) 1979, *Political Economy of the Raj 1914–1947: The Economics of Decolonization in India*, London, Macmillan.

Torri (Michelguglielmo) 1989, "'Westernized Middle Class', Intellectuals and Society in Late Colonial India", in *La modernizzazione in Asia e Africa, Problemi di storia e di metodo*, Pavie, Viscontea (= 1990, *Economic and Political Weekly* 25/4, p. PE2-PE11 (http://www.jstor.org/ stable/4395867; = Hill (J. L.) [ed.] 1991, *The Congress and Indian Nationalism: Historical Perspectives*, Londres, Curzon Press, p. 18–55).

Torri (Michelguglielmo) 1991, "Colonialismo e nazionalismo in India, il modello interpretativo degli storici di Cambridge", *Rivista di storia contemporanea*, CIII, II, p. 483–527.

Torri (Michelguglielmo) 1996, *Regime coloniale, intellettuali e notabili in India. Politica e società nell'era del nazionalismo*, Milano, CSPEE/Franco Angeli.

Torri (Michelguglielmo) 2007, *Storia dell'India*, Bari, Editori Laterza.

Touchaleaume (Éric) et Moreau (Gérald) 2010, *Le Corbusier, Pierre Jeanneret: L'aventure indienne / The Indian Adventure*, Montreuil, Gourcuff Gradenigo / Paris, Galerie 54.

Tuker (Francis) 1950, *While Memory Serves*, London, Cassel.

Upadhyay (Shashi Bhushan) 2004, *Identity, Existence and Mobilization: The Cotton Millworkers of Bombay, 1890–1911*, New Delhi, Manohar.

Van Schendel (Willem) 2009, *A History of Bangladesh*, New Delhi, Cambridge University Press.

Vogt (Adolf Max) 1998, *Le Corbusier, the Noble Savage. Toward an Archaelogy of Modernism*, translated from the German by Radka Donnell, Cambridge (Mass.) / London, MIT Press.

Volwahsen (Andreas) 2004, *Imperial Delhi: The British Capital of the Indian Empire*, Prestel, Munich, Berlin, London, New York and New Delhi, Timeless Books.

Walter (Michael) 1979, "The U.S. Naval Demonstration in the Bay of Bengal During the 1971 India-Pakistan War", *World Affairs* 141/4, p. 293–306.

Warner (Geoffrey) 2005, "Nixon, Kissinger and the Breakup of Pakistan, 1971" *International Affairs* 81/5, p. 1097–1118.

Wattas (Rajnish) 2003, "An Icon of Modern Architecture", *The Tribune*, Oct. 7, Chandigarh.

Wavell 1973, *The Viceroy's Journal*, ed Penderel Moon, Oxford University Press.

Weigold (Auriol) 2008, *Churchill, Roosevelt and India: Propaganda during WW2*, Abingdon, Routledge.

Wheeler (A. H.) [ed.] 1918, *The Montagu-Chelmsford proposals for Indian Constitutional Reform: Their scope and object*, Allahabad.

Witzel (Michael) 1989, "Tracing the Vedic Dialects", *Dialectes dans les littératures indo-aryennes*, Paris, Collège de France, p. 249–251.

Younghusband (Francis) 1927, *The Light of Experience: A review of some men and events of my time*, Londres, Constable and Co.

Yusufi (Khurshid Ahmad Khan) [ed.] 1996, *Speeches, Statements & Messages of the Quaid-e-Azam*, vol. 1 (1934–1937), Lahore, Bazm-e-Iqbal.

Yusufi (Khurshid Ahmad Khan) [ed.] 1996, *Speeches, Statements & Messages of the Quaid-e-Azam*, vol. 2 (1938–1941), Lahore, Bazm-e-Iqbal.

Yusufi (Khurshid Ahmad Khan) [ed.] 1996, *Speeches, Statements & Messages of the Quaid-e-Azam*, vol. 3 (1941–1945), Lahore, Bazm-e-Iqbal.

Yusufi (Khurshid Ahmad Khan) [ed.] 1996, *Speeches, Statements & Messages of the Quaid-e-Azam*, vol. 4 (1946–1948), Lahore, Bazm-e-Iqbal.

Zaheer (Hasan) 1994, *The Separation of East Pakistan: The Rise and Realization of Bengali Muslim Nationalism*, Karachi, Oxford University Press.

Zaidi (Z. H.) [ed] 1993-, *Qaid-e- Azam Mahomed Ali Jinnah Papers*, edited, vols. 1-, Islamabad.

Zecchini (Laetitia) 2009, « Enquête sur les postcolonialismes, ou l'analyse d'un malentendu », in Castaing (Anne), Guilhamon (Lise) et Zecchini (Laetitia) [sous la dir.] 2009, *La modernité littéraire indienne: perspectives postcoloniales*, Paris, Presses Universitaires de Rennes, p. 239–245.

Zecchini (Laetitia) 2011, « Les études postcoloniales colonisent-elles les sciences sociales ? », in *La vie des idées*, 27 janvier 2011 (http://www.laviedesidees.fr/Les-etudes-postcoloniales.html, consulté le 13 septembre 2013).

ANGLO-AMERIKANISCHE STUDIEN – ANGLO-AMERICAN STUDIES

Herausgegeben von
Rüdiger Ahrens, Maria Eisenmann und Laurenz Volkmann

Band 21 Andrew Parkin: The Rendez-Vous. Poems of Multicultural Experience. 2003.

Band 22 Götz Ahrendt: *For our father's sake, and mother's care*. Zur Eltern-Kind-Beziehung in den Dramen Shakespeares unter Berücksichtigung zeitgenössischer Traktatliteratur und Porträts. 2003.

Band 23 Brian Hooper: Voices in the Heart. Postcolonialism and Identity in Hong Kong Literature. 2003.

Band 24 Alexander Bidell: Das Konzept des Bösen in *Paradise Lost*. Analyse und Interpretation. 2003.

Band 25 Isolde Schmidt: Shakespeare im Leistungskurs Englisch. Eine empirische Untersuchung. 2004.

Band 26 Claudia Schemberg: Achieving 'At-one-ment'. Storytelling and the Concept of the *Self* in Ian McEwan's *The Child in Time, Black Dogs, Enduring Love,* and *Atonement*. 2004.

Band 27 Wing-chi Ki: Jane Austen and the Dialectic of Misrecognition. 2005.

Band 28 Daniela Carpi (ed.): Property Law in Renaissance Literature. 2005.

Band 29 Ina-Patricia Bellinger-Bischoff: Die *New Woman* und das suffragistische Propagandadrama der edwardianischen Zeit. 2005.

Band 30 Sabine Jackson: Robertson Davies and the Quest for a Canadian National Identity. 2006.

Band 31 Sidia Fiorato: The Relationship between Literature and Science in John Banville's Scientific Tetralogy. 2007.

Band 32 Shu-Fang Lai: Charles Reade, George Meredith and Harriet Martineau as Serial Writers of *Once a Week* (1859–1865). 2008.

Band 33 Lyndsay Lunan / Kirsty A. Macdonald / Carla Sassi (eds.): Re-Visioning Scotland. New Readings of the Cultural Canon. 2008.

Band 34 Valentina Adami: Trauma Studies and Literature. Martin Amis's *Time's Arrow* As Trauma Fiction. 2008.

Band 35 Zuzanna Ladyga: Rethinking Postmodern Subjectivity. Emmanuel Levinas and the Ethics of Referentiality in the Work of Donald Barthelme. 2009.

Band 36 Alma Budurlean: Otherness in the Novels of Patrick White. 2009.

Band 37 Martina Deny: Lost in the Postmodern Metropolis. Studien zu (Des-)Orientierung und Identitätskonstruktion im zeitgenössischen Londonroman. 2009.

Band 38 Catharine Walker Bergström: Intuition of an Infinite Obligation. Narrative Ethics and Postmodern Gnostics in the Fiction of E. L. Doctorow. 2010.

Band 39 Pavlina Ferfeli: Poetics of Identity: Mina Loy Voicing the Fluid Female Body. 2011.

Band 40 Theresa Staab-Schultes: Feste als didaktischer Lerngegenstand im Englischunterricht der Grundschule. Eine Untersuchung landeskundlicher und sprachlicher Aspekte in Englischlehrwerken der dritten und vierten Jahrgangsstufe. 2011.

Band 41 Jesús López-Peláez (ed.): Strangers in Early Modern English Texts. 2011.

Band 42 Thierry Di Costanzo: L'idée séparatiste dans la presse anglo-musulmane du Bengale. Le cas du *Star of India*, 1937–1947. 2011.

Band 43 Andrew Parkin: Another Rendez-Vous. Poetry and Prose from Cultural Crossroads. 2011.

Band 44 Renée Dickason / Rüdiger Ahrens (eds.): Screening and Depicting Cultural Diversity in the English-speaking World and Beyond. 2013.

Band 45 Katharina Glas: Teaching English in Chile. A Study of Teacher Perceptions of their Professional Identity, Student Motivation and Pertinent Learning Contents. 2013.

Band 46 Stefanie Fuchs: Geschlechtsunterschiede bei motivationalen Faktoren im Kontext des Englischunterrichts. Eine empirische Studie zu Motivation, Selbstkonzept und Interesse im Fach Englisch in der Sekundarstufe I. 2013.

Band 47 Charlott Falkenhagen: *Content and Language Integrated Learning* (CLIL) im Musikunterricht. Eine Studie zu CLIL-Musikmodulen. 2014.

Band 48 Thierry Di Costanzo / Guillaume Ducœur (eds.): Decolonization and the Struggle for National Liberation in India (1909–1971). Historical, Political, Economic, Religious and Architectural Aspects. 2014.

www.peterlang.com